Contents

Introduction   iv

Unit 1

Chapter 1   Sex and Gender   1

  Key Concepts   1

  Core Theory: Biological Approach   3

  An Alternative Theory: the Psychodynamic
    Approach   6

  Core Study: Diamond and Sigmundson (1997)   7

  Application of Research into Sex and Gender   9

  Topic 1 Exam Café   12

Chapter 2   Memory   15

  Key Concepts   15

  Core Theory: Multi-Store Model   18

  An Alternative Theory: Levels of Processing   23

  Core Study: Terry (2005)   25

  Application of Research into Memory:
    Memory Aids   27

  Topic 2 Exam Café   30

Chapter 3   Attachment   33

  Key Concepts   33

  Core Theory: Bowlby's Theory   36

  An Alternative Theory: the Behaviourist Theory   39

  Core Study: Hazen and Shaver (1987)   40

  Application of Research into Attachment:
    Care of Children   42

  Topic 3 Exam Café   46

Chapter 4   Obedience   49

  Key Concepts   49

  Core Theory: Theory of Situational Factors   51

  Criticisms of the 'Situational Factors'
    Explanation of Obedience   54

  An Alternative Theory: Dispositional Factors   54

  Core Study: Bickman (1974)   55

Application of Research into Keeping
  Order in Institutions and Situations   57

  Topic 4 Exam Café   60

Chapter 5   Atypical Behaviour   63

  Key Concepts   63

  Core Theory: Behaviourist Theory   66

  An Alternative Theory: Evolutionary Theory   70

  Core Study: Watson and Rayner (1920)   71

  Application of Research into Atypical Behaviour   73

  Topic 5 Exam Café   76

Unit 2

Chapter 6   Criminal Behaviour   79

  Key Concepts   79

  Core Theory: Biological Theory   81

  An Alternative Theory: Social Learning Theory   83

  Core Study: Mednick *et al.* (1984)   85

  Application of Research into Criminal Behaviour:
    Crime Reduction   87

  Topic 6 Exam Café   90

Chapter 7   Perception   93

  Key Concepts   93

  Core Theory: The Constructivist Theory of
    Perception   97

  An Alternative Theory: Nativist Theory   98

  Core Study: Haber and Levin (2001)   100

  Application of Research into Perception:
    Advertising   101

  Topic 7 Exam Café   104

Chapter 8   Cognitive Development   107

  Key Concepts   107

  Core Theory: Piaget's Theory   108

  An Alternative Theory: Vygotsky   113

Core Study: Piaget and Conservation of
   Number (1952)   114

Application of Research into Cognitive
   Development: Educating Children   115

Topic 8 Exam Café   118

Chapter 9   Non-verbal Communication   **121**

Key Concepts   122

Core Theory: Social Learning Theory   125

An Alternative Theory: Evolutionary Theory   127

Core Study: Yuki *et al.* (2007)   128

Application of Research into Non-verbal
   Communication: Social Skills Training   130

Topic 9 Exam Café   132

Chapter 10   The Self   **135**

Key Concepts   135

Core Theory: Humanistic Theory of Self   136

An Alternative Theory: Trait Theory   140

Core Study: Van Houtte and Jarvis (1995)   143

Applications of Research into the Self:
   Counselling   145

Topic 10 Exam Café   148

Unit 3

Chapter 11   Research in Psychology   **151**

Planning Research   151

Doing Research   159

Analysing Research   167

Planning an Investigation   173

Topic 11 Exam Café   174

Glossary   *180*

Index   *184*

Introduction

Congratulations on choosing to study Psychology GCSE with OCR! This book is designed to support you as you work through this fascinating course, and closely follows the specification and the ways that you will be assessed.

Psychology is essentially the study of mind and behaviour. At the core of Psychology GCSE are five key approaches:

- Biological Psychology
- Cognitive Psychology
- Developmental Psychology
- Social Psychology
- Individual Differences.

Biological Psychology looks at how biological factors, such as genes and chemicals, influence behaviour. Cognitive Psychology focuses specifically on the functioning of the mind and looks at mental processes. Developmental Psychology is concerned with how people's minds and behaviour change over time. Social Psychology looks at how we respond to and are affected by others. Finally, research into Individual Differences reminds us that we are not all the same and how each individual is unique.

OCR's Psychology GCSE course has been designed around the five key perspectives. Each approach is represented by two topics, giving ten topics in total.

The first five topics are covered by Chapters 1 to 5 in this book: Sex and Gender, Memory, Attachment, Obedience and Atypical Behaviour. These topics represent all five approaches and are assessed in Unit 1 of the examination. This unit is called 'Studies and Applications 1' and is worth 40% of the final grade.

The remaining five topics are covered by Chapters 6 to 10 in this book: Criminal Behaviour, Perception, Cognitive Development, Non-Verbal Communication and The Self. These topics also represent all five approaches and are assessed in Unit 2 of the examination. This unit is called 'Studies and Applications 2' and is worth 40% of the final grade.

The ten topics listed focus on important aspects of Psychology, such as theories, evidence and how findings are used in real-life.

Another key part of Psychology is actually doing research and this is covered by Chapter 11: Research in Psychology. The content of Chapter 11 is assessed in Unit 3 of the examination. This unit is called 'Research in Psychology' and is worth 20% of the final grade.

This book encourages you to develop the three skills assessed in the GCSE Psychology examinations. One of these is *demonstrating knowledge and understanding*. Here you will need to recall, select and communicate knowledge and understanding of key concepts, core theories and core studies which are all clearly identified in the book. A second skill is *applying knowledge and understanding*. Here you need to be evaluate theories and concepts, as well as be aware of how they are used in real-life situations. Look out for evaluation and application sections in the book to help you with this. The final skill is *interpretation, evaluation and analysis of psychological data and practice*. The last chapter on Research in Psychology is dedicated to this but also pay attention to other parts of the book where the limitations of studies are discussed.

We have not just written a book to cover the content of the GCSE Psychology specification. Along the way, we have added other features to help you go beyond what you need to know and also prepare for the examinations. The features include the following:

Buzzwords

These are basically all of the terms listed in the specification. The examinations can ask questions about any of these terms so they have been highlighted for you along with definitions that you can learn.

Hints

These are our ideas, tips or pieces of advice on ways that you can enhance your understanding or learning, including memory techniques.

Grade Studio

These are specific pieces of advice that relate to doing well in the examination, including tips on examination technique, deconstructing questions and how to hit higher marks.

Activities

These are designed to reinforce and support the text by getting you to test your knowledge and understanding through various tasks including interpreting sources, groupwork, discussion points, Internet research, and completing tables and diagrams.

How Science Works

These are links made between the main topics and psychological research that help to enhance understanding of 'Research in Psychology'.

Doing Research

These are opportunities to do actual research through suggested investigations. This is good preparation for the Unit 3 examination where you not only have to answer questions about doing research but also have to design your own investigation. It is also a chance to put into practice concepts that you have learned about within topics.

Exam Café

Each chapter also ends with an Exam Café section. This has two main objectives:

- to suggest ways of revising for the examinations, including highlighting common mistakes
- to prepare you for the examinations by identifying exam-style questions, considering how they might be answered, and sharing how they would be assessed by an examiner.

We hope that you find this book a useful tool for learning about Psychology and how it works. It is something that you can use individually to develop your own personal understanding of the subject, but it has also been written so that you can work with fellow students and your teachers.

Good luck and enjoy your studies.

Sex and Gender

In everyday life, people tend to use the terms 'sex' and 'gender' interchangeably. For example, some job application forms ask for your sex and others for your gender, but they are essentially asking for the same thing – whether you are male or female. However, in psychology, we tend to make a clear distinction between sex and gender.

Psychologists are particularly interested in gender. They are especially interested in why there are gender differences in some behaviours.

There is not much debate about what determines a person's sex. Sex is physical, and people are *born* either male or female. However, there is more debate about what determines gender, as gender is psychological rather than physical. The biological approach says that we are also born with our gender and that it is related to sex. However, not all psychologists agree with this approach.

LEARNING OBJECTIVES:

By the end of this topic, you should be able to:

1 Understand the key concepts of
   • *sex and gender*
   • *masculinity, femininity and androgyny*.

2 Understand the *biological* and *psychoanalytic* approach to gender development.

3 Demonstrate knowledge of *Diamond and Sigmundson's case study* of the castrated twin boy raised as a girl, and its limitations.

4 Show awareness of *applications of research* into sex and gender by considering equal opportunities in education, work and leisure.

Key Concepts

Sex and gender

Sex is a biological term which tells us whether someone is male or female. This is determined at conception, when a sperm fertilises an egg.

A person's sex is obvious through characteristics present from birth, for example the penis or vagina. It is also obvious from other characteristics that develop as a person gets older, such as breasts or facial hair. Since these characteristics are fixed, a person's sex cannot change. Even people who undergo so-called 'sex-change' operations have not really changed their sex. Their internal organs, such as the

BUZZWORDS

Sex – A biological term that tells us whether an individual is male or female

ovaries and the brain, will still be the same, and these also determine sex. A person who has had a sex change still has to have their original sex on their passport.

Gender is a psychological term and is more to do with how a person behaves or thinks. There are three main categories for gender: **masculine**, **feminine** and **androgynous**. Masculinity refers to typical male traits or roles, such as being aggressive, going out to work or playing football. Femininity refers to typical female traits or roles, such as being sensitive, staying at home to care for children, or playing with dolls. Androgyny refers to both masculine and feminine traits and roles. An androgynous person is someone who displays many masculine behaviours and many feminine behaviours. There is some evidence that androgynous people are psychologically healthier than people who are just masculine or just feminine.

Grade Studio

'A girl who likes fighting'

In the exam, many candidates give examples like the one above to illustrate androgyny. However, it is not clear enough. Just because the character is a girl does not automatically mean she is feminine. The example should also include a feminine behaviour as well. For example, 'A girl who likes fighting but also enjoys ballet'. This shows both sides of androgyny and should earn two marks.

ACTIVITY

1.1

Complete the following task in groups of two or three.

1 Read the following traits. Put them into two categories: masculine or feminine traits. If there are traits that you think are neither particularly, you may decide to have a group of neutral traits too.

assertive	athletic	big-headed	bitchy
caring	competitive	considerate	creative
daring	flirtatious	forgiving	gossip
humorous	immature	intelligent	logical
patronising	shy	sly	sympathetic

Ask yourself the following questions. Did you agree on which traits were masculine and feminine? Which ones, if any, did you disagree on? Why did you disagree?

2 When you have categorised the traits, read the group of masculine traits. Decide how many of them describe you. If many apply to you, this would suggest that you see yourself as masculine. Read the list of feminine traits. Decide how many of these describe you. If many apply to you, this would suggest that you see yourself as feminine. If many traits in both groups apply to you, this would suggest that you see yourself as androgynous.

Behaviour, sex and gender

Sex and gender are often related. Most males behave in more masculine ways than feminine ways. It is the opposite for most females. Both sexes can display androgynous behaviours. There is evidence that more people are androgynous now than in the past, which suggests that gender roles can change. As well as gender changing across generations, some psychologists believe that a person can change their own gender within their lifetime. For example, a girl may be a 'tomboy' as a child but grow up to be a very feminine woman.

ACTIVITY

1.2

Can you think of any evidence that shows that gender roles have changed over time? How convincing is this evidence?

To what extent do you think an individual can change their own gender?

ACTIVITY

1.3

Read the following case and then answer the questions below.

Claire is a 4-year-old girl who enjoys playing with train sets and helping her dad to service his car. Claire's mother is concerned that her daughter is not very 'lady-like'. Her mother thinks they should make a greater effort to bring up Claire to be more feminine. Claire's father is not so bothered, and even argues that they cannot change the way Claire is. 'It's in her nature,' he says.

Using the stimulus:

1 Identify Claire's sex.

2 Identify Claire's gender.

3 State which parent believes in the biological approach to gender development.

Although sex and gender are often related, this is not always the case. It is possible for an individual to be female but display masculine behaviour. Similarly, an individual can be male but display feminine behaviour. This shows us why it is important to distinguish between sex and gender as they do not always match as might be expected.

Core Theory: Biological Approach

The biological approach believes that an individual's gender is decided at the same time as their sex is decided – at conception. When a new foetus is formed, it has two sex **chromosomes** as part of its genetic make-up. This pair of chromosomes decides whether it will be male or female. The biological approach also argues that they decide whether the individual will grow up to be masculine or feminine.

The sex chromosome pair associated with females is XX. The sex chromosome pair associated with males is XY. The chromosome pairs are labelled this way because of their shape.

Although it is very unusual, babies can be born with atypical (abnormal) sex chromosomes. For example, some baby boys have an extra X chromosome (XXY). Interestingly, such boys grow up to have more feminine traits as well as more female looking bodies. This shows that chromosomes can have a significant effect on gender.

Development of the foetus

Up to about 6 weeks into a pregnancy, male and female foetuses look the same. Their gonads (i.e. sexual organs) are no different. However, around the sixth week, the sex chromosomes begin to have an effect on the development of the gonads. The Y chromosome 'switches on' a **hormone** in the male foetus. This hormone makes the gonads develop into testes. Meanwhile, without this hormone, a female foetus's gonads will automatically turn into ovaries.

Even within the womb, the testes and ovaries begin to produce different levels of sex hormones which affect gender development.

BUZZWORDS

Chromosome – A part of a cell that contains genetic information

HINT

Students sometimes get the chromosome pairs mixed up between the sexes. It might help if you remember that males wear Y-fronts and they are the ones with the Y chromosome!

BUZZWORDS

Hormone – A chemical produced by the body that affects cells and organs

The effects of hormones

Testes produce high levels of testosterone. This hormone is said to affect the brain and the behaviour of the child after it is born. For example, testosterone is thought to make boys more aggressive and to give them superior mathematical and spatial skills. Meanwhile, the ovaries produce high levels of oestrogen. It is said that this hormone has different effects on the brain and behaviour. For example, oestrogen is thought to make girls more sensitive and a lack of testosterone gives them superior verbal skills.

The effects of hormones on gender-related behaviour can be seen in cases where individuals are injected with substances that affect hormone levels. For example, some female athletes have injected themselves with steroids to try and improve their sporting performance. These steroids increase levels of testosterone and as a consequence, they often report feeling more aggressive. Similarly, men undergoing sex-change operations use drugs to raise their oestrogen levels. There is evidence that this improves their verbal ability on tests. However, they actually do worse on tests of visual-spatial ability.

ACTIVITY

1.4

Below is a flow diagram to summarise the stages of gender development according to the biological approach.

Copy and complete the diagram by filling in the gaps.

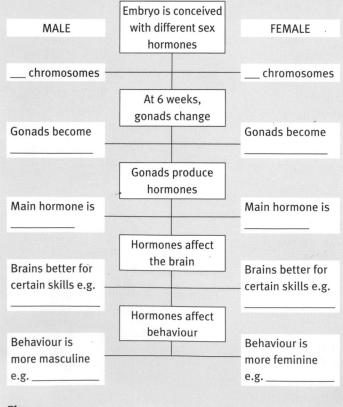

Figure 1.1

Instincts, evolution and the biological approach

The biological approach believes that human behaviour is instinctive, and that instincts have developed to help us to survive and to reproduce. Therefore, the biological approach says gender roles are instinctive. In the same way that males and females have physical differences which help them to reproduce (e.g. having a penis or a vagina), they also have *psychological* differences that help them to reproduce.

The biological approach also states that males and females have evolved with different levels of hormones which, in turn, affect their psychological characteristics. For example, it is thought that females are coyer than males. This means they are thought to be choosier about who they mate with. The approach says that because females only have about 400 eggs they can use to reproduce, they do not want to waste them on a poor mate. Males, however, produce millions of sperm per day so they are less choosy. They can afford to 'waste' them on a poor mate. This is why males are thought to be more promiscuous and 'play the field'.

Evolution may also explain why females appear naturally more caring and sensitive. Since they have to carry and then raise the young, and breast-feed,

BUZZWORDS

Evolution – A process by which species adapt to their environment in order to survive and reproduce

they need to be better equipped to deal with needy babies. Males, meanwhile, are more aggressive and competitive because they have to fight for the resources to provide for their partner and their children.

Finally, evolution may explain the different skills that males and females seem to naturally possess. For example, males' superior visual-spatial skills may be necessary (or at least have been necessary) to help them to hunt (such as aim a spear) and to find their way back home. Meanwhile, females' superior communication skills may be necessary for teaching their young, or for sharing childcare with other mothers.

ACTIVITY

1.5
Choose two masculine and two feminine traits from Activity 1.1, for example: athletic (masculine), daring (masculine); flirtatious (feminine), sly (feminine).

For each trait, explain how evolution might explain why these traits are associated with one sex more than the other.

Figure 1.2 *The biological approach would argue that men are instinctively more aggressive and women are instinctively more communicative.*

Evaluating the biological approach

There are a number of criticisms of the biological approach to gender development, including the following:

- **The biological approach ignores the idea that gender roles may be learnt.** There is a lot of evidence that shows that families and communities socialise males and females differently. Perhaps this is why the two sexes end up with different gender roles. For example, boys are rewarded for being tough whereas girls are rewarded for being 'lady-like'. Similarly, if a child behaves like the opposite sex, they are often punished by being ridiculed or shunned.

- **If all men are biologically similar and all women are biologically similar, why do the two sexes show such a range of behaviours?** For example, two men will have the same chromosome pattern and similar levels of testosterone, yet one could be very masculine and one very feminine. How does the biological approach explain this?

Sometimes a criticism is only worth 1 mark in the exam, so a brief statement will do. However, criticisms are usually worth 2 or more marks, so you have to be able to expand on the first point you make. Remember to stick to the same point but explain it further. You cannot pick up more marks by just introducing another, different criticism.

BUZZWORDS

Oedipus complex – A conflict that occurs when boys unconsciously desire their mother but fear their father finding out

Electra complex – A conflict that occurs when girls unconsciously desire their father but worry about losing their mother's love

Figure 1.3 *A girl who wants to marry her father may be going through the Electra complex.*

Biology is relatively fixed, yet gender roles can change. This would, again, suggest that it is more to do with socialisation. Gender roles can change across time. For example, both females and males are more androgynous now than in the past, yet human biology has not changed. Gender roles can also change across cultures. Females and males may have different gender roles in different cultures despite human biology being the same around the world. For example, in Japan both males and females show high levels of what would be seen as feminine behaviour in the UK. In the past, psychologists have also studied tribes in which the sexes take on different roles compared with what we see in the West. For example, in some tribes both women and men were warriors. In other tribes, roles were reversed; for example, women dealt with economic affairs while men sat around gossiping and preening themselves.

An Alternative Theory: the Psychodynamic Approach

The psychodynamic approach says that gender is less to do with biology and nature, and more to do with upbringing. It particularly focuses on the role of parents.

Parental relationships

Freud is the most famous psychologist behind the psychodynamic approach. He believed that children develop in stages. Between the ages of three and six, a child develops a strong attachment to the opposite sex parent (boys to their mother, girls to their father). However, this causes problems for their relationship with the same sex parent. In boys, Freud called this the **Oedipus complex**. In girls, it is called the **Electra complex**.

In the Oedipus complex, boys fear their father finding out about their desire for their mother. Boys are afraid their fathers will be so angry that they will cut off their penises – this leads to castration anxiety. The way this is resolved is by boys identifying with their fathers. This is when boys develop a masculine gender identity.

In the Electra complex, girls desire their fathers because they desire a penis – this is known as penis envy. They blame their mothers for not having a penis and believe they have been castrated already. They come to realise that they will never get a penis and so instead desire a baby. The baby is a penis substitute. When they reach this point, girls recognise that they are in the same position as their mother. They then identify with their mother. This is when they develop a feminine gender identity.

The Oedipus complex, Electra complex and identification all occur in the unconscious mind according to the psychodynamic approach. The unconscious mind is the part of the mind that we are not consciously aware of, yet still has a big influence on our actions.

The psychodynamic approach argues that if a parent is not around or is a weak model, then a child's gender identity does not develop properly.

ACTIVITY

1.6

Copy out the following boxes. Match the psychodynamic idea to the example.

Figure 1.4

Oedipus complex	A boy wants to sleep in between his mother and father.
Electra complex	A girl dreams about living in a big tower.
Penis envy	A boy hides his 'privates' from his father.
Castration anxiety	A boy helps his father to wash the car.
Identification	A girl wants to marry her father.

Grade Studio

When you are writing about the psychodynamic theory in an exam, use appropriate words and phrases. It doesn't sound very good when candidates write things such as 'boys fancy their mums' or 'girls really want a willy'! You may not get the highest marks if your quality of written communication does not include psychological terminology.

Core Study: Diamond and Sigmundson (1997)

The biological approach is supported by a case study reported on by Diamond and Sigmundson in 1997. They aimed to show that a child cannot be socialised to take on the role of the opposite sex.

Procedure

Diamond and Sigmundson researched the case of a boy who had been raised as a girl. They conducted interviews to help them to describe the life history of this boy.

The boy was one of a pair of twins born in Canada in 1965. When they were 8 months old, the boys went to hospital for a routine circumcision operation. However, one of the twins, Bruce, suffered a terrible accident. During the operation, most of his penis was accidentally burnt off. At this time, reconstructing a new penis was not an option. So his parents took advice from a number of experts. A psychologist named Money recommended that Bruce was raised as a girl instead. He believed that babies were not born with their gender, and that it was upbringing that made them masculine or feminine.

When Bruce was 17 months old, he had his testes removed. He was re-named Brenda by his parents, who then began to treat him as a girl. The plan was that they would bring up Bruce as their daughter, not their son. Brenda was too young to know what had happened. As 'she' got older, she was led to believe that she had been born a girl.

HOW SCIENCE WORKS

See Research in Psychology for more information on:

- **Case study**, page 165
- **Interviews**, page 162.

Grade Studio

Candidates sometimes struggle to work out what the procedure is in a case study. Because case studies are not set up like other investigations, there is not always an obvious design. To earn marks in an exam, it is fine to describe the background to a case study as this comes before the findings.

Results

At first, Money was heavily involved in the case. He frequently interviewed and observed Brenda. He reported that she had adapted to her new gender role well. For example, he claimed that she enjoyed playing with girls' toys and had no reason to believe she was any different from other girls of her age.

However, when Brenda reached puberty, there were some problems. To begin with, she needed to be given hormones to help her to develop a more female shape (e.g. breasts and hips). Despite this, she was said to have quite a masculine appearance and masculine mannerisms. Brenda later reported that she had felt like a man inside. For example, she found other girls attractive and rejected boys who were interested in her. She preferred more masculine activities, such as sports, and wanted to 'hang out' with her brother.

At the age of 13, life had become so difficult for Brenda that her parents decided to tell her the truth about her past. When Brenda found out she had been born a boy she was actually quite relieved. It helped to explain the strange feelings she had about her gender. Soon after finding out about her true sex, Brenda decided to live the rest of her life as a man. She renamed herself David. Eventually, David ended up having a penis reconstructed, married a woman and became a father by adopting her children.

Diamond and Sigmundson concluded that the effect of David's chromosomes had outweighed the attempts to socialise him as a girl. In other words, gender is more a product of nature than nurture.

Figure 1.5 *This book cover shows an early picture of Bruce, after his parents had started to raise him as a 'girl'.*

Methodological limitations

- **Case studies rely on small samples, so it is difficult to generalise.** In this case, the sample is one individual. Just because Bruce could not adapt to his new gender role does not mean that other boys would not be able to. Bruce may have been the exception to the rule.

- **Case studies are based on naturally occurring situations, so it is not possible to control key variables.** The case of Bruce was complicated by certain factors. For example, he had a twin brother who looked just like him. This gave him a masculine role model that he could easily imitate. In addition, Bruce was raised as a boy for over a year and a half. Ideally, he should have been socialised as a girl from birth. Finally, his parents obviously knew that he was a boy really so they may not have treated him exactly as they would have done if he was truly their daughter.

- **Case studies are very thorough investigations, so researchers may become too involved in what they are studying. When this happens, researchers may stop being objective.** Money, for example, was accused of interpreting Brenda's behaviour to suit his approach. He was so keen to show that a boy could be raised as a girl that he failed to report on the fact that Brenda was struggling with her feminine gender identity.

Applications of Research into Sex and Gender

Equal opportunities for the sexes

Research into sex and gender is important for real-life situations. It is crucial that psychologists discover which gender differences, if any, children are born with. The point is that if males and females naturally have different strengths or abilities then there is little we can do about this. However, if males and females are born more or less the same, then they can potentially achieve the same kinds of things.

Equal opportunities in education

There is still a lot of debate about how different females and males are. As we have seen in this chapter, there is also still a lot of debate about whether any differences are natural or socialised. This debate is particularly relevant to equal opportunities for the sexes. If males and females are essentially the same, then we just need to give them the same opportunities to succeed. However, what happens if one sex has a natural advantage

1.7

Questions on the core study

Answer the following questions on Diamond and Sigmundson's case of the boy raised as a girl.

1 Give the sex of the child in the case study. [1]

2 Outline what Money believed about a person's gender. [2]

3 Give one piece of evidence that suggested Brenda's gender was feminine. [1]

4 Give the gender of Brenda after puberty. [1]

5 Outline how the study supports the biological approach. [2]

6 Briefly explain why it was useful for the researchers that Bruce had a twin brother. [3]

7 Describe the ethical problems raised by this study. [4]

8 Explain why the findings from the case may be unreliable. [6]

over the other sex? We may need to use positive discrimination to create better opportunities for the disadvantaged sex. For example, what if boys naturally struggle with reading and writing more than girls do? It may be that schools need to put more resources into helping boys with their literacy. Similarly, if girls struggle more with mathematical tasks, then schools may need to put more resources into helping them.

A lot of the evidence shows there are very few natural differences between females' and males' abilities. Despite this, females are doing significantly better than males in both GCSEs and A-Levels. This is sometimes known as 'the gender gap' in education.

How do we explain the gender gap in education? If females are performing better than boys in education yet they are not naturally better – then what is it down to? A lot of psychologists would argue that it must be to do with socialisation. In other words, we bring up girls and teach girls to be more successful at school. Interestingly, before the 1980s, it was the other way round in the UK. Males used to do much better than females in secondary education and beyond. Is this because girls were not encouraged to be successful in education? Or does the school curriculum now take into account girls' natural interests and abilities more than it used to?

We have suggested that there aren't that many natural differences between male and female ability. However, there is evidence of some. There is a lot of reliable evidence to suggest that males have better visual-spatial skills than females. This would suggest that teachers need to spend more time developing these skills in female students to give them the same opportunities as boys. For example, female students may need more instruction in map reading skills in Geography, more support in doing transformations in Mathematics, and more coaching in hand–eye co-ordination in PE. Meanwhile, there is reliable evidence to suggest that females are stronger verbally. This means that teachers may need to find other ways of testing and assessing male students, besides getting them to talk about what they know.

Equal opportunities in work

Despite the fact that females perform better than males in education, it is men that seem to do better in the workplace in terms of promotion and pay. This might suggest that there is a need for more equal opportunities in the workplace (see Activity 8.1).

ACTIVITY

1.8

Use the website www.direct.gov.uk and search for information on 'sex discrimination'.

When you have read the laws about sex discrimination, consider the two questions below.

1 Do you think that sex discrimination laws assume that males and females are born equal? Justify your answer.

2 Can you think of any circumstances in which male and female employees would have to be treated differently because of natural differences?

Equal opportunities in leisure and play

ACTIVITY

1.9

Imagine you are a teacher in charge of organising a fun activity day for a group of 10- to 11-year-olds. The idea is to think up lots of games they could play, both outdoors and indoors. One of your colleagues suggests that you might want to organise different games for boys and girls because, in his words, 'they naturally like different things'.

How would you argue that boys and girls are capable of taking part in the same activities? What activities would you choose and why?

DOING RESEARCH

This topic started by assuming that there were differences between females and males. The debate is about where these differences come from. However, it might be worth investigating whether gender differences exist in the first place. What would your hypothesis be? Would you predict there are gender differences between the sexes, or not?

Your brief is to carry out an investigation into gender differences between the sexes. You should do this using the questionnaire method. You will need to survey a sample of males and a sample of females, and ask them the same set of questions. Your aim is to discover whether they score differently on different traits. It might be that they score differently on some traits and not others.

Remember, when you carry out the questionnaire you should make sure that anything you find out is confidential. People can be sensitive about their gender and you are probably going to be asking them about some very personal characteristics. Think about the ways in which you can ensure confidentiality.

It is up to you how you design your questionnaire. You can also decide how many traits you ask about and what they are. If you need some help designing your questionnaire, here are some ideas:

HOW SCIENCE WORKS

See Research in Psychology for more information on:

- **Hypotheses**, page 151
- **Questionnaire**, page 161
- **Confidentiality**, page 158
- **Closed questions**, page 161
- **Mode**, **median** and **mean**, page 168
- **Bar charts**, page 169

- Simply ask your respondents to rate themselves on a list of traits, using a scale (e.g. 1 to 10). Remember to explain how to use the scale.

- You could give respondents a small scenario and ask them what they would do in that situation (e.g. a violent situation).

- You could give them multi-choice answers. Each answer can be given a different score and the answers given can then be rated using these scores.

- You could write statements (e.g. 'I like to gossip with others') and ask them to say whether they 'strongly agree', 'agree', etc. 'Strongly agree' would score higher than 'strongly disagree'.

You will notice that all of the examples use closed questions because there are pre-set answers.

As you are scoring respondents in some way, you should also be able to present your findings using averages: either a mode, a median or a mean. For example, you could calculate the males' mean score for aggression and compare it with the females' mean score for aggression.

You should also be able to present your results using bar charts. You should use these charts to show the difference between male and female responses.

Looking at your results, was your hypothesis right?

Summary

- Sex and gender are different terms: sex is biological and gender is more psychological. Gender can be categorised as masculine, feminine or androgynous.

- The biological approach suggests that gender, like sex, is naturally determined by chromosomes and hormones. Gender roles are instinctive and a product of evolution.

- The psychodynamic approach offers an alternative explanation for gender development. It says that gender is determined by the relationships children have with their parents. Gender roles develop when boys resolve the Oedipus complex with their fathers, and girls resolve the Electra complex with their mothers.

- Diamond and Sigmundson's case study of Bruce supports the biological approach. The case shows that psychologists were unable to raise a male child as a girl, after his penis had been accidentally removed.

- Research into sex and gender provides useful insights into equal opportunities for males and females.

ExamCafé

Revision

Summarise Content

The following key terms have their consonants missing. Can you work out what they are?

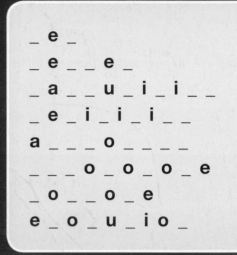

```
_ e _
_ e _ _ e _
_ a _ _ u _ i _ i _ _
_ e _ i _ i _ i _ _
a _ _ _ o _ _ _ _
_ _ _ o _ o _ o _ e
_ o _ _ o _ e
e _ o _ u _ i o _
```

Common Mistakes

It is easy to mix up similar terms in this topic, such as XX and XY chromosomes, and the Oedipus and Electra complexes. It may help to colour code terms. When you write down a definition of a female term (e.g. oestrogen), perhaps put it on a pink Post-it. When you write down a male term (e.g. testosterone), use a blue Post-it. It might be a bit stereotypical, but it could help you to remember which terms are associated with females, and which are associated with males.

Revision Checklist

Draw up a table as shown below.

	Males	Females
Biological approach	Have XY chromosomes	
Psychodynamic approach		Experience Electra complex

Complete the table to summarise the biological approach and the psychodynamic approach of gender development.

For each approach, list what it says about males' development and females' development. Part of the table has been completed for you as examples.

Exam Preparation

Time is precious in the exam. For that reason, you do not want to write any more than you have to. Equally, you do want to write enough for the marks available. Indeed, it is the 'marks' that are key. Get used to looking at the marks at the end of a question and working out how much you need to write. For example, a 1-mark question may only require one word, phrase or sentence. If a question is worth 3 marks but requires three things (e.g. three categories of gender), each of those will also only be worth a mark each. At the other end of the scale, a question worth 6 or 10 marks requires a more detailed response. It will often require you to 'describe' or 'explain' or 'evaluate'. This will need to be written in sentences, and you should attempt to go into some depth.

Practice Questions

Here are some examples of questions covering a range of marks.

1 From the options below, identify the male sex chromosomes. [1]

XX

XY

YY

2 Name the hormone associated with females. [1]

3 Outline what is meant by the Oedipus complex. [3]

4 Explain the difference between sex and gender. [3]

5 Describe and evaluate the biological approach of gender development. [10]

Examiner's Tip:
Q3. For 3 marks, you would need to make 3 separate points about this concept. If it was worth 2 marks, then 2 points would be enough.

Examiner's Tip:
Q4. This question requires a balanced answer. You need to say as much about 'sex' as you do about 'gender'. You can assume that a description of each concept is worth 2 marks. However, to guarantee 3 marks, you need to demonstrate in some way how the concepts are different (or opposites of each other).

Sample Student Answer

Q5. The biological approach of gender development states that sex and gender are inter-related. Since sex is biologically determined by genetics, the approach believes the same is true of gender.

In terms of genetics, it is the sex chromosomes that decide a person's sex and gender. XX gives a female baby who will grow up to be feminine and XY gives a male baby who will grow up to be masculine. This means that boys are instinctively more aggressive than girls, for example. On the other hand, girls are instinctively more sensitive than boys.

Examiner says:
A good general introduction which identifies some broad assumptions in the biological approach.

Examiner says:
This paragraph includes some useful ideas, such as the effects of chromosomes and instinct. However, it would have been better if the candidate had made some reference to hormones. This would have helped to show the link between genes and behaviour.

The biological approach is supported by the Diamond and Sigmundson case study. This case study describes a boy who was castrated when he was young because he had lost his penis in a nasty accident. Because he did not look like a boy any more, a psychologist advised his parents to bring him up as a girl. However, this did not work because the 'girl' always felt like a boy inside. This shows we cannot change a person's gender just by how we treat them. Gender is much more to do with biology.

Examiner says:
This counts as evaluation. Presenting evidence for an approach is an effective way of showing that an approach might be right.

However, in contrast to the above, there are cases where children have been successfully raised as the opposite sex, for example in cases where babies are born with ambiguous genitals so it is not clear what sex they are. Sometimes they are raised as the wrong sex but still adapt to their gender role.

Examiner says:
Looking at 'evidence against' as well as 'evidence for' helps to balance the discussion.

Another problem for the biological approach is the fact that some people do not behave as expected for their sex. If gender was just about chromosomes, then wouldn't all men and all women just behave in more or less the same way? You can have two men, both with XY chromosomes, but one may be masculine and the other may be feminine.

Examiner says:
This is not the best evaluation point to make. Men may be different because of different hormone levels. However, this candidate has forgotten to discuss hormones.

Examiner says:
Overall, a good essay that demonstrates understanding. The candidate has attempted to look at both sides of the approach.

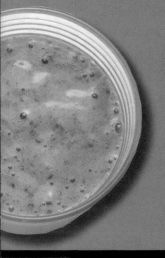

Memory

The cognitive approach in psychology focuses on studying the mind rather than just behaviour. Cognitive psychologists are interested in understanding thought processes. Memory is central to thinking and therefore is a popular area of investigation in cognitive psychology.

Indeed, people in general are interested in understanding how their memory works. For example, an understanding of memory is useful for students wanting to revise for exams. It is also useful for those of us who tend to forget everyday things, such as what we came to the shop to buy, or the name of a person we have just met!

LEARNING OBJECTIVES:

By the end of this topic, you should be able to:

1 Understand the key concepts of
 - *information processing*, including input, encoding, storage, retrieval and output
 - *accessibility* problems and *availability* problems.

2 Have insight into the *multi-store model of memory*, including considering the *levels of processing theory* as an alternative explanation of memory.

3 Demonstrate knowledge of Terry's experiment into the *serial position effect* in the recall of television commercials.

4 Show awareness of applications of research into memory.

Key Concepts

Information processing

Many cognitive psychologists take an **information processing** approach to studying memory. They believe that the human memory processes bits of information *in stages*, much like a computer processes data. Indeed, a lot of cognitive psychologists find it useful to compare the human memory with a computer memory. They believe that this helps them to explain how the human memory works.

According to cognitive psychologists, there are five main stages to information processing. These are shown in Figure 2.1.

BUZZWORDS

Information processing – The idea that information is processed through a number of stages

Figure 2.1

Grade Studio

Candidates are often good at learning the stages of information processing and getting them in the right order. However, this shows knowledge but not understanding. It is important that you can describe each stage as well as state it. You may have to answer questions in which you outline the meanings of such terms as 'input' and 'encoding'.

ACTIVITY

2.1

Look at the following stages of memory. Using the information-processing approach, put them in the correct order and label them as input, encoding, storage, retrieval and output.

- The student searches for possible answers to the question.

- The student makes sense of the teacher's question.

- The student tells the teacher what they think the answer is.

- The student thinks they have found the answer to the question.

- A teacher asks a student a question about who carried out a particular study.

These five stages apply to both the human memory and the computer memory:

1 **Input** is the first stage, and involves information entering the memory from the environment. In computer terms, this is like typing something into a keyboard or clicking the mouse. In human terms, inputs come through the senses. For example, most data entering the human memory is visual and therefore comes through the eyes.

2 **Encoding** is the stage after input. Encoding involves putting information into a format that the memory system can recognise. In computer terms, most data is encoded into binary code (a code that only uses zeros and ones). For example, when we type the letter 'Q' on a keyboard it is represented in the memory system as 01010001. In human terms, we have to represent data in a format that the mind can cope with. For example, if we see a skyscraper in front of us, we cannot store it in that form if we want to remember it. We have to represent it as 2D (rather than 3D) and have to scale it down. In other words, we have an *image* of the skyscraper in our memory rather than the skyscraper itself. When visual data is turned into an image it has been encoded. In the same way that images are a reflection of what we see, then echoes are a reflection of what we hear. Therefore, we use echoes to encode sounds into memory.

3 **Storage** follows encoding. This is how information is 'filed away' to be used at a later date. In computer terms, this may involve saving a document. In human terms, we place information somewhere in a memory store so that it is available to be used again.

4 **Retrieval** happens after storage. Information has to be stored somewhere in order for it to be retrieved. In computer terms, retrieval may involve searching for a file, or opening the last document you saved. In human terms, we are literally searching the memory store for information – sometimes this is easy and sometimes quite hard! Sometimes we simply cannot find the piece of information we are trying to retrieve – in which case, we say we have forgotten it.

5 **Output** is the final stage, after retrieval. In computer terms, this may involve opening a file on screen or printing off a document you have retrieved. In human terms, it might be saying something or writing it down. However, outputs do not have to be that literal. When we conjure up an image in our minds, or recall a song we heard earlier, or simply have a thought – these are outputs too.

Accessibility and availability

It has already been suggested that retrieval, and therefore output, are not always straightforward. Computers may be very good at finding stored information and finding it quickly but human beings are not so efficient. We experience 'forgetting' every day of our lives.

There are two main problems associated with forgetting: **accessibility problems** and **availability problems**.

Accessibility problems occur when we cannot get to a piece of information in the memory. In other words, we know it is there but we just cannot retrieve it. You may have experienced the 'tip of the tongue' phenomenon, when you feel sure you know something but just cannot recall it there and then. This is a good example of inaccessible information. Another is when you see someone you have not seen for a long time and cannot remember their name. However, later in the day it comes back to you. In other words, you have accessed the information at last.

The following activity should illustrate that some information is inaccessible rather than unavailable.

ACTIVITY

2.2

Look at the following list of countries and see how many of their capital cities you can recall.

1	Portugal	6	Thailand
2	Denmark	7	Kenya
3	Egypt	8	Iraq
4	Canada	9	Australia
5	Venezuela	10	Czech Republic

You may have just experienced that 'tip of the tongue' phenomenon – you feel sure you *know* the answers but cannot quite recall them. In other words, the answers are inaccessible.

A good way to access information is by using cues. In this case, the initial letter of each capital city may help you to recall them. These are given below.

1 L   2 C   3 C   4 O   5 C   6 B   7 N   8 B   9 C   10 P

Did the above cues help? If so, it means that some of the information was inaccessible rather than unavailable.

Availability problems are more serious, as this suggests that information is no longer in the memory at all. Some psychologists believe that we lose information if we do not use it enough, or if there is not enough room for it. For example, you may know all the names of your teachers now, but when you do not have to see them every day, you will eventually forget them for good because they are not necessary to hold in storage. It is almost like deleting a file in a computer memory. Not all psychologists agree that memories become unavailable. Some psychologists believe that once a piece of information has been stored long term, it is in the memory forever.

ACTIVITY

2.3
Think about the kind of things you forget. From your own experience, do you think you suffer more accessibility problems or more availability problems? What kind of information becomes unavailable? Is it different from information that becomes inaccessible?

HINT

It is easy to get availability and accessibility problems muddled. Think of a way of distinguishing between them. For example, you may notice that unavailable has the letter 'v' in it. If you think of 'v' for 'vacant' and know that vacant can mean 'empty' – it might help you to remember the idea of an empty store with nothing in it anymore.

Core Theory: Multi-Store Model

There are a number of theories that cognitive psychologists have put forward to explain how the human memory works. One of the most well-known theories is the multi-store model of memory.

The main idea behind the multi-store model is that the human memory system is made up a number of *separate* and *distinct* stores. It also believes that memory is affected by two main factors: time and space. The importance of time can be seen by the labels given to the two main stores: the **short-term memory** (STM) and the **long-term memory** (LTM).

The multi-store model can be illustrated using a diagram, as shown in Figure 2.2.

2

COGNITIVE PSYCHOLOGY

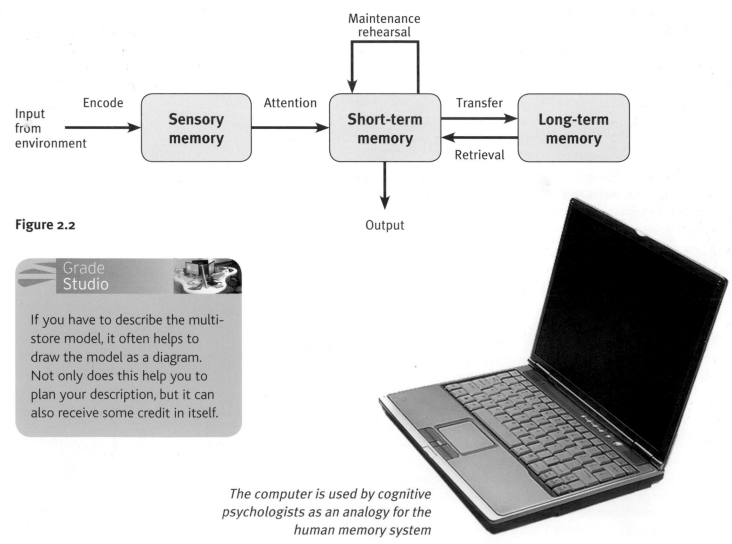

Figure 2.2

Grade
Studio

If you have to describe the multi-store model, it often helps to draw the model as a diagram. Not only does this help you to plan your description, but it can also receive some credit in itself.

The computer is used by cognitive psychologists as an analogy for the human memory system

According to the multi-store model:

- The human memory system needs an input. Without an input, there is nothing to store in the memory. This input comes from the environment.
- This input needs to be encoded so that it can enter the memory stores.
- The first store that information enters is the **sensory store**. This store holds all the information that is immediately around us (e.g. sights, sounds, smells) but only for a few seconds.
- If we do not pay **attention** to the information in the sensory store, the information simply **decays**.
- If we do pay attention to information it is processed into STM. Psychologists believe that only about one per cent of all information waiting in the sensory store actually reaches STM at any one time. This is because there is so much going on around us that we can only give our attention to a small amount of it. Sometimes, we give our attention to information because we have to (e.g. a teacher tells us it is important to listen) or sometimes we give our attention to information because it just 'grabs us' (e.g. when someone attractive walks past us). Either way, when we are *conscious* of something (because it has our attention), it is then in STM.
- STM has a limited **capacity** and a limited **duration**, so information will not be held for very long in this store. Very soon, information will either decay (because time has run out) or will be **displaced** (when STM has run out of space because of other items coming in). If decay or displacement happens, then the information becomes unavailable (i.e. it is gone for good).
- To keep information in STM, we need to keep repeating or practising it (e.g. repeating a phone number, constantly looking at someone's face). This is known as **maintenance rehearsal**. This puts information into a 'loop' so that it can be maintained. If we rehearse information for about 30 seconds then it should transfer into LTM.
- LTM has an unlimited capacity and an unlimited duration. This means that once information is in LTM, it is supposedly there forever. Psychologists estimate that about 25 per cent of the information that reaches STM goes on to LTM.
- Even though information is stored in LTM permanently – and should never be displaced – we do not automatically remember it. Information still needs to be retrieved from LTM and brought back into STM so that it can be output.
- Retrieval is not always possible (i.e. when information is inaccessible). In other words, it is in LTM but we cannot find or reach it. However, it may be retrievable at a later date or when someone or something gives us a cue.

As stated already, the LTM has an unlimited capacity and an unlimited duration. Meanwhile, the STM has a limited capacity and limited duration. But what are the limits?

BUZZWORDS

Sensory store – The store where all immediate information is briefly held unless it is paid attention to

Attention – A process that makes people aware of information in the memory

Decay – This is the fading of information over time until it is forgotten

Capacity – This refers to the amount of space in the memory

Duration – This refers to how long information lasts in the memory

Displacement – A process in which information is 'shunted out' of storage by new information, and so becomes forgotten

Maintenance rehearsal – A process that basically involves repeating information so that it stays in storage, either temporarily or permanently

ACTIVITY

2.4

Use the description of the multi-store model to explain how you would go about learning and remembering a new mobile number.

The capacity of STM is measured in something called 'chunks'. The multi-store model argues that the capacity of STM is 7 ± 2 chunks. This means that the average person can hold 7 chunks in their STM. However, some people can only hold as few as 5 chunks (7–2), whereas others can hold as many as nine chunks (7 + 2).

However, research shows that it is impossible to hold 10 or more chunks of information at the same time in STM. Some of us may think that we can hold many more than ten bits of information at once – for example, all of the words in this sentence! This is why it is important to understand what a 'chunk' is. A chunk can be one piece of data or it can be a group of related pieces of information. For example, the letters D, A, R, L, I, N and G may take up the 7 spaces in the average person's STM. However, if you recognise that the letters spell the word 'DARLING', then this only takes up 1 chunk. For example, the digit string 1819665236512 has too many single digits for anyone's STM. However, if you recognise it as 18 (voting age), 1966 (when the England football team won the World Cup), 52 (number of playing cards in a pack), 365 (days in a year) and 12 (a dozen), then this only requires 5 chunks (1 for each piece of information). Performers who claim to have amazing memory capacities could just be very good at chunking! In other words, when they are given a long list of items to remember they are just able to relate them to each other so that they can be stored in one chunk or space.

ACTIVITY

2.5

In real life we seem to recognise the importance of the limited capacity of short-term memory.

1 Explain why car registration plates are not any longer than seven characters.

2 List other real-life examples in which items are blocked into seven.

The duration of STM is measured using more familiar units: seconds. The multi-store model argues that the duration of STM is between 10 and 20 seconds. In other words, if a person was given some information but did not or could not rehearse it, then it would stay in STM for around 15 seconds on average. For example, imagine a teacher telling you what page number to turn to (and you pay attention of course!), but then you are distracted by a friend talking to you. In theory, as long as it has not been displaced, the information should still be there about 15 seconds later. Of course, if information is rehearsed in STM it will last for longer than 20 seconds and may even transfer to LTM.

The multi-store model mainly focuses on how the human memory system works. Of course, it does not always work and this is when forgetting occurs.

Figure 2.3 *The fact that car registration plates are only seven characters long can be related to the capacity of STM.*

Forgetting

Displacement is one theory of forgetting. As mentioned above, this happens when a memory store runs out of space because it is overloaded. For example, if a waiter has a long list of drinks to remember, the earlier ones may get 'shunted out' by any new ones entering STM from the end of the order. Another example might be if we are introduced to a lot a new people, one after the other, at a party. We may well forget the names of the first couple of people that we were introduced to.

HOW SCIENCE WORKS

See Research in Psychology for more information on:

- **Hypotheses,** page 151
- **Independent variables** and **dependent variables,** page 153.

ACTIVITY

2.6

To test displacement theory, work with a small group of other students and carry out the following experiment on each other.

- Each of you needs to write down a list of digit spans (strings of different numbers e.g. 7345031).

- Start with a 5-digit span, then write down a 6-digit span, then 7, and up to a 10-digit span. Don't just add a digit each time – put the digits in a different order.

- When you have done this, test each other by reading out your digit spans one at a time. As soon as you have finished reading each digit span, the others have to write it down as they heard it (with the digits in the right order and no digits missing).

- At the end of the whole experiment, see how many people recalled each digit span correctly. If there is a single digit error then their answer is wrong.

1 What do you predict will happen – that is, what is your hypothesis?

2 What are the independent variable and the dependent variable in this experiment?

3 Look at your findings. What patterns can you see in people's answers? What seems to determine whether people recall a digit span or not?

4 Can you see how your findings relate to displacement theory, or *should have* related to displacement theory?

Decay is another theory of forgetting. To re-cap, this happens over time when a piece of information has not been rehearsed at all or not enough. Decay happens in a matter of seconds in STM. Some psychologists also believe that decay can happen in LTM. Decay occurs because we don't use, or we stop using the information. For example, if we learn French for an exam but never actually practise it or need it afterwards, then it may decay through disuse. Or, someone may have really fond memories of their sixteenth birthday but if they do not think about it for a number of years, they may eventually forget lots of details about it.

2.7

To test the decay theory, work with a small group of other students and carry out the following experiment on each other.

- Each of you needs to have a set of ten trigrams. Trigrams are made up of three different letters that do not mean anything when put together, such as XHT, LGR but *not* DOG or ITV.

- Each of your trigrams should be different and written on a separate piece of card or paper.

- On the other side of each piece, write a different 3-digit number.

When you have done this, test each other in the following way.

One at a time, show your first trigram to each other by holding it up for everyone to see. Only hold it up for 1 second. As you hold it up, say out loud the 3-digit number on the back. As soon as you have said that digit (and put the trigram face down), the others have to count backwards in 3s from the number you have said (e.g. if you say 317, they say 314, 311, etc). You need to time them as they count backwards. After they have been counting backwards for 3 seconds, stop them and ask them to write down your first trigram.

Once you have gone around the group once, repeat the task using your second trigram. However, on the second round, ask the others to count backwards for 6 seconds. In the next round, it should be for 9 seconds, then 12 seconds, and so on. In other words, they count backwards for an additional 3 seconds each time. This means that on the last round of trigrams, they will be counting backwards for 30 seconds.

At the end of the whole experiment, see how many people recalled each of your trigrams exactly.

1 What do you predict will happen – that is, what is your hypothesis?

2 What are the independent variables and the dependent variables in this experiment?

3 Why do you think the trigrams have to be meaningless groups of letters?

4 Why do you think people need to count backwards in 3s before you test their recall?

5 Look at your findings. What patterns can you see in people's answers? What seems to determine whether people recall a trigram or not?

6 Can you see how your findings relate to the decay theory, or *should have* related to the decay theory?

It is easy to confuse the terms 'displacement' and 'decay', so think about them logically. 'Decay' is a word we use in everyday life for when something 'runs out' or 'wears out', which is what happens to information over time. In the same way that your teeth will decay if you do not look after them, pieces of information in the memory will decay if you do not look after (or rehearse) them! You may also notice that the word di**space**ment has the word 'space' within it – which is useful since it is all about running out of space.

Criticisms of the multi-store model

There are a number of criticisms of the multi-store model of memory, including the following:

- **The model is too rigid and ignores individual differences.** It assumes that each person's memory system has the same structure. It does not easily explain why some people have a much better memory than others. Critics argue that some people must have a greater capacity for memory than others. They also argue that some people have good memories for certain types of information, while others have better memories for other types.

- **The model over-simplifies the STM and the LTM.** Critics argue that the STM is not a passive store where information just passes through. They say that the STM is more active than this, and can actually deal with different types of inputs at the same time. Critics also say that there are different types of long-term stores: one for storing general knowledge, one for storing autobiographical events, and one for storing procedures.

- **The model over-emphasises the role of rehearsal.** The point is that not all information stored in LTM has to be rehearsed. For example, we may rehearse something like a telephone number or a person's name to help us remember it. However, do we really rehearse smells and tastes to store them in LTM? In addition, there is a lot of information which is in LTM not because it has been rehearsed but because it has meaning.

An Alternative Theory: Levels of Processing

As stated above, one criticism of the multi-store model is that it over-emphasises the role of *rehearsal* in memory. Critics suggest that we remember things long term because they have meaning, not because we rehearse them. For example, if we are involved in a bad accident or have a brilliant birthday party, we don't remember these events because we rehearse them over in our minds, we remember them because they are significant and meaningful. Similarly, we remember details from lessons more easily when we are interested in them (i.e. because they have meaning), or because we have tried to associate them with something that has meaning (e.g. remembering a list of words using a rhyme). The levels of processing (LOP) theory supports this idea.

The theory says that there are different levels of processing in the memory, from shallow to deep. If we only shallow-process information, then we are not really thinking about its meaning. For example, **shallow processing** includes noticing only the colour a slogan is in, or only recognising whether a person's voice is male or female. We are not processing what the slogan or the person says, so are less likely to recall it. **Deep processing** includes thinking about what a piece of writing means, or trying to understand what a person is saying. If we process information for meaning, we are more likely to recall it.

Grade Studio

When you are evaluating in an extended answer, the examiner is more likely to give you higher marks if you elaborate on points. So rather than just list criticisms of the multi-store model, try to explain them.

MEMORY 2

BUZZWORDS

Shallow processing – Only coding information based on its physical characteristics

Deep processing – Coding information for meaning

Figure 2.4 *Deep processing leads to better recall than shallow processing.*

Grade
Studio

The specification only refers to 'deep processing' under the levels of processing theory. However, it will help you in the exam if you can also describe shallow processing. This is because it allows you to *compare* different levels of processing and how they affect recall.

The LOP theory contrasts with the multi-store model. The LOP theory does not believe that there are different stores in memory. In fact, the LOP theory is not interested in the structures of memory. The theory argues that it is wrong to assume that memory is so limited by structures such as time and space. It states that we can remember vast amounts of information in a short time-span if we can find a way of giving it meaning, or if it already had meaning for us. This is supported by a study in which a group of participants were asked to memorise a large number of real football scores in a short amount of time. Half the participants were non-football fans and the other half were football fans.

The findings showed that the football fans were much better at recalling the match scores than the non-football fans. The LOP theory can explain this. It would say that the scores meant something to the football fans (e.g. it affected where their club was in the league) and so they were able to deep process the information and recall it later. However, because the non-football fans were not really interested in the scores they were simply memorising pairs of meaningless digits. They were therefore shallow processing the information and could not recall it very well later.

2.8

Copy out Table 2.1. Look at the examples in the first column and decide whether they are examples of deep processing or shallow processing. Write your response in the second column.

Table 2.1

Example	Deep or shallow processing?
A student remembers a list of the researcher's names by attaching each name to the face of someone she knows.	
A customer registers what font a logo is written in but not what it was.	
A teacher recognises a series of faces because she rated each one for how pleasant it was.	
A victim recalls that a nuisance caller spoke in a southern accent, but not what was actually said.	
A student says that she can recall what she did last lesson because she thought it was a 'fun' lesson.	

Core Study: Terry (2005)

The multi-store model is supported by a laboratory experiment carried out by Terry in 2005. He aimed to show that a person's memory is affected by factors such as time and space.

Procedure

Terry decided to test people's memories for television commercials. The commercials were about 10 months old at the time of the experiment, and each commercial was for a different product. The commercials were no more than 30 seconds long and were presented in groups of fifteen. Terry varied the order in which the commercials were presented.

Terry used 39 students as his participants. He used a repeated measures design, which meant that the participants took part in both conditions. The independent variable was whether the participants recalled the commercials *immediately* after they were presented or whether they recalled them after a *delay*. During this delay they were doing a written task for 3 minutes. The dependent variable was how many brand names the participants could recall. They could recall them in any order they wished in both conditions.

Results

The results generally showed a *serial position effect*. This means that whether a commercial was recalled depended on where it was in the list (its serial position), not on what the product was.

In the condition where participants recalled the brand names straight away, there was a *primacy effect* and a *recency effect*. Overall, the participants showed good recall of the first few commercials (the

HOW SCIENCE WORKS

See Research in Psychology for more information on:

- **Experiments,** page 159
- **Repeated measures,** page 154
- **Independent** and **dependent variables,** page 153.

primacy effect) and good recall of the last few commercials (the recency effect). This supports the multi-store model because it shows the importance of time and space. The first few brands were remembered well because there was the time to rehearse them and put them in LTM. More recent brands were also remembered well because they were still in STM and could either be recalled instantly or transferred into LTM.

The middle commercials (from the fourth to the twelfth) were not remembered very well – in most cases they had been forgotten. Some of the middle products had been displaced from STM because there wasn't the space for them. Other products had decayed because there was no opportunity to rehearse them in order to transfer them into LTM.

In the delayed recall condition (where the participants had to carry out a written task before recall), there was a primacy effect but no recency effect. The first few brands were still remembered well because they had been transferred to LTM (through rehearsal) before the written task. However, the written task had stopped participants from rehearsing the last few commercials in STM. Doing the task had displaced the products and/or allowed them to decay (see Figure 2.5).

Terry concluded that memory for the television commercials was affected by their serial position in the list and not by their meaning. Whatever product was being advertised, it was poorly recalled if it was presented in the middle of the list. This was because commercials in the middle had been lost due to running out of time and/or space.

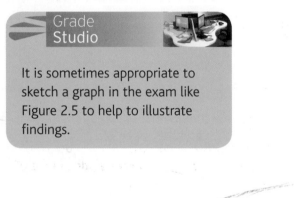

Grade Studio

It is sometimes appropriate to sketch a graph in the exam like Figure 2.5 to help to illustrate findings.

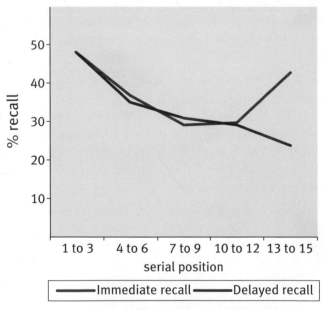

Figure 2.5 *The graph shows the effect of the serial position of television commercials on immediate and delayed recall.*

The limitations of Terry's experiment

- **Laboratory experiments lack ecological validity.** This is because they are carried out in artificial settings that do not reflect real life. In real life, there is a good chance that people would watch television commercials with many other distractions going on around them. They probably would not give commercials the same attention that they are able to under controlled conditions.

- **Experiments often lack construct validity.** This is because experiments often take a narrow measure of what is being investigated – in this case, memory. There is much more to memory than remembering commercials. And even if the experiment only claims to be about memory for commercials, it is artificial to make them all a certain length and for them to all be ten months old.

- **Experiments have the problem of demand characteristics.** This is when it is clear from cues in the study what the researcher is trying to investigate. The participants obviously knew they were being experimented on and may have tried to help Terry achieve the results he wanted. After the written task, they could have realised that he was trying to affect their memory. They may not have recalled the last few products on purpose.

Applications of Research into Memory: Memory Aids

Research into memory aids is important for real-life situations. Memory aids can be used in many areas, but an obvious one is education. Although learning is not always about memorising information, a large part of it is. As you will know, remembering information is particularly important for examinations!

As psychologists have discovered more about how the human memory works (and when it does not work!), they have been able to suggest techniques for improving memory (i.e. memory aids).

Use of cues

When we have learnt something and transferred it to long-term memory, using cues is one way of aiding memory. Cues work on the assumption that 'lost' information is just inaccessible and can be retrieved. Cues help to trigger and therefore access lost information. Cues can trigger memories through any of the senses; for example, the smell of Plasticine may remind someone of an event from their childhood.

Cues can be used very formally as memory aids. For example, a police reconstruction of a crime scene aims to provide visual and verbal cues. By recreating the context of a crime, police hope to trigger witnesses' memories of events. We also use cues more informally. For example, when we mislay something (e.g. a bag) we may 'retrace our footsteps'. As we move from room to room, either literally or in our minds, we are trying to look for

ACTIVITY

2.9

Questions on the core study

Answer the following questions on Terry's laboratory experiment into the serial position effect on the recall of television commercials.

1. State the type of experiment used in the study. [1]
2. Identify the items that had to be recalled. [1]
3. Give the size of the sample. [1]
4. Outline what is meant by the primacy effect. [2]
5. Outline what is meant by the recency effect. [2]
6. Explain why participants were poor at recalling products from television commercials presented in the middle of a block. [4]
7. Terry used a repeated measures design. Give one advantage and one disadvantage of this experimental design. [2]
8. Explain why Terry decided to vary the order in which the television commercials were presented to different participants. [3]

ACTIVITY

2.10

The primacy/recency effect should happen with any list of items, whatever the length of the list and whatever the items (visual or otherwise).

You should put this to the test by compiling your own list of items (e.g. written words, spoken words, pieces of music, pictures, famous faces, flavours).

When you have done this, test as many of your classmates as you can. Remember, you are presenting them with your list and immediately afterwards asking them to recall your items in any order they want.

Plot your findings on to a graph, with 'serial position' on the x-axis and 'frequency of recall 'on the y-axis.

Have you also got a primacy/recency effect? If not, why not? Or are there some items that are well remembered in the middle? Why might this be?

cues to remind us whether we had the bag or not, or where we left it.

Cues can be used in similar ways in education. On a simple level, teachers may use cues in questioning. They may be looking for a specific answer to a question that a student cannot remember. To help the students, a teacher might give them the initial letter of the answer (e.g. 'It begins with F.') or may remind them when they learnt it (e.g. 'I introduced you to it last Thursday when we were in the lab.').

Cues can be used in more sophisticated ways. For example, colour-coding topics gives students a colour cue to trigger the content of the topic (e.g. key concepts in Memory are put on yellow card). Mnemonics also provide cues. This is when a rhyme or sentence is used, so that the initials of the words in the rhyme or sentence correspond to the initials of a list of items that need to be learnt, for example '**N**ever **E**at **S**hredded **W**heat' is commonly used for remembering the order of the points of a compass.

There is evidence that people recall information better if they are in the same context or situation in which they learnt it. This is because there may be lots of visual and other cues around them that help to trigger memories. If we relate this to education, then ideally a student should try to sit their Psychology exam in the classroom in which they had their Psychology lessons! However, this would generally not be allowed. There are ways around this. For example, if a student knew the room they were going to take the exam in, they could try to do some revision in there beforehand. This is not always practical or possible of course. A possible solution is to create cues during revision that can be taken into and used in the exam. For example, a student could wear different perfumes when revising different subjects. On the day of her Mathematics exam, she could wear the perfume that she wore when revising Mathematics. The idea is that the smell would help to trigger memories of what she revised!

Mind mapping

Mind maps help us to revise and remember materials because they are supposed to reflect the way that memory is organised.

ACTIVITY

2.11

Use the website www.bbc.co.uk/schools/gcsebitesize and search for information on 'mind maps'. When you have read about how to construct a mind map, then complete the following activity.

Choose a topic you have studied in Psychology. Put the topic title (e.g. Memory) in the middle and then construct a mind map around it. Remember, whatever topic you choose, it will always branch off into:

- Key concepts
- Core theory
- Core study
- Applications.

Use of imagery

If you have to learn and remember written material, it has been found that relating it to images (or pictures) will help. Not only does it give the material more meaning, it also 'doubles your chances' of remembering it (i.e. by having a word *and* an image).

ACTIVITY

2.12

Imagine you have been asked to make a revision poster for another GCSE topic you have recently studied. Each point needs to be illustrated. Think of images to match the ideas presented.

Either write down or, if you are feeling artistic, draw the types of images you would use to help the ideas to become more memorable.

DOING RESEARCH

Cognitive psychologists have offered a number of ways to improve memory, based on their research.

Your brief is to test a memory aid by setting up your own experiment. You will need an experimental condition (through which you test the technique) and a control condition (to compare it with). You will therefore need to use an independent groups design. This is because you need to test how well some material is recalled with the memory technique, and how well the same material is recalled without the technique. You cannot have the same people looking at the same material twice.

You will need to decide on the memory technique you are going to test. For example, you could test the effect of imagery, mind mapping, cues, chunking or rehearsal. Once you have decided this, you will need to decide what material you are going to use to test the technique. For example, you might use a passage of text to test rehearsal, but you might use a shopping list to test chunking. Obviously, the material needs to be appropriate to the technique.

You will need to test at least five participants in each condition, in order to make a reliable comparison. In your experimental condition, you will need to give clear instructions on how you want them to use the technique. In the control condition, you simply instruct participants to memorise the material you give them.

You need to think about the controls you should or could use. Important controls may include using timings (for presentation and recall), using the same environment (if appropriate) and giving the same instructions each time.

You also need to think about how you are going to measure recall. It is easy if it is a list of words – you simply count how many words are remembered correctly. However, if you give your participants a passage to read, then how are you going to measure the recall? Do they have to recall the whole passage word for word, and you reduce the score if they make a mistake? Or do you ask them questions on the passage, and see how many they get right? Perhaps consider testing recognition rather than recall. Whatever your method of measuring memory, you need to find some way of *quantifying* it so that each participant has a score.

When you have run your experiment, you should be able to calculate an average for each condition. This could be a *mode*, *median* or *mean*. You are checking to see if the participants who use a memory aid do recall more on average than participants who do not.

Look at your results. Do they suggest that the memory aid works?

HOW SCIENCE WORKS

See Research in Psychology for more information on:

- **Experiments**, page 159
- **Independent groups designs**, page 154
- **Modes**, **medians** and **means**, page 168.

MEMORY 2

Summary

- The human memory is like a computer memory – information goes through the stages of input, encoding, storage, retrieval and output. However, it is not always easy to retrieve information from memory. It might just be inaccessible but sometimes it has become unavailable.

- The multi-store model states that memory is made up of three stores: sensory store, short-term memory (STM) and long-term memory (LTM). Each one differs in terms of duration and capacity. Information enters STM through the process of attention and transfers to LTM through the process of rehearsal. According to the multi-store model a lot of information is lost through decay and displacement.

- The levels of processing theory disagrees with the multi-store model, and says that memory is not that limited by time or space. The theory argues that recall is affected by the level to which information is processed. If information is deeply processed (i.e. given meaning) it will be remembered well.

- Terry's experiment into the recall of television commercials supports the multi-store model. This is because the findings show the effect of time and space. However, the findings lacked ecological validity because of the laboratory conditions.

- One application of research into memory is the use of memory aids. These are mainly used in education to help students prepare for exams, and can include techniques involving, for example, cues, mind maps and imagery.

Revision

Revision Tips

Some students learn a lot from actually doing things. Sometimes this can be difficult in Psychology. However, it is possible to *do* something while learning about the multi-store model at the same time. Consider building your own multi-store model with different types of boxes for stores, and materials like string and wires to show the processes in between. You can have a go at deciding how to do it for yourself. Later, remembering what you built may help you to remember the multi-store model.

You have to learn about memory aids because it might be in the exam. Use common sense – if you've got to know how memory aids work then why not use them as part of your revision! You can use the memory aids you are studying to help to revise this topic as well as all the others!

Summarising Content

Label the diagram of the multi-store model of memory, to test your knowledge of the model's key features.

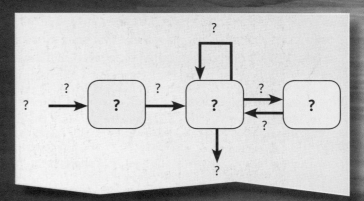

The following statements refer to Terry's experiment into the serial position effect. Decide whether they are true or false.

'Terry carried out his experiment in a natural environment.'

'He used students as his participants.'

'Participants had to recall billboard posters.'

'He used an independent groups design.'

'Terry found that items at the beginning of his presentation were recalled better than those in the middle.'

'When participants' recall was delayed, they remembered fewer of the last items in the list compared with when they could recall items immediately.'

Exam Preparation

Practice Questions

Here are some practice questions and examiner's advice to support you.

1 Outline one memory aid. **[2]**

2 Complete the figure to show the *information processing approach* in memory. **[3]**

3 | **Questions for the teacher**

> **Ross**: Sir, did you say that information gets displaced from short-term memory if it is overloaded?
>
> **Psychology teacher**: Yes, that's right.
>
> **Ross**: And did you say that information decays quickly in short-term memory as well?
>
> **Psychology teacher**: Yes, if you don't have the chance to rehearse it.
>
> **Ross**: Sir, then why do you dictate so much so quickly?

Using the source:

a) Identify the **two** features of short-term memory that Ross and his teacher were discussing.

   i) _____

   ii) _____ **[2]**

b) Give the **two** reasons for forgetting that Ross refers to.

   i) _____

   ii) _____ **[2]**

4 Describe and evaluate **one** study into memory. **[10]**

Examiner's Tip:

Q1. You can answer this question in one of two ways. Either identify a memory aid (e.g. use of cues) and then briefly describe it, or describe a memory aid by covering two features of it.

Examiner's Tip:

Q4. Each of the Unit 1 and Unit 2 exams will end with an essay that asks you to describe and evaluate something. The mark allocation is always the same – 5 marks for demonstrating knowledge and understanding (the description bit) and 5 marks for demonstrating the ability to be analytical, interpretative and critical (the evaluation bit). So do make sure that your essays reflect this balance of skills.

ExamCafé

Sample Student Answer

Craik and Lockhart (1972) carried out an experiment to test the levels of processing theory.

Craik and Lockhart used an independent groups design, in which they divided the participants into three conditions. In each condition, the participants were presented with the same set of words in the same way and at the same rate – these were controls. However, the participants were asked to do something different depending on what condition they were in.

In the first condition, the participants were asked to count how many letter were Es in each word. In the second condition, the participants were asked to think of words that rhymed with each of the words presented. In the last condition, participants were asked to think of words that had similar meanings to the words presented. Just after this, they were given a surprise recall test.

Craik and Lockhart found that participants in the last condition recalled the most words because they had to think of the meaning of the words to do their task. This meant they had been deep processing. Participants in the first condition did worse because they had only been shallow processing the words.

The problem with Craik and Lockhart's research is that it lacks ecological validity. It might also be that participants in the last condition just had better memories than the others. It was also unethical to deceive the participants – they did not know it was a memory experiment.

Examiner says:
This is a good start. If you choose to describe a study which is not the core study, it is worth identifying it clearly in case the examiner is not familiar with it.

Examiner says:
This reads well because the candidate is using technical terms, such as 'independent groups design' and 'controls'.

Examiner says:
The findings are covered quite briefly compared with the procedure. However, at least the candidate does cover them, while a significant proportion of candidates forget to describe findings.

Examiner says:
It is pleasing that the candidate attempts to evaluate the study. However, all of the points are quite brief. If he had attempted to explain each one in more detail, then the evaluation would be as good as the description.

Attachment

Developmental psychology looks at how individuals' thinking and behaviour develops over time. There is a lot of evidence to show that childhood experiences have an effect on how people develop as adults. This can be seen in the area of attachment.

Attachment is an important idea, especially to new parents who want to develop lasting bonds with their babies. There is a great deal of research that suggests babies are affected long term if parents do not bond with them properly. No wonder parents-to-be invest so much money in books and classes in their attempt to 'get it right'. But should they be so anxious? This chapter will try to address this question.

LEARNING OBJECTIVES:

By the end of this topic, you should be able to:

1 Understand the key concepts of
   • *separation protest* and *stranger anxiety*
   • *secure* attachment, *insecure-avoidant* attachment and *insecure-ambivalent* attachment.

2 Have insight into *Bowlby's theory of attachment*, and consider the *behaviourist theory* as an alternative theory of attachment.

3 Demonstrate knowledge of *Hazen and Shaver's survey* of the relationship between attachment types and adult relationships.

4 Show awareness of the applications of research into attachment.

Key Concepts

Attachment

Attachment is sometimes known as bonding. In other words, it describes a relatively strong and lasting emotional tie to another person. Most individuals' first attachment is to their parents or carers. After that, attachments can occur between brothers and sisters, between friends, lovers and with your own children. We seek to stay close to the people we have become attached to.

Research suggests that newborn babies do not show many signs of attachment in the first six months of their lives. Although newborns appear to enjoy being around others, they are not particularly fussy about who those 'others' are!

BUZZWORDS

Attachment – An enduring bond formed with a significant other

ACTIVITY

3.1

Imagine you have been asked to test the following hypothesis:

'nine-month-old infants are more likely to form an attachment compared with three-month-old infants'.

Outline how you would set up an investigation to test this hypothesis.

Grade Studio

In an exam, you may be asked about 'ways of measuring attachment'. Faced with this phrase, candidates can make the mistake of detailing studies into attachment. However, if you remember that 'separation protest' and 'stranger anxiety' are essentially ways of measuring attachment, then you will be able to give a clear and concise answer if it comes up in your exam.

It is at about six months that babies begin to show a strong attachment – usually to their primary caregiver(s). There are well-known ways of investigating whether a child has developed an attachment or not. There are two main measures of attachment: **separation protest** and **stranger anxiety**.

Separation protest measures how much a child is upset when they are left by their primary caregiver(s). If a child has formed an attachment to their primary caregiver, then they will show high levels of distress on separation, such as sobbing, searching for the caregiver and reaching after the caregiver. A child who has not formed an attachment will show little emotion when separated from the caregiver.

Stranger anxiety measures how much a child is afraid when they are in the presence of a stranger. If a child has formed an attachment to their primary caregiver(s), then they will express fear when approached by or left with a stranger. For example, they will start screaming, try to get away from the stranger or appear tense. A child who has not formed an attachment will show little emotion in the presence of a stranger.

Secure, insecure-avoidant and insecure-ambivalent

Not all young infants react in the same way when they have formed an attachment to a caregiver. In the 1960s, an American psychologist named Ainsworth developed a procedure to show that infants formed different types of attachment. She called her procedure the 'strange situation'.

The strange situation involved observing mothers and their children in a laboratory via a one-way mirror. The children were between 12 and 18 months old and so should have easily formed attachments by then.

The strange situation involved a series of stages:

- Mothers and their infants entered the lab.
- The infant played with some toys while the mother was still there.
- A stranger then entered the lab and the mother left.
- The stranger tried to comfort the infant.
- The mother returned and the stranger then left.
- The mother comforted the infant and then left for a second time.
- The child was left alone for a short period of time.
- The stranger returned and tried to interact with the child.
- Finally, the mother returned and picked up the infant, while the stranger left.

Throughout the strange situation, the children were observed to see how they reacted at the different stages. From her observations, Ainsworth was able to identify three distinct attachment types:

- a **secure attachment**
- an **insecure avoidant attachment**
- an **insecure ambivalent attachment**.

Children who showed secure attachments would explore while playing with toys in the lab. They used the mother as a safe base. When the mother left, they showed signs of distress and were easily comforted on her return. They allowed the stranger to comfort them, but much preferred being with the mother. This is described as the best type of attachment because it is one based on trust and security. In total, 70 per cent of infants were securely attached.

Children who showed insecure avoidant attachments did not pay much attention to the mother when playing. Similarly, they were not too distressed when she left the lab. The children were easily comforted by the stranger when they were upset. They tended to ignore the mother whenever she returned to the lab. This is described as a weak attachment because the infant is showing high levels of independence. It was found that 15 per cent of infants were insecure avoidant in their attachments.

Children who showed insecure ambivalent attachments did not stray far from the mother when playing. However, as well as seeking her out, the children would also resist their mothers. These children were extremely distressed when their mothers left, and it was very difficult for strangers to comfort them. Interestingly, when mothers returned to the lab, children were desperate for their attention but would also sometimes push their mothers away once they got it. This is described as a poor attachment because the infants show little trust or security. It was found that 15 per cent of infants were insecure ambivalent in their attachments.

A child's attachment type appears to depend on the way he or she is cared for. This would explain why the most common attachment type differs from country to country. Different cultures have different

Figure 3.1 *There are three types of attachment in infancy.*

3.2

Look at the following examples, and decide which attachment type each child is.

1 Violet hates being left by her parents at nursery. She clings to their legs when they try to leave, and it is very difficult for the nursery workers to calm her down after her parents have gone.

2 Callum does not like it when his parents leave him at the nursery and he likes to have a big hug before they go. However, once they have gone, he soon settles into playing. When his parents pick him up, he is always excited to see them.

3 Anjeli seems to like nursery. As soon as she arrives, she goes straight to the toys and starts playing. She hardly pays attention to the fact that her parents are leaving, and sometimes it is hard even to get her to say goodbye.

3.3

List the people that cared for you in the first three years of your life. Go down this list and highlight the ones you think you formed strong attachments with.

How many did you highlight? Compare your list with other people's. What is the evidence for monotropy?

Monotropy – An attachment to one primary caregiver

Critical period – The first three years of a child's life, when attachment has to take place or there will be long-term consequences

3.4

Are you convinced that there is a critical period for forming an attachment? Can you think of any evidence or examples that support this? Can you think of any evidence or examples that you could use to argue against the idea of a critical period?

Privation – When a child forms no attachment to a caregiver

ideas on how children should be raised. In the UK, as in Ainsworth's study, the most common type of attachment is a secure one. However, in Germany, the most common attachment is insecure avoidant as carers tend to encourage more independence in their children. Meanwhile, in Japan, the most common attachment is insecure ambivalent as carers tend to develop more intense relationships with their children. So, although infant–carer attachments seem to occur across all cultures, we should remember that the nature of those attachments may differ.

Core Theory: Bowlby's Theory

In the 1950s, a famous psychologist named Bowlby developed a very influential theory of attachment. Although it has been criticised in many different ways since then, its key ideas are still valued.

Bowlby believed that humans and other animals are very similar in terms of attachment. His theory was that infants instinctively bond with one key figure. He said that in non-human animals this is nearly always the mother but he argued that it was the same for human beings too.

It is worth noting that Bowlby developed his theory at a time when the primary caregiver was typically the mother. However, the more important point is that Bowlby believed that babies formed a special attachment to just one particular person. He went on to say that this was probably the mother but it could be the person who cared for them the most. The idea of having one special attachment is known as **monotropy**.

Bowlby also believed that the attachment between an infant and its caregiver had to happen at least in the first three years of the infant's life, and preferably in the first year. He described this as the **critical period** for attachment. He said that it was critical in the sense that if children did not form an attachment they would suffer negative psychological effects, particularly in adulthood.

Although unusual, it is possible for a child to not form an attachment. For example, children who are placed in many different foster homes in early childhood may not form a lasting bond with anyone. Alternatively, a child who suffers extreme neglect from their parents, and experiences no love or care, will not have the opportunity to form an attachment. When a child does not form any attachment with any significant person it is known as **privation**.

Research shows that the effects of privation can be extreme. There are distressing cases of children who have been essentially locked away by their parents from birth. In these cases, children develop poor social skills, poor language skills and even poor motor skills (e.g. co-ordination problems). More worryingly, these negative effects seem to persist even when children are found, taken into care and given support and treatment. This means that they also suffer as adults. This fits in with Bowlby's idea that the effects of privation are irreversible.

As well as privation, children can experience **deprivation**. This occurs when an attachment is formed but then broken at a later date. Bowlby called this 'maternal deprivation', but the bond can be broken with any primary caregiver. He said that children experience deprivation if they are separated from the caregiver for a week or longer within the first five years of life. For example, if a father leaves home and loses contact with his children, they may suffer from the effects of deprivation. Other examples of deprivation include parents dying or spending a period of time in hospital.

Although the effects of deprivation tend to be less extreme compared with privation, they are still damaging. Research has shown that deprivation can make children over-demanding and clingy, and they may develop a phobia of going to school. In adulthood, deprivation has been associated with depression and aggression. Bowlby carried out some research himself on deprivation. He studied a group of teenage

BUZZWORDS

Deprivation – When a child has formed an attachment to a caregiver, but this attachment is broken through separation

Figure 3.2 *A child who is neglected may suffer the effects of privation.*

Grade
Studio

In the exam, you may be asked to explain the difference between privation and deprivation. Remember that as well as identifying the difference, you will need to say which is which. This will be important if there are 3 marks available (i.e. 1 mark for stating what privation is, 1 mark for stating what deprivation is and 1 mark for labelling them correctly). This is means you can still get 2 marks if you muddle them up, but the aim is to get full marks!

3.5

Look at the following scenarios, and decide whether they are examples of privation or deprivation.

Child A is a five-year-old who has come to his headteacher's attention after developing behavioural problems. His behaviour seems to be related to the fact that his father was sent to prison last year to serve an 18-month sentence.

Child B's mother died in childbirth. Tragically, her father committed suicide just two weeks later. For the past year she has been waiting to be adopted. In that time, she has had three different foster carers.

Child C is two years old. Her mother has recently had a second child but, because of severe post-natal depression, the mother has been admitted to hospital with the baby boy. She has already been there for three weeks. The father has contacted the health visitor because he is concerned that his daughter's development is being affected.

Child D is a three-year-old who has been taken into care. This happened after it was discovered that her parents had left her to go on holiday for two weeks. Her fifteen-year-old auntie was looking her after.

Child E is a twelve-month-old infant who has just been taken from his mother, who is an alcoholic. She is a single parent, living alone, who has basically put him in danger, as well as neglected him by paying him little attention and giving him no affection.

GradeStudio

If you have to evaluate Bowlby's theory in the exam, make sure you are actually being critical of his theory rather than just describing it. Do not write, 'he said effects of deprivation were irreversible' when what you mean is 'he was wrong for stating that the effects of deprivation were irreversible'. For example, writing that 'he believed we had one primary caregiver' is descriptive but saying 'he ignored multiple attachments' is evaluative. Or writing 'he stated there was a critical period for attachment' is descriptive but writing 'he was too inflexible on when attachment should take place' is evaluative.

boys and found that those that had experienced maternal deprivation were more likely to be 'affectionless psychopaths'. This was a term he used to describe criminals who were not only deviant but showed a lack of remorse and guilt.

In the same way that problems in attachment can lead to negative effects, then successful attachment can have positive effects. Basically, children who develop secure attachments as infants are more likely to have effective relationships throughout their lives, whether they are family relationships, intimate relationships or relationships with friends and peers.

Criticisms of Bowlby's theory

There are a number of criticisms of Bowlby's theory of attachment, including the following:

- **Bowlby believed in monotropy but his critics say that children can develop multiple attachments.** There is a lot of evidence, particularly in this day and age, that children can have a number of attachment figures. As well as attaching to mothers, children can bond with fathers, grandparents and paid carers (e.g. nannies or child-minders).

- **Bowlby believed that there was a critical period for forming attachments but his critics say that this was too extreme.** More recent research suggests that there may be a sensitive period for attachment rather than a critical period. This means that the first three years may be the best time to form an attachment but it is not the only time. In other words, there is evidence that children can form healthy bonds with others even after the age of 3 (e.g. with an adoptive parent).

- **Bowlby believed that the effects of deprivation were irreversible but his critics say that they can be reversed.** For example, there is a famous case of two Czech twins who spent the early years of their life locked in a cellar after their mother had died. They were cruelly treated by their father and stepmother to the point of suffering deprivation. However, when they were taken into care they gradually got over the abuse and neglect. They formed strong bonds with the family that fostered them and both twins went on to have successful marriages.

- **Bowlby's theory states that attachment is primarily instinctive, whereas others believe that it is a learnt behaviour.** In other words, babies do not naturally bond with caregivers but instead learn to bond with them. This is explained by the behaviourist theory of attachment.

An Alternative Theory: the Behaviourist Theory

The behaviourist theory says that attachment is not an **instinctive** process but relies on learning and experience (i.e. on nurture).

Infants learn to attach to people through a process of reinforcement. Reinforcement refers to learning by consequences. If the consequence of a behaviour is positive, then a person will repeat that behaviour. For example, if a child gets a sticker (a reward) for using a potty, they are more likely to use the potty again. Or if a child gets attention (which can be rewarding) for being naughty, then they are more likely to be naughty again. The same logic can be applied to attachment behaviours.

If an infant interacts with its caregiver (e.g. by gazing at them, smiling, cooing, or even crying) then they will get attention and this is rewarding for him or her. More importantly, the caregiver will also feed, comfort and keep the child safe, which

is particularly rewarding. This reinforces the bond between caregiver and infant, which means that attachment behaviours become more common. Of course, attachment is a two-way process and so caregivers also form an attachment because it is rewarding for them, too. Having a child that interacts with you, relies on you and is generally happier in your company is also reinforcing. In short, the infant and the caregiver learn to bond with each other because they both benefit from the relationship. This also explains why children do not bond with caregivers who neglect and abuse them – there is nothing rewarding about the relationship. They may even see relationships as punishing and so avoid them.

ACTIVITY

3.6
Make a list of the things that carers might do that reinforce attachment behaviours in babies.

BUZZWORDS

Instinctive – Natural and automatic

Figure 3.3 *Attachments may develop because they are reinforcing for both infants and their caregivers.*

ATTACHMENT **3**

Remember, you do not need to know the 'alternative theory' (in this case, the behaviourist theory) in as much detail as the 'core theory'. In an exam, you may use it to evaluate the core theory, in which case it is important to know how it contrasts with the alternative theory. For example, the contrast between Bowlby and behaviourists is whether attachment is more down to nature or nurture.

HOW SCIENCE WORKS

See Research in Psychology for more information on:

- **Questionnaires**, page 161
- **Opportunity sampling**, page 157.

In general terms, the behaviourist theory suggests that whether a child attaches or not, or how well they attach, depends on experience. This can be seen in research on the relationship between attachment types and parenting styles:

- Securely attached children tend to have caregivers who are very sensitive to their child's needs. The sensitive caregiver sees things from their child's perspective and correctly interprets their signals. The caregivers are co-operative, accepting and accessible.
- Insecure avoidant children tend to have caregivers who are generally uninterested in their child. These caregivers often reject their child, and can be self-centred and strict.
- Insecure ambivalent children tend to have caregivers who are interested in them but who tend to misunderstand their child's behaviour. As a result, their child cannot really rely on the caregiver's emotional support.

As mentioned previously, upbringing does not only affect the child in the short term but goes on to affect them later in life. For example, research shows that secure infants are less likely to be involved in bullying at school. However, insecure ambivalent children are more likely to end up being bullies whereas insecure avoidant children are more likely to end up being the victims of bullies. There is also an association between attachment type and the quality of people's intimate relationships in adulthood. This is detailed in the core study below.

Core Study: Hazen and Shaver (1987)

The idea that attachment types in infancy affect adult relationships was investigated by Hazen and Shaver using a questionnaire.

Procedure

A questionnaire was used to collect information from an opportunity sample of a group of people aged between 14 and 82. The questionnaire was carried out in the USA, and was advertised as a 'love quiz' in a local newspaper.

Two variables were measured. The first variable was a person's infant attachment type: secure, insecure avoidant or insecure ambivalent. This was assessed using a checklist. The second variable was a person's attitude to their most important love relationship. This was assessed using a series of multi-choice questions.

Readers were asked to send in their completed love quizzes.

1200 replies were received, and of these 620 were analysed.

Results

The first measure showed the distribution of people's attachment types. As expected, most people reported secure attachment types in childhood, as shown in the pie chart on the opposite page (Figure 3.4).

Attachment types were then analysed against attitudes to adult relationships. Findings showed that:

- Adults with secure infant attachments had happy, friendly relationships. They were also more accepting and supportive of their partners despite faults. They were the least likely to be divorced out of the three groups.

- Adults with avoidant infant attachments were afraid of intimacy. They also experienced more highs and lows in their relationships, and were prone to jealousy. They were most likely to say they could get along fine by themselves.

- Adults with ambivalent infant attachments were more prone to obsession. They experienced extreme sexual attraction but also extreme jealousy. They were the most likely to be divorced out of the three groups.

The findings also showed a difference in the average lengths of people's most important intimate relationship between the attachment types (Figure 3.5).

Overall, Hazen and Shaver concluded that there was a clear relationship between the type of attachments that people have developed in infancy and the type of intimate relationships they had in adulthood. This generally shows the long-term effect of attachment.

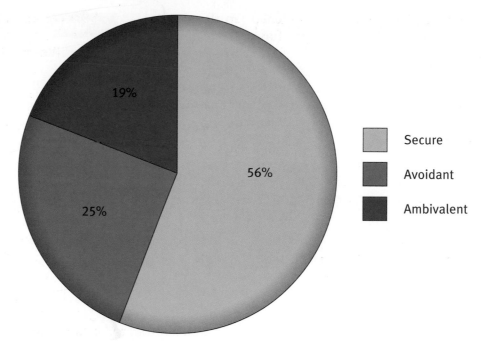

Figure 3.4 *The distribution of attachment types in infancy.*

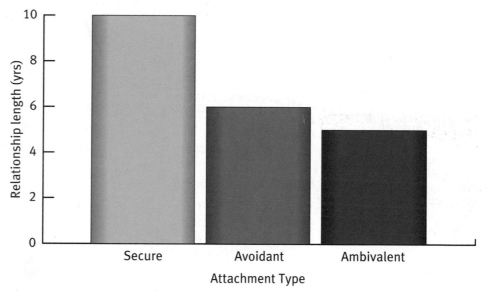

Figure 3.5 *The average length of intimate relationship against attachment type.*

Limitations of Hazen and Shaver's survey

- **The sampling method may have given an unrepresentative sample.** This is because only certain types of people may have responded to the questionnaire, or bothered to send it back. For example, people with particularly poor relationships may not want to do the 'love quiz', so they are missing from the results. In addition, many more females than males did the quiz and so the results are gender-biased. The fact that the quiz only appeared in one newspaper in one locality may also mean that the researchers only accessed a certain class or culture of people.

- **Questionnaires rely too much on respondents giving honest and accurate answers.** Asking people about their upbringing and then about their intimate relationships is quite sensitive, so they may be likely to lie, exaggerate or cover up. It is easier to do this when the questionnaire is anonymous as there is no 'come-back' for people. This questionnaire also relied on people reporting on their childhoods. This may make the results unreliable as people may not have accurate memories of their upbringing. In addition, their perspective on their childhood may be too subjective. Were their infant attachments really as they thought? Compare this to an observation, in which researchers can see things for themselves.

- **The questionnaire used closed (multi-choice) questions which may not have gone into enough depth.** Intimate relationships are complex so it may not be valid to ask about them by getting people to simply select an answer to a question. It may be that people wanted to elaborate or explain their responses, but were not able to.

HOW SCIENCE WORKS

See Research in Psychology for more information on:

- **Gender bias,** see page 172
- **Closed questions,** see page 161.

Applications of Research into Attachment: Care of Children

Most parents and carers want the best for their children, and want them to grow up to be healthy and happy individuals. The research into attachment suggests that the way they care for their children can have a significant impact on the children's development throughout life. On this basis, it is important to look at what counts as good and bad parenting. However, not all childcare takes place in the home, and so it is important to consider other care settings, too, such as nurseries and hospitals.

Care of children in hospitals

Before research was carried out into attachment, it was traditional for hospitals to consider only the physical factors involved in treating and caring for children in hospital. However, the research showed that it is important to consider psychological factors too.

About 50 years ago, it was standard practice in hospitals for newborn babies to be taken away from their mothers almost immediately after their birth. Babies were kept in separate wards in the hospital, usually for over a week. In some cases, mothers did not have contact with their children for the first 24 hours after birth. Even after that, contact was often limited – especially if the baby was in intensive care. One idea was that it protected the mother and baby from infection. Another idea was that it gave the mother a chance to recover from giving birth. However, hospital policies began to change when research showed how important it was for mothers and babies to have the opportunity to bond.

ACTIVITY

3.7
Questions on the core study

Answer the following questions on Hazen and Shaver's survey of the relationship between attachment types and adult relationships.

1 Give the method used to conduct the survey. [1]

2 Identify the two variables measured in the study. [2]

3 Outline how the sample was drawn for this study. [2]

4 State the percentage of the sample that reported having an insecure avoidant attachment in infancy. [1]

5 Calculate the difference in the average length of intimate relationship between people with secure infant attachments and ambivalent infant attachments. [2]

6 Outline one way in which the study was culturally biased. [2]

7 Explain the advantage of Hazen and Shaver using closed questions in their questionnaire. [3]

8 Critics suggest that because Hazen and Shaver's questionnaire was anonymous, it was easier to lie. Explain how an anonymous questionnaire may actually give more valid results. [3]

Findings showed that the more contact a baby had with its mother in the days immediately after their birth, then the better the quality of their attachment. On this basis, hospitals now try hard to encourage bonding between mother and child. For example, as long as there are no problems, babies are given to their mothers to hold straightaway so that they make skin-to-skin contact – the beginning of bonding. In addition, the baby is put at the mother's bedside, so that they can have continual contact.

Bowlby carried out some research in the 1950s, which looked at the effects of hospitalisation on children. Traditionally, parents were not given much access to children who were hospital patients. However, Bowlby disagreed with the limited contact that parents were allowed. He observed that children seemed to go through a number of damaging stages because they were essentially separated from their caregivers. The first stage was protest, in which children were panic-stricken and visibly upset. The second stage was despair, in which children were less upset but became uninterested and apathetic. The final stage was detachment, in which children began to reject their caregiver.

Based on research like Bowlby's, there was a change in hospital policies which still hold today. For example, hospitals tend to have more flexible and more frequent visiting hours for parents and carers with children in hospital. It is also often possible for parents and carers to have a bed in the room with their children and sleep over. Practices like these try to ensure that children do not experience the negative effects of separation.

Care of children in nurseries

Increasingly, parents are using nurseries to help them with their childcare. There is a big debate about whether this is good or bad for children, or about who or how many people should contribute to a child's development or whether it simply makes no difference at all.

ACTIVITY

3.8

Go to the website www.bbc.co.uk and enter 'nurseries risk' into the search engine. You should see an article from 21 October 2006 listed.

Read the article. Based on what you know about attachment, do you agree or disagree with the article?

Draw up a table of the advantages and disadvantages of using nurseries for childcare.

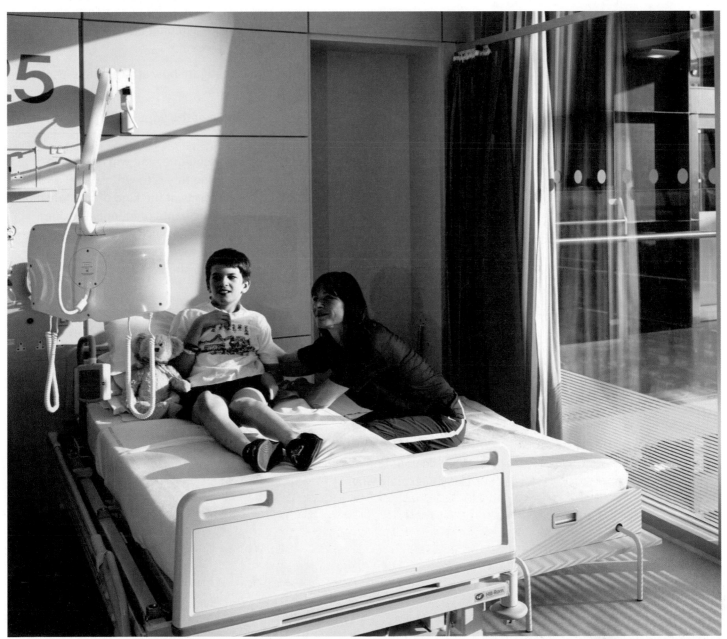

Figure 3.6 *Parents are now allowed to stay in hospitals with children because of research into attachment.*

Care of children in the family

Once upon a time, parents were left very much to their own devices when it came to bringing up children. This also meant it was difficult for them to get help and advice. Nowadays, not only are there organisations that help with child rearing but sometimes they even insist on intervening (e.g. social services).

ACTIVITY

3.9

Imagine that you have been approached by a government organisation which is constructing a website with tips for parenting.

You are the 'attachment' expert, and have been asked to come up with five tips for parents based on research in this area.

What would your five tips be?

HOW SCIENCE WORKS

See Research in Psychology for more information on:

- **Right to withdraw**, page 158
- **Confidentiality**, page 158
- **Questionnaire**, page 161.

DOING RESEARCH

Ainsworth identified three attachment types: secure, insecure avoidant and insecure ambivalent. In the UK population, we would expect most people to show secure attachments (about 70%) and the remaining people to show insecure attachments (about 15% of insecure avoidant and 15% of insecure ambivalent).

Your brief is to use a questionnaire to investigate how attachment types are distributed in the population.

You will need to get a representative sample of the population. Think about how you are going to achieve this.

When you have decided on your sampling technique, you will then need to devise your questionnaire. One way of doing this is to write a brief description of each attachment type (i.e. in terms of the kind of relationships they have with others) and then ask your participants to identify the one which is most like them. You may have other ideas, such as listing traits and getting your participant to rate themselves on each one. Whatever you do, when you survey each of your participants, you should have a reliable way of assessing their attachment type.

Remember, people may be sensitive about discussing themselves and their relationships so do give them the right to withdraw even if they have consented to take part. On the same basis, it is important to keep any information you do collect confidential.

When you have collected your data, you should be able to calculate the percentage of people that show secure, avoidant or ambivalent attachments.

You can then present this data in a pie chart or bar chart.

What do your findings show? Are they different from what is expected? If so, can you explain why?

Summary

- Infants tend to form an attachment to their primary caregiver(s) by the age of 6 months. This can be seen when they display separation protest and stranger anxiety.

- Although most children form attachments, there are different types of attachment: secure, insecure avoidant and insecure ambivalent.

- Bowlby's theory states that attachment is an instinctive process which occurs with one primary caregiver (known as monotropy). The theory goes on to state that the attachment has to happen within a critical period (the first three years of a child's life) otherwise there are serious negative consequences for a child. If no attachment is formed it is known as privation and can lead to problems with development. Even when there is an attachment, children can suffer from deprivation if the attachment is broken. Bowlby's theory states that the effects of privation and deprivation are irreversible.

- Behaviourist theory disagrees with Bowlby's theory and states that attachment is learnt through reinforcement rather than being instinctive. It also states that the effects of deprivation are not irreversible.

- Hazen and Shaver's survey showed that attachment types in infancy have a bearing on the kind of intimate relationships people have as adults. This shows the long-term effects of attachment.

- Applications of research into attachment include childcare practices in settings such as the family home, nurseries and hospitals.

ExamCafé

Revision

Revision Tips

Students can get confused between the different types of attachment. One idea is to make them more 'real', which should help you to remember the differences. For example, if you think that you were a securely attached baby, get a baby photograph of yourself and stick it on your wall. Try pinning words around it, like 'trust' and 'caregiver is safe base', to help remember the features of the securely attached baby. Then do a similar thing with a photograph of a baby who you think is insecure ambivalent (e.g. a family member perhaps?). Finally, get a photograph of a baby who you think is insecure avoidant – it might be someone you babysit for (if you are unlucky!). If you can find a way of using pictures of real children, it may help you to remember the terms associated with their attachment type.

You may find the attachment topic quite difficult if you do not have a lot of experience of children and if there are no babies in your family. However, consider the idea of talking to your parents or carers about it. They may be able to relate the topic to things that you did or they did with you when you were younger. The theory is that it could help you to make more sense of the topic.

Summarising Content

1   Decide what key terms from the attachment topic are being defined below:

- When a child is fearful on being left alone with someone they do not know
- When a caregiver–child bond is based on trust and security
- The idea of attaching to one primary caregiver
- The time limit (the first three years) in which a child should attach to a caregiver
- When a child is upset at being left by the caregiver
- When a caregiver–child bond is based on the child being clingy yet resistant
- When a child forms no attachment at all
- When a caregiver–child bond is weak because of the child's independence
- When a child's attachment to the caregiver is broken
- The strengthening of a caregiver–child bond.

2   Draw up a table as shown below.

Table 3.1

BOWLBY	VS	CRITICS
Instinct		
Monotropy		
Critical period		
Effects of privation/deprivation are irreversible		

Complete the table to show how critics disagree with each of the features of Bowlby's theory.

Exam Preparation

Look at the following questions and the examiner's tips that support them.

1 State what is meant by 'privation' in attachment. [1]

2 Outline what is meant by 'separation protest'. [2]

3 Match the attachment type to its correct definition. [3]

Insecure avoidant	When the infant operates independently of the caregiver
Secure	When the infant makes many demands on the caregiver
Insecure ambivalent	When the infant trusts the caregiver

4 Explain the concept of a 'critical period' in attachment. [3]

5 Describe and evaluate Hazen and Shaver's study into attachment types. [10]

Examiner's tip
Q2. To earn 2 marks you will have to find a way of defining the term without simply using the terms 'separation' and 'protest'.

Examiner's tip
Q4. To earn 3 marks, you have to make three points about the critical period. You could say what is supposed to happen in this period (1 mark), when it is supposed to happen by (1 mark), and why it needs to happen (1 mark).

Sample Student Answer

Q5 Hazen and Shaver used a questionnaire to study attachment types. They put the questionnaire in a newspaper and waited for people to reply. The questionnaire asked them about their attachment type and also about the most important romantic relationship they had. This was done using closed questions. Over 600 responses were analysed.

The results showed there was an association between a person's attachment type and the kind of romantic relationship they had. Securely attached babies grew up to have secure romantic relationships. Insecurely attached babies grew up to have insecure romantic relationships.

Examiner says:
The candidate has covered most of the main points of the procedure here. However, they could have gone into more detail on some of these points.

Examiner says:
It is good to see the findings included but they have been outlined rather basically. For example, the candidate could have said what a secure relationship was like.

The problem with Hazen and Shaver's research is:

- Only certain types of people may have replied to the questionnaire.
- People can lie on questionnaires quite easily.
- It is not possible to accurately judge someone's attachment type by using a simple checklist (which is what they did).
- It is not reliable to judge all romantic relationships just by asking about only one.
- The research was only carried out in the USA.

Examiner says:
A broad range of evaluation points are offered. However, it might have been better to explain some of them, even if it meant covering fewer points.

Examiner says:
Overall, the essay covers a wide range of ideas. However, it would have greater depth if more ideas were explained.

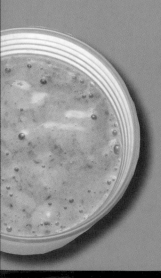

Obedience

Social psychology focuses on the idea that human beings are *social animals*. This means that we generally spend our days and lives in the company of others. A poet once wrote, 'no man is an island'. He meant that we function fully as people in the company of, and with the help of, others.

One way in which this can be seen is when other people control our behaviour (i.e. when we do what we are told, or submit to the authority of another person). An example is when we obey an order from someone in a uniform that carries authority, as Bickman discovered (see below).

However, of course, we are not machines – our own personality, the place or the circumstances can all play an important part in how we react to others' orders.

LEARNING OBJECTIVES:

By the end of this topic, you should be able to:

1 Understand the difference between *obedience* and *defiance*.

2 Explain what is meant by the term *denial of responsibility*.

3 Develop insights into a number of *situational factors* affecting obedience, and the criticisms of these factors.

4 Identify *dispositional factors*, including the role of the *authoritarian personality* in obedience.

5 Explain and outline Bickman's research into obedience and the power of uniform.

6 Show an awareness of applications of *research* into obedience for *understanding institutions*, such as schools, prisons and the armed forces.

OBEDIENCE 4

Key Concepts

Obedience

Many social psychologists are intrigued by the process of **obedience**. It is a classic example of social influence because it describes situations in which we often do something we do not want to do. Why? Because many of us tend to 'do as we are told'. We will follow an order, instruction or command if we regard the person who gives it to us as a person who has **authority** over us.

BUZZWORDS

Obedience – Following orders or commands from people in authority

Authority – A level of status or power

4.1

Make a list of the people you think are figures of authority over you.

Identify:

a) why they are authority figures, and

b) what makes one authority figure good and another 'a pain'?

Discuss your personal list with others in the group.

Grade Studio

In the exam, you may be asked to distinguish between obedience and defiance. You will earn some marks for knowing what each term means. However, to get higher marks you will also need to be able to say how they differ. This would involve comparing their meanings.

When defining terms like 'obedience', 'defiance' and 'denial of responsibility', it is tempting to use the words themselves (e.g. obey, defy, responsibility). However, you need to find alternative words to put in your definitions.

Defiance

Defiance is the opposite of obedience. It refers to an attitude of mind that can decide to resist authority. There is nothing automatic about defiance. Sometimes a person says 'no' literally or in their head and refuses to do as they have been ordered or instructed. It is not about throwing a tantrum but about *deciding* not to go along with an instruction. This is sometimes called *resistance*. It involves being 'your own person' and not being 'a puppet on a string' that jumps at the command of someone else. You *know* that it's not right to follow the order, so you don't.

4.2

Discuss the following situation with a partner.

It is the first GCSE Psychology lesson, a new subject with a new teacher, and you are uncertain of what lies ahead. The teacher starts by going over a permanent seating plan, some classroom rules, such as 'no talking in class', how you must bring your textbook to every lesson, and so on. It all seems okay so far – just. Then you are told that notes in class must be written in green, that everyone must put their watches on the desks, and that you must 'now put two fingers in your ears and bark like a dog'! Would you do it? Would you obey the teacher or would you be defiant and refuse?

Psychologists have identified some of the reasons why someone might resist, or be defiant. For example: they might just have a high personal moral sense, arguing that 'It's wrong to... .'; they may have been brought up by their parent(s) to always think for themselves; they may have had an experience like the one facing them and think, 'I've been there before, and I don't want anyone else to order me around.'

Denial of responsibility

Although defiance of authority is common, obedience seems to be the usual state of affairs. Obedience is not necessarily a bad thing as it helps to avoid chaos and anarchy. However, obedience can sometimes result in damage and destruction. Often, in this situation a person explains and defends their behaviour as simply carrying out orders from a higher authority. This is known as **denial of responsibility**. It refers to the state of mind when someone insists, for example, that 'I was only doing as I was told. It was not my fault that something nasty happened.'

Milgram, in his research (see page 51), put forward the idea that when a person feels they are acting out the wishes or orders of another person, they feel less responsible for their own actions than if they were following their own wishes.

This situation is known as someone being in the *agentic state*, that is, being another person's agent – just as an estate agent acts on behalf of a house seller or a travel agent sells holidays for a tour operator. The evidence from research suggests that taking away a person's personal responsibility encourages obedience.

Core Theory: Theory of Situational Factors

It might seem from what you have already read that the psychology of obedience and defiance is all to do with a person's state of mind and the role of authority figures. However, it is not as easy or straightforward as that. There are a number of *variables*, which influence the process one way or another.

These variables can be best understood against the background of a small number of well-known research studies into obedience.

A psychologist called Milgram showed that *social influence* can trigger off obedience to instructions that are apparently dangerous or hurtful to others. Volunteers from the general public took part in his experiment at a famous American university. They were told that they were taking part in a study about punishment and memory. They met the 'learner', a Mr Wallace, who was actually a colleague of Milgram's. Mr Wallace had been briefed to give lots of wrong answers. Real participants were told that the task was to get Mr Wallace to give correct answers to questions by giving him an electric shock. The shock increased in strength if Mr Wallace gave a wrong answer. If the participant hesitated to give the electric shock, the experimenter (who was dressed in a white lab coat) would say, 'Please go on. It is important for the research.'

Every participant went up to the level of 'intense shock', 300 volts. Sixty-five per cent continued to the highest 'danger' level of 450 volts. (There was no electricity in the experiment. Mr Wallace just acted as if the shocks were applied, while in fact he was safe and well.)

Hofling *et al.* showed that obedience is also a fact of life in the real world (it has *high ecological validity*). In this case, 'the real world' was a number of psychiatric hospitals in the USA. The participants were 22 staff nurses on night duty. The nurses on the ward were phoned by an unknown 'Dr Smith' who told them to give 20 milligrams of a drug called Astrofen from a bottle in the medicine cabinet to a particular patient. (The bottle had a label saying the maximum daily dosage was 10 milligrams.) All but one of the 22 nurses who had been phoned obeyed the fake doctor's orders and went on to administer twice the safe level of the drug. (The drug, of course, was a harmless substance.) The nurses were prepared, on the authority of a doctor, to break a number of basic hospital rules and procedures.

We return now to the theory of *situational factors* in obedience.

The possible effect of the setting

The effect of **setting** refers to the fact that at times people act obediently because of *where* they are. For example, at the dentist or in a post office, or in a place of worship people behave appropriately (i.e. they obey the unwritten or unspoken rules of the place or event).

In the Milgram research the study was transferred away from the famous American university to a run-down office building in downtown Bridgeport. The level of obedience measured by participants giving Mr Wallace the maximum 450-volt lethal voltage fell from 65 per cent to 47.5 per cent. This showed that the prestige or fame of the university had played some part in the level of obedience in the first experiment.

ACTIVITY

4.3

Work with a group of fellow students and devise a role-play to demonstrate 'denial of responsibility'. Think of a situation In which someone may follow orders but where the consequences of the actions are bad. What is the situation? Who is in authority? How does the person following the orders deny responsibility?

HOW SCIENCE WORKS

See Research in Psychology for more information on:

- **Ecological validity,** page 171.

BUZZWORDS

Setting – The physical environment in which something takes place

ACTIVITY

4.4

Describe the 'rules' about how to behave in one of the following settings:

- at the dentist
- in the post office
- in a place of worship.

It is important to note that in the Hofling research with the nurses, the command to administer the medication was given by a doctor in the medical environment of a hospital. The nurses saw it as their job to do as the doctor said when on the ward. Would they have been so obedient outside their work setting?

The possible effect of the cultural setting

Most of the studies into obedience, as you will have spotted, were carried out in the USA. Many of the participants were white, middle-class males who were keen to earn $4 plus 50 cents car-fare for an hour's work at a university. Questions then arise: Can the results be generalised to other groups or other societies or **cultures**? Is what we now know about obedience true for everyone wherever they live?

Milgram's research was carried out in a number of countries. In Australia it was found that male participants' level of complete obedience was down to 40 per cent. Other research showed the levels at 80 per cent in Italy and 85 per cent in Austria. Generally, psychologists do distinguish between *collectivist* cultures, in which individuals share tasks, belongings and income, and *individualist* societies, which put the emphasis on the rights and interests of the individual. This distinction also affects the general level of obedience – a person is more likely, on average, to be able to be disobedient in an individualist culture.

The power of an authority figure with the power to punish disobedience

It seems to be true that in situations of obedience people do as someone tells them if the person is seen to have authority. With authority comes the power to punish. In countries where there was a dictator (a single all-powerful political leader running the country), it was noted that, unsurprisingly, obedience levels rose to very high levels, suggesting that the political situation can affect obedience in ordinary people.

Milgram did a variation of his study in which a different assistant was used to give orders to the real participants. This time, the assistant was presented as another 'participant' (and did not wear a lab coat). When the real participants believed that they were being given orders by someone who had no more authority than they did, their obedience rates went down to 20 per cent.

The power of authority can also be seen in the Hofling *et al.* study. Many of the nurses justified their actions by saying that if they did not obey orders then they could be reprimanded, and some even feared losing their job. In other words, they were avoiding punishment.

4

SOCIAL PSYCHOLOGY

ACTIVITY

4.5

Think about what you have learnt so far about obedience. Read the passage below and identify examples from it that relate to the theories and research so far.

It doesn't always have to be a political dictatorship. In the jungle of Guyana, in 1978, 913 members of a religious cult obeyed the order from their leader, Jim Jones, to commit suicide by drinking a soft drink laced with cyanide. Jones had created a religious dictatorship controlling all sources of information, social rewards and punishments, and in the process eliminated any opposing views of his followers.

The infamous incident known as the My Lai massacre in Vietnam in 1969 is another example of how a person of authority can affect obedience. American soldiers rounded up over 300 unarmed women, children and elderly people in the village of My Lai and killed them by putting them into a ditch and shooting them in the back of the head. The officer in charge, Lieutenant William Calley, who gave the order to kill, was eventually charged and tried. His defence was that a Captain Medina had given him the order to kill everyone in the village; his men had just obeyed the same order through him.

The impact of consensus on obedience

The impact of **consensus** describes the sheer presence and behaviour of others that makes it impossible for us not to obey: 'the more of them there are the more obedient we are …'. However, in the same way that people 'follow each other like sheep' and obey, the same may happen with disobedience. Milgram carried out another variation of his experiment in which groups of participants tested 'Mr Wallace'. Participants were in groups of three, but only one was a genuine participant. Milgram had arranged for the other two 'participants' (his assistants) to disobey orders to shock Mr Wallace. In this scenario, only 10 per cent of real participants carried on giving a shock up to 450 volts. It seems that support from peers or others often gives a person the confidence to say no – to disobey an order. There is strength in numbers, including the strength to resist what you see as an unfair command or order.

HINT

The specification gives a list of situational factors you should know about: **s**etting, **c**ulture, **a**uthority, **p**unishment, **c**onsensus. You may find that using a mnemonic helps you to remember a list like this. For example, in the spirit of Milgram, you may use the phrase '**s**hocking **c**uddly **a**merican **p**eople **c**onstantly'.

ACTIVITY

4.6

An example of the effect of consensus can be seen at football matches. Sometimes, supporters end up rioting, harming other fans, and fighting with the police. Some of these people are often law-abiding in other areas of their lives. However, in a crowd situation, they lose their identity and do as others do.

Can you identify two other examples of situations in everyday life when the sheer presence of others may have a real influence on your behaviour?

BUZZWORDS

Consensus – When everybody agrees on something

HOW SCIENCE WORKS

See Research in Psychology for
more information on:

- **Demand characteristics**, page
  171

- **Ethical considerations**, page
  158.

Criticisms of the 'Situational Factors' Explanation of Obedience

None of the situational factors described above are foolproof and beyond comment. The research by Milgram appears to suggest that people may only reluctantly do unpleasant or harmful things to others while acting under orders from superiors.

- **A lot of research into situational factors in obedience lacks ecological validity.** For example, Milgram's set-up in the laboratory was simply unbelievable – participants must have wondered why they had to punish Mr Wallace when the researcher could test his recall himself and punish him. They may have been 'playing along' and responding to demand characteristics.

- **A lot of research into situational factors has ethical problems.** This is because research involves manipulating situations to see which factors have an effect on obedience rates. By manipulating factors, many researchers end up causing distress and embarrassment, deceiving people, and potentially causing long-term harm.

- **The main criticism to be made about explaining obedience in terms of the situation is that it has not given enough weight to the role of personality.** It tends to suggest that our behaviour is nearly always just a reflex or reaction to something or someone. It is as if we live our lives on 'automatic pilot', ignoring parts of our human make-up, such as our feelings, ambition, frustrations, imagination, sense of right and wrong, and so on.

An Alternative Theory: Dispositional Factors

Rather than assuming that all or most people will obey in any given situation, an alternative is to assume that the situation is irrelevant and that the *disposition of the person* is more important. **Dispositional factors** refer to factors about a person themselves, their personality traits. So now we will move away from thinking of obedience in terms of circumstances, setting and culture, and instead insist that some people are more likely than others to obey because of their personality.

BUZZWORDS

Dispositional factors – Factors
associated with an individual's
personality

The theory of the authoritarian personality appeared on the psychological scene shortly after the Second World War (1939–45). Adorno and his colleagues were really driven to try and understand the anti-Semitism in Nazi Germany which had produced the Holocaust, and the state of mind that allowed so many to go along with Hitler's belief that people should 'submit to the overwhelming need to obey'. In 1950, Adorno *et al.* went on to claim that there is a certain personality type – **authoritarian personality** – which is more prone to obedience than others. People with this personality are more likely than others to be obedient and also to be bigoted and prejudiced.

BUZZWORDS

Authoritarian personality – A
personality type which is prone to
obedience

HOW SCIENCE WORKS

For more information on **interviews**
see Research in Psychology, page
162.

The research involved interviews and the use of personality tests with over 2000 college students in the USA, as well as other American white, non-Jewish middle-class people, such as teachers, nurses and psychiatric patients. One of the scales devised by Adorno became know as the F-scale ('F' stands for fascism – a form of government or belief that praises the virtues of obedience, strong leadership, and law and order). Participants were required to indicate their support or opposition on a sliding scale, from slight to strong, in relation to a number of statements; for example: 'Obedience and respect for authority are the most important virtues children should learn'. Adorno classified people who scored high on the F-scale as authoritarian personalities.

An analysis of the F-scale and typical responses revealed the characteristics of the typical authoritarian personality; for example:

- someone who feels an active dislike of people from lower social classes
- someone with fixed and conventional ideas of right and wrong, good and evil
- someone who cannot deal with any ambiguity or uncertainty about the right way to behave, and acceptable attitudes or beliefs
- someone who is always willing to be 'bossed' by those of a higher status than themselves.

In simple terms, people with an authoritarian personality are great supporters of obedience.

The interesting psychology, of course, is about the origins of such a personality. Adorno claimed that it all went back to childhood and upbringing, when the child learnt to fear and obey authority (i.e. it was all down to the parent). If a child's experiences included being dominated and bullied by strict and harsh parents, they may come to hate them. Some people repress the hatred for their parents, only to displace it later towards minority groups who are seen as deviant and bad, and in need of punishment. For them, life is all about obeying, just as they had obeyed their controlling parent.

Core Study: Bickman (1974)

So far, you have read claims that there are a number of differences or variables which have the effect of making people obey; for example:

- the setting
- the number of people around
- the culture.

In the following Core Study your attention is switched to a quite different issue, the potential effect of the appearance of the person giving the orders.

Procedure

Bickman carried out a **field experiment** into obedience in which he manipulated the appearance of three male experimenters who gave orders to 153 randomly occurring pedestrians on a street in Brooklyn, New York.

The three experimenters each took turns dressing in each of the three different styles of dress: a sports coat and tie (a civilian), a milkman's uniform and a guard's uniform closely resembling that of a police officer. In this way, the pedestrians' reactions would, for the most part, be reactions to the uniform and not the individual.

ACTIVITY

4.7
Carry out an investigation on some fellow students to investigate any relationship between how obedient they are and how strict their parents/carers are.

You can ask each person to rate how obedient they are (on a scale of 1 to 10) and how strict their parents/carers are (on a scale of 1 to 10). These are quite personal questions, so it may be appropriate to do it as a confidential questionnaire.

When you have collected the data, plot it on a scatter graph to see if there is a positive correlation between obedience levels and strictness of upbringing.

4

OBEDIENCE

HOW SCIENCE WORKS

For more information on **field experiments,** see Research in Psychology page 160.

The research involved one of the experimenters giving one of the following orders to each passing pedestrian:

- **Picking up litter** – The experimenter pointed to a bag lying on the ground and ordered, 'Pick up this bag for me.'
- **Coin and parking meter** – The experimenter nodded in the direction of a helper who stood nearby at a parking meter, and said, 'This man is overparked at the meter but doesn't have any change – give him a dime.'
- **Bus stop** – The experimenter approached a subject waiting for a bus and exclaimed, 'Don't you know you have to stand on the other side of the pole? This sign says "No standing".'

Results

People were nearly two to three times as likely to obey orders given by an experimenter dressed as a guard compared with an experimenter dressed as a civilian. Figure 4.1 shows the results for the 'coin and parking meter' condition where there were significant differences between obedience rates. Bickman concluded that this demonstrated the power of certain types of uniform. Dress alone can suggest authority and when people think someone has authority to punish them, they are more likely to obey.

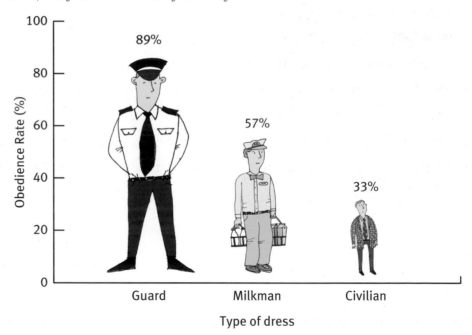

Figure 4.1 *A bar graph showing the obedience rates depending on appearance of the person giving the order when participants were asked to give a coin to a stranger.*

Methodological limitations

Various criticisms have been made of Bickman's research:

- **Because it was a field experiment there was a lack of control over extraneous variables.** Obvious extraneous variables would have been 'street' variables, such as crowding, noise, weather, etc.
- **The pedestrians were selected by opportunity sampling.** There was no prior knowledge of the personality or circumstance of each participant. For example, they might have been in a hurry, depressed or just absent-minded.

HOW SCIENCE WORKS

See Research in Psychology for more information on:

- **Extraneous variables,** page 154
- **Opportunity sampling,** page 157
- **Gender bias,** page 172
- **Cultural bias,** page 172.

- **The study was unethical for a number of reasons.** It was not possible to get the consent of participants for obvious reasons, but neither were they debriefed afterwards. Distress or embarrassment could have been caused by the orders.
- **As all the experimenters were male, gender might have played a part in the results.** For example, people may have been more inclined to take an order from a man than from a woman.
- **The study was only carried out in one city in one country.** As we know, there is evidence that culture affects obedience levels. Therefore, we cannot be sure that passers-by in other cities or countries would be as obedient. In this sense, the research is culturally biased.

ACTIVITY

4.8

Questions on the core study

Answer the following questions on Bickman's research into obedience.

1 Name the method Bickman used in his investigation into obedience. [1]

2 Identify the sample in this study. [1]

3 Identify the independent variable in this study. [1]

4 Identify the **three** dependent variables in this study. [1]

5 Give the percentage of the participants who did as they were told by the ordinary civilian. [1]

6 Give the percentage of the participants who did as they were told by the guard. [1]

7 Explain how the 'street' variables could have affected the results of the study. [6]

8 Describe how you would carry out a study similar to Bickman's but without the limitations identified above. [6]

Applications of Research into Obedience: Keeping Order in Institutions and Situations

There is obedience and there is disobedience or defiance, and sanctions or punishment, and psychologists have been researching it all experimentally for over half a century. Finally, what remains to be considered is how all or some of that research can be put to use or applied. Here, we will look at a number of organised groups of people, each with a particular purpose.

Most groups in our society share one important feature, known as a hierarchy. A hierarchy is the structure of an organisation or group, which starts with a person at the top with the most authority, and with a sliding or descending line of command and decision making. Conversely, there is an ascending line of obedience from bottom to top.

For example, think about your local supermarket. The hierarchy is probably:

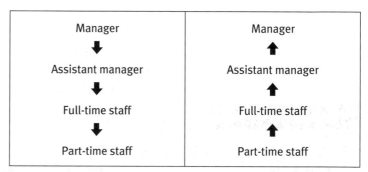

Arrows pointing down: this line of command is about giving orders, making business decisions, exercising discipline.

Arrows pointing up: this line from bottom to top is about following instructions, obeying or else 'you're fired'.

Figure 4.2 *Hierarchy of a local supermarket.*

4.9

To do this activity, you will need to go to the armed forces website (www.army.mod.uk).

On this website, click on 'Joining the Army' at the top of the page, and then select 'Discipline, Values and Standards'. You will find a document, 'A British Soldier's Values and Standards', that outlines what is expected of a British soldier.

Analyse the words and pictures in this document. Identify all the ways in which this document encourages obedience in potential recruits.

4.10

Imagine that you are a new headteacher who has just taken over a school. The school has a bad reputation for the poor behaviour of its pupils.

Draw up a document to introduce ten ideas you have for making your pupils more obedient. For each idea, try to explain the psychology behind it.

Keeping order in prisons

Can you imagine a prison with no hierarchy or rules? A prison where the prisoners decide for themselves about getting up and eating and using the facilities, where the prison staff have no sense of being in charge and arranging things, and no responsibility to the prison governor?

In the end, these would be the ingredients for a riot! Rules and procedures make prison life possible, with almost everyone – staff and inmates – obeying. For example, staff see to it that the inmates 'toe the linc' in terms of a daily timetable.

So how is order kept in prison? A number of situational factors can be used to promote obedience. For example, prison guards wear uniforms which gives them automatic power and status. Interestingly, inmates often have uniforms too. This may be for practical reasons – so that it is easy to distinguish a prisoner from a guard. However, there may also be psychological reasons behind this. Dressing people the same makes them lose their identity, so they become easier to control. Using numbers for prisoners rather than names helps with this process.

However, there is a danger in people losing their identity. They may not feel as identifiable and may take less responsibility for their actions. This means that they may get more involved in disruptive and disobedient behaviour. Dressing guards in uniforms means that they also lose their identity. This may make it easier to carry out orders, such as locking inmates in cells or making them do tasks, as they do not feel so personally responsible.

Imprisonment is a punishment in itself, but within prisons there are further punishments for inmates who break rules, such as loss of privileges, having to do certain duties, or solitary confinement. The fact that prison staff have the power to punish inmates in this way means that they can expect inmates to obey more than if they had no powers.

We also know that consensus can encourage obedience and disobedience. With reference to disobedience, it is important that prison inmates are not given the opportunity to 'gang up' and agree to disobey a rule or set of rules. When prisons have riots, it is often because this has been allowed to happen. So, to keep order, it helps if the prison inmates are kept separate a lot of the time (e.g. by locking them in their cells for periods) and when they are together they need to be closely monitored.

Keeping order in the armed forces

Can you imagine an army, navy or air force with no rules? In fact, the military would become a farce if there were no top brass generals to decide action, officers to get the action going, and soldiers, sailors and aircrew to 'jump to it' by obeying orders or commands. But how do the armed forces encourage obedience? (See Activity 4.9.)

Keeping order in schools

Just like prisons and the armed forces, schools need a level of obedience to make them function effectively. (See Activity 4.10.)

Your brief is to carry out an interview to investigate the factors that affect obedience. This is going to be an unstructured interview so although you may have some idea of the questions you would like to ask, you also need to be prepared to ask questions 'on the spot' depending on what your interviewee tells you. This needs to be an in-depth interview so open questions would be appropriate. It would be useful to prepare about five questions.

Your interview needs to be with someone who is in a position of authority. This might be a police officer, a football referee, a doctor, a shop manager, a security guard – even a teacher!

Your aim is to try to find out:

- What commands or orders your interviewee is able to make

- How they can punish any disobedience

- When their power or authority is effective

- When their power or authority is less effective

- How they feel about their power or authority.

Think about how you are going to record your interviewee's responses. Are you going to take notes, or an audio recording? Whatever you do, you will need to *summarise* your findings afterwards rather than present what was said word for word.

What were your main findings? How do these compare with other students' findings?

HOW SCIENCE WORKS

See Research in Psychology for more information on:

- **Unstructured interviews**, page 162

- **Open questions**, page 161.

Summary

- Obedience describes the situation where people follow the commands of others. Defiance is the opposite of this and occurs where people refuse to follow orders. When people do obey they often argue that they were just doing as they were instructed, leading to the denial of responsibility.

- One theory is that people obey depending on situational factors. For example, factors such as setting, culture, level of authority, threat of punishment and consensus can all have an impact on how much an individual obeys.

- An alternative theory is that obedience levels are affected by an individual's disposition (or personality) rather than the situation they are in. Put simply, some people are more obedient than others regardless of the situation.

- Bickman's study into the effect of uniform demonstrated the impact of the situation. If a person is dressed formally in a uniform then others are more likely to obey.

- Research into obedience can be used to increase (or even decrease) levels of obedience. Therefore it is useful to apply to institutions including schools, prisons and the armed forces.

OBEDIENCE **4**

ExamCafé

Common Mistakes

Remember that an exam question about research in any topic in Psychology is probably directed at the **Core Study**, which you need to know like the back of your hand! With obedience, however, there are other well-known studies, for example, Milgram, which you *might* be able to use if Bickman is not specified.

One of the problems with research into obedience is that you can get obsessed with the shocking details (literally in Milgram's research) – just remember that in an exam if you are asked about a study you should try to offer:

Procedure ➜ Results ➜ Conclusion

Procedure and Results are essential to earn full marks.

And remember – a 'study' in an exam means research, not real world incidents from page 3 in your local newspaper.

Quiz

Check up on Bickman's (1974) study of obedience

	Yes	No
Unethical		
Low in ecological validity		
Culturally biased		
Representative sample		
High level of control		

If you are struggling perhaps you need to re-read the **Core Study** section in the topic.

Summarising Content

Find a partner and draw a large poster diagram of Bickman's research. For example, you could draw three street scenes with the three cartoon figures and speech bubbles.

Exam Preparation

Understanding Exam Language

The essays at the end of each exam paper will always use the commands 'Describe and evaluate'. There are 5 marks for describing and this is where you show your knowledge and understanding of a theory or study. There are also 5 marks for evaluating. In simple terms, this means looking for limitations or criticisms of the theory or study you are describing.

a) Look at the examination question below, and the candidate's response to it.

b) Identify ways in which the response could be improved to get a higher mark.

> Describe and evaluate Bickman's (1974) study into obedience.   **[10]**

Student Answer A

Bickman did a study where he got confederates to pose as different types of people and give out orders. Sometimes the confederates dressed as security guards, or as milkmen, or as civilians. Bickman found that passers-by would follow orders more when the confederate was dressed as a security guard.

Examiner says:
The description of the study would be better if the candidate had stated the method used, detailed some of the orders given out, quoted some data in the findings, and given the conclusion of the study. This would give the description more breadth and depth; something the examiner is looking for to award full marks.

Examiner's tip
Make sure you know the kind of situational factors that encourage obedience (e.g. a prestigious setting) and that reduce obedience (e.g. lack of authority). This is because you may be presented with a stimulus in the exam where you have to decide what factors would increase or decrease people's level of obedience.

Examiner's tip
Students are often quite good at understanding the explanations behind obedience. If someone is very obedient, they understand that one theory is that it is because of the context they are in and that the other theory is that they are simply an obedient person (whatever the context). This is the difference between a theory of situational factors and a theory of dispositional factors. You need to be aware that the phrases 'situational factors' and 'dispositional factors' will be used in the exam because they are on the specification. So, try not to get them muddled up and try to remember what they mean. Students often forget what dispositional factors refer to – it is basically talking about the personality of an individual. To help you to remember, it might be useful to make the link between **dis**position and personality with a phrase like 'stop **dis**sing my personality!'

Limitations of this study are:

- it was gender biased
- there were too many extraneous variables
- it wasn't a very ethical piece of research.

Student Answer B

Bickman did a field experiment where he got confederates to pose as different types of people and give out orders, such as asking people to pick up litter or donate a coin to someone. Sometimes the confederates dressed as security guards, or as milkmen, or as civilians. Bickman found that approximately 80% of passers-by would follow orders more when the confederate was dressed as a security guard compared with approximately 40% when he was a dressed as a civilian.

Limitations of this study include the fact that it was gender biased because only male confederates were used. There were also too many extraneous variables, such as time of day or the nature of the weather. Finally, it wasn't a very ethical piece of research since passers-by did not actually know they were participating in an experiment.

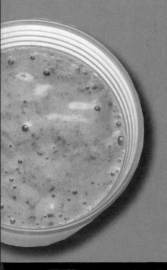

Atypical Behaviour

Many psychologists and much of psychology focuses on people *in general*. There is an assumption that people are more or less the same and do things for similar reasons. For example, cognitive psychologists continue to search for a model of human memory while assuming that human memories work the *same* way. Social psychologists are still interested in what makes the *average* person obey or disobey orders rather than looking at each individual's reasons. Biological psychologists tend to see males as *generally* behaving one way and females *generally* behaving another way – again, leaving no room for individual differences.

However, there are psychologists who are more interested in individual differences, and who focus on ways in which people are different rather than the same. Instead of researching typical behaviour, they research atypical behaviour. One obvious example of atypical behaviour is mental disorder, in which people behave and think differently from the norm.

LEARNING OBJECTIVES:

By the end of this topic, you should be able to:

1 Distinguish between the concepts of *atypical* and *typical* behaviour in relation to *fear*.

2 Outline the following *common phobias*:
- agoraphobia
- social phobia
- school phobia
- acrophobia
- arachnophobia.

3 Have an understanding of the *behaviourist theory* of phobias, including considering *evolutionary theory* as an alternative theory for explaining phobias.

4 Demonstrate knowledge of Watson and Rayner's experiment to *induce a phobia* in a young child.

5 Show awareness of the applications of research into atypical behaviour and phobias more specifically.

Key Concepts

Typical and atypical behaviour

There are many behaviours which can be described as **typical behaviours**. These are behaviours that all or most of us do or experience. For example, it is typical for most of us to obey at certain

BUZZWORDS

Typical behaviour – A behaviour which is considered normal, usually because it applies to the majority of people

5.1

Decide whether the following are examples of typical or atypical behaviours:

1 walking down the street naked

2 avoiding eye contact in a crowded lift

3 sharing a secret with a friend

4 queue jumping in a shop

5 breaking the speed limit on the motorway.

Compare your answers with your classmates and see how much you agree on what are typical and atypical behaviours.

points in our life. It is also typical (or normal) to forget things or to form an attachment to a caregiver. **Atypical behaviours** are behaviours that are unusual because they go against the norm, for example rarely obeying, forgetting much less than the average person, or never forming an attachment.

Mental disorders are good examples of atypical behaviours because, fortunately, they affect a minority of people and are reasonably rare. For example, schizophrenia affects only one per cent of the population. People suffering from this disorder have symptoms which are considered abnormal or atypical, for example hearing voices that do not really exist, or believing that outside forces are manipulating their thoughts.

Common phobias

Phobias are another example of atypical behaviour, this time related to fear. They are intense, persistent and irrational fears of objects (e.g. snakes, needles), contexts (e.g. confined spaces, hospitals) or activities (e.g. flying, speaking on the phone). It is quite typical or common to experience fear (we all know what it feels like to be frightened or anxious) but it becomes atypical when people show extreme fear in a non-threatening situation (e.g. a cat crossing their path) or mildly threatening situation (e.g. going to a party). In other words, the fear is out of proportion to the situation.

Some common phobias are detailed below.

1 **Agoraphobia.** This is a fear of being in a place or situation where the sufferer feels escape would be difficult or where they feel trapped. This might be places such as shopping centres, public transport or even the workplace. It is not simply a fear of open spaces as many people believe. People suffering from agoraphobia often end up confined to their homes because it is the only place they feel safe. It is one of the worst phobias to suffer from because it restricts people's lives greatly.

2 **Social phobia.** This is a fear or dread of social situations. It is more than just shyness – sufferers are very anxious about what others may think of them or how they will be judged. They worry that they will act in an embarrassing way when in public. This could relate to a specific situation, such as doing a presentation, meeting a stranger or eating in front of others. However, social phobias can be more general and apply to any situation in which there is contact with others. Interestingly, most sufferers know their behaviour is irrational. However, they still panic about situations days or weeks in advance, and avoid them if they can.

3 **School phobia.** This is a fear of attending school. It is not the same as truanting, because non-attendance is related to anxiety. Like people with agoraphobia, it can sometimes be a fear of leaving the safety of home, or the safety of being with parents/carers. Like social phobia, it can sometimes be fear of embarrassing oneself in public, for example when speaking in class, getting undressed in the changing room or saying something stupid in front of friends. Unsurprisingly, school phobia is only diagnosed amongst school-aged children. It is most commonly diagnosed in eleven- to twelve-year-old boys.

4 **Acrophobia.** This is a fear of heights. It is true that many people feel anxious about being high up somewhere, but a person suffering from acrophobia may have a more extreme response to, say, being on top of a tall building. For example, they may respond by closing their eyes, kneeling down or even crawling on all fours. This is often because they fear losing their sense of balance. A person suffering from acrophobia may also avoid situations where they are not even especially high – for example, climbing a ladder or being in a first-floor hotel room.

Figure 5.1 *It is quite rational to be scared of heights when our safety is under threat, but at what point should a fear of heights be diagnosed as a phobia?*

ACTIVITY

5.2
Discuss in pairs how each phobia might affect your everyday routine if you had it. For example, from getting up in the morning, going to school, to going to bed at night.

5 **Arachnophobia.** This is an irrational fear of spiders. It is thought to be the most common animal-based phobia. As with all phobias, sufferers' reactions will differ. In extreme cases, sufferers may not even be able to cope with a cartoon picture of a spider or even read the word. In less extreme cases, an actual spider may need to be present to trigger the fear response. However, for a lot of sufferers there is also the fear of coming across a spider. For example, they may check their bed carefully before getting into it at night, or they may inspect the shower cubicle before entering it. Interestingly, arachnophobia is much more likely to be diagnosed in women than men.

The above phobias are just a small percentage of the thousands of different ones that people have been diagnosed with. However, although there are many different stimuli that cause a phobia, reactions are often very similar. Symptoms of phobias include

- heart pounding
- sweating
- feeling sick
- dizziness
- difficulty concentrating
- loss of control.

It is also worth noting that a phobia is not just about a fear of a particular stimulus. It is about *avoiding* it as well, and this is when it can really begin to impact on people's lives.

HINT

A lot of names of phobias are hard to spell. Some of them also have similar spellings, which makes it even more difficult. Try to use tricks to distinguish between different words. For example, for a**gor**aphobia think of someone called **Gor**don who does not like to leave his home. For a**cro**phobia think of a **cro**w flying 'high' for fear of heights.

ACTIVITY

5.3
We have looked at some of the most common phobias. However, there are many more phobias, including very unusual ones.

Hold a competition with your classmates to see who can find the strangest example of a phobia. You may have to put it to the vote!

5

INDIVIDUAL DIFFERENCES

BUZZWORDS

Behaviourists – A group of psychologists who believe that human behaviours are learnt rather than natural

Classical conditioning – Learning by association, so that certain stimuli are associated with certain responses

Unconditioned response (UCR) – A response which is natural and does not need to be learnt

Unconditioned stimulus (UCS) – Something that triggers a natural (unconditioned) response

Neutral stimulus (NS) – Something that would not normally trigger a reaction

Conditioned stimulus (CS) – Something that triggers a learnt response; something we have been conditioned to respond to

Conditioned response (CR) – A response which has been learnt (or conditioned) through association

Core Theory: Behaviourist Theory

Behaviourists are a group of psychologists who believe that behaviours are learnt rather than natural. So, they believe that people *learn* to be phobic rather than are born phobic. This would fit in with the fact that many people can relate their fear of an object or situation to something bad they have experienced; for example, someone who is afraid of needles may report having been badly hurt when given an injection as a child. To understand how this happens, we first need to look at the behaviourist principles of **classical conditioning**.

Classical conditioning is also known as 'learning by association', and is when people learn to associate a particular response with a particular stimulus.

Even behaviourists accept that some behaviours are *not* learnt and are instinctive instead. They call these **unconditioned responses (UCR)**. This includes instinctive responses such as vomiting, sexual arousal and anxiety.

These unconditioned responses are triggered by **unconditioned stimuli (UCS)** – that is, objects and events that naturally cause the reaction. For example, poison causes us to vomit, stimulating genitals may cause arousal, and a threat makes us anxious.

However, sometimes these responses happen in the presence of a **neutral stimulus (NS)** – one that would not normally cause any reaction. Examples of neutral stimuli might be a plate of chips, a piece of music or the inside of a bus. In other words, if a person is sick after a plate of chips, they may associate the plate of chips (originally a neutral stimulus) with the response (vomiting). Similarly, a person could be sexually aroused when listening to a certain piece of music, or be threatened by someone on a bus. So, to take the last example – if the person gets anxious when getting on a bus, we can say that they have been classically conditioned.

Each of the neutral stimuli is now described as a **conditioned stimulus (CS)** because they trigger a learnt response. The response itself does not change (e.g. being sexually aroused) but if it is a response to a conditioned stimulus (e.g. a piece of music), we now call it a **conditioned response (CR)**.

ACTIVITY

5.4

Copy out the following examples of unconditioned stimuli. In each case, write down what your unconditional (instinctive) response might be.

You should label the list 'UCS' and label your answers 'UCR'.

1 Someone blowing into your eye

2 Something knocking you on the knee when you are sitting down

3 Someone tickling you under the chin

4 Someone shouting 'Boo!' behind you when you are not expecting it

5 Someone holding a tray of rotten eggs beneath your nose

5.5

Copy out the table:

Conditioned stimulus	Conditioned response

For each of the following examples, use the table to show which is the CS and which is the CR.

1 Terence feels sick whenever he has a sip of cider.

2 Sam flinches whenever his Dad takes his coat off the hook.

3 Whenever 'Tom and Jerry' comes on the television, Azra cries.

4 When Caroline hears the theme tune to 'Who Wants to be Millionaire?', it now makes her feel anxious.

5 The smell of candyfloss makes Petra feel all excited inside.

Behaviourists believe that animals, as well as humans, can be classically conditioned. This can be seen in the following example, in which a dog was conditioned to salivate to the sound of a bell.

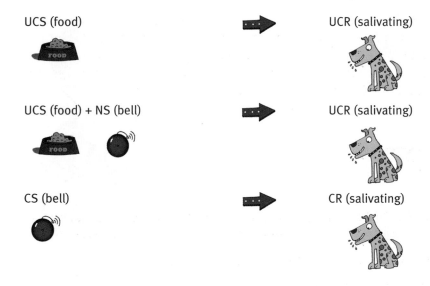

UCS (food) → UCR (salivating)

UCS (food) + NS (bell) → UCR (salivating)

CS (bell) → CR (salivating)

Figure 5.2 *Dogs respond naturally to food by salivating.*

In the previous example, dogs would be conditioned over a number of trials. However, one-trial learning can take place when an association is formed after one event, for example if a person is aroused enough or anxious enough, as with a phobia.

5.6

Look at the examples in Activity 5.5 again.

Describe how each one may have occurred as a result of classical conditioning.

In the exam, you can only be asked to describe classical conditioning in relation to phobias. This means that, whatever phobia you are writing about or you are asked about, the UCR and CR will always be fear. The UCS is also going to be some kind of threat, as this is what naturally triggers the fear response. The only thing that really changes depending on the phobia is the CS. The CS is simply the object or situation which causes the phobia, such as open spaces, heights and spiders.

Grade Studio

It is acceptable to use a classical conditioning diagram to show the behavourist theory's view of how a phobia starts. This could earn 2 or 3 marks alone, depending on the total for the question. However, if the question requires you to *describe* the behaviourist theory of phobias then you will need to include some sentences as well as the diagram. The diagram could be your starting point, then you should attempt to describe what the diagram shows. Also remember to apply the theory and diagram to phobias. For example, it would *not* be relevant to phobias if you used the example of the dogs being conditioned to salivate at the ring of a bell.

Classical conditioning normally involves stimulus generalisation in which similar conditioned stimuli will trigger the same conditioned response; for example, the dog may salivate to the sound of other bells, or a person will vomit when they see any plate of chips and not just the one that made them sick!

Conditioned responses will become extinguished over time if the association does not continue. For example, if the dog does not receive food when the bell is rung, after a while it will stop salivating. If the person is not hassled on the bus for a number of journeys, then they will stop getting anxious. In other words, the association dies out.

You can perhaps now see how classical conditioning might be used to explain the onset of a phobia. The behaviourist theory is that phobias are the result of a negative experience with the feared object, context or activity. For example, a person who has apiphobia (a fear of bees) may once have been attacked by a bee. We will use this example to illustrate the behaviourist theory of phobias. However, whatever the phobia, the conditioned response is always going to be fear.

Fear is an unconditioned response when it is a reaction to an unconditioned stimulus. For example, being stung may cause a fear response because it potentially threatens your survival (e.g. if poisoned) or because it causes pain. If it is a bee that stings you, then you could associate the stinging with the actual bee. Before this event, a bee might appear quite harmless (a neutral stimulus). However, the bee becomes a conditioned stimulus because it triggers a conditioned response: fear. This will probably happen after one bad experience (one trial learning) if it is frightening enough.

This is summarised in Figure 5.3.

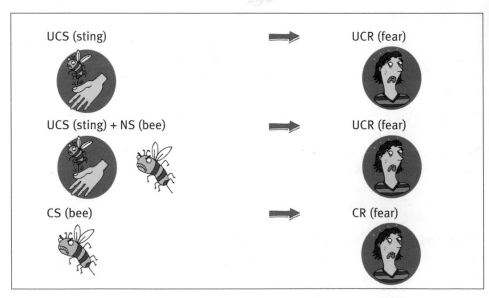

Figure 5.3 *A diagram to show the classical conditioning of phobias.*

Figure 5.3 explains how the phobia starts, but there are two more steps to developing an actual phobia.

1   Stimulus generalisation is also important in the explanation. This means we tend to associate the conditioned response with stimuli similar to the original conditioned stimulus. In the case of phobias, people do not just fear the original object, context or activity that triggered the fear. They also fear similar objects, contexts or activities. In the example of apiphobia, the person does not just fear the original bee that stung them, but fears all bees. Because of stimulus generalisation, the fear may go beyond bees and include other similar insects, such as wasps.

2   As well as classical conditioning, **operant conditioning** is used by behaviourists to explain phobias. Whereas classical conditioning is 'learning by association', operant conditioning is 'learning by consequences'. Put simply, if the consequences of an action are rewarding, we learn to do them again. However, if the consequences are negative, we tend not to repeat the action. But how does this apply to phobias?

BUZZWORDS

Operant conditioning – Learning by consequences. If the consequences of an action are rewarding, we learn to do them again. However, if the consequences are negative, we tend not to repeat the action

You may remember earlier that we referred to extinction. This is the idea that associations become *extinguished* over time. In the case of phobias, we could ask: Why doesn't the person eventually learn that not all bees are going to sting them? The problem is that people only learn this when they 'face their fear'. For example, they stay in the garden when a bee is buzzing around and (hopefully!) do not get stung again. However, a phobia is not just about fearing an object or situation – it is about *avoiding* it too. If a person avoids the object or situation that they are scared of then they feel relieved. Relief is rewarding, so they keep on avoiding the object or situation. However, if they do try to, or have to, face their fear (e.g. they are stuck in a bus with a bee) this will cause a lot of anxiety. Anxiety is punishing, so they don't want to 'face their fear' again.

To conclude, the behaviourist principles of classical conditioning can be used to explain the onset of a phobia, and then the behaviourist principles of operant conditioning can be used to explain why it continues.

One final point to note is that, according to behaviourists, atypical behaviours are learnt in just the same way as typical behaviours. Typical behaviours are classically conditioned too; for example, babies learn to associate carers with comfort and drivers learn to associate red with danger. Atypical behaviours are just more unusual examples of classical conditioning.

Criticisms of behaviourist theory

There are a number of criticisms of the behaviourist theory of phobias, including the following:

*   **By only focusing on behaviour, behaviourists ignore the mind and the *thinking* behind behaviour.** For example, two people may have been attacked on a dark night. One person may think about it rationally and realise that they are unlikely to be a victim of an attack again, especially if they 'play safe'. However, another person may think about it irrationally and decide that there are lots of potential attackers lurking in the dark. Therefore, they may develop

HINT

If you are summarising the criticisms of behaviourist theory, you will see they are all points about what the theory ignores. The behaviourist theory:

- ignores thinking behind phobias
- ignores indirect experience with phobia
- ignores the role of nature in developing phobias.

BUZZWORDS

Evolutionary theory – The theory that animals have evolved over time and instinctively behave in ways that allow them to survive and reproduce

ACTIVITY

5·7

Look at the following examples of phobias. In each case, explain why it would be natural to fear these objects/situations according to the evolutionary theory.

- Fear of the dark
- Fear of heights
- Fear of flying
- Fear of closed spaces
- Fear of rats

a phobia of the dark. The point is that two people can have the same experience but may not form the same associations. We do not just respond passively to the stimuli around us, we actually think about what is happening to us too.

- **Behaviourists assume that you need direct experience with the feared object or situation; however, others argue that phobias can be learnt more indirectly.** In other words, phobias may develop through social learning. This means that people (often children) learn their phobias through observing and imitating their roles models' (e.g. parents') behaviours. So if a parent hides under the stairs during a thunderstorm, a child may copy this behaviour and develop a phobia of storms too. This would also explain why some phobias seem to run in families.
- **Behaviourists cannot explain the fact that some people have phobias of objects and situations that they have no direct (or indirect) experience of.** For example, a number of British people have a phobia of snakes even though they are unlikely to have come across one! It might be that some phobias are more to do with nature, and that people are simply born with them.

An Alternative Theory: Evolutionary Theory

As stated above, behaviourists tend to ignore the role of nature in their theory of phobias. **Evolutionary theory**, however, focuses more on nature to explain phobias. This theory generally argues that human beings, and other animals, are governed by nature. It is natural for animals to want to survive, and to survive long enough to reproduce and pass on their genes.

With reference to phobias, the evolutionary theory would first argue that fear is instinctive because it helps us to survive. If we had no sense of fear then we would keep putting ourselves in dangerous situations that could potentially harm or kill us.

Evolutionary theory would then argue that certain objects or situations are more threatening to our survival than others (e.g. the dark, heights, flying, closed spaces, rats). Interestingly, these objects and situations give us some of the most common phobias. In terms of animal phobias, the evolutionary theory would argue that we instinctively fear animals that are more unlike us in shape or form. This is because they are less closely related to us in terms of genes, and therefore more likely to attack us. For example, we are more likely to develop phobias of limbless animals (e.g. snakes), animals with many limbs (e.g. spiders) and flying animals (e.g. birds), rather than animals that look similar to us (e.g. chimpanzees).

It is important to note that the evolutionary theory does not necessarily argue that people are born with their phobias. What we are born with is a biological *preparedness* to fear certain objects and situations more than others because they are a greater threat to our survival. Phobias still require a negative experience with that object or situation, but if we are prepared to fear it, it will not take much to develop a phobia of it. For example, it would be easy to develop a phobia of being in water (where we could drown) rather than being in a field of flowers (where nothing dangerous is likely to happen to us).

Interestingly, evidence suggests that it is more difficult to treat and get rid of phobias of objects or situations which are a greater threat to our survival. This would suggest that they are more in-built and not just learnt.

To conclude, a preparedness to fear certain objects or situations is something that has evolved over thousands of years. Our ancestors may have been seriously under threat from animals such as snakes and spiders in their day, and without modern technology situations such as being out in the dark or being up high would have been dangerous too. People in the past who feared these things were more likely to survive. These are the people who therefore managed to reproduce as well. In reproducing, they passed on their fears. These fears, or at least a preparedness to fear, have been inherited by each new generation. This also explains why we do not often have phobias of things that really do threaten our survival today, such as fast cars, guns and cigarettes. These objects were not around in our ancestors' past and so we have not evolved an innate mechanism to fear them.

Core Study: Watson and Rayner (1920)

The idea that phobias can be learnt through the principles of classical conditioning is supported by a now infamous experiment carried out almost a hundred years ago by early psychologists, John Watson and Rosalie Rayner.

Procedure

Watson and Rayner's subject was a baby known as Little Albert, who was described as 'healthy from birth'. At nine months old, they tested his reactions to a range of different stimuli, including live animals (e.g. a rat, a rabbit, a dog, a monkey) and other objects (e.g. burning newspaper, cotton, human masks). None of these stimuli frightened him. They were neutral stimuli. The only stimulus that triggered a natural fear reaction was a hammer striking a steel bar.

When Albert was just over eleven months old, Watson and Rayner brought him back to their laboratory. Their aim was to condition him to fear a white rat. They did this by offering the rat to the boy. As Albert reached out to stroke the rat, Watson crept behind the baby and brought the hammer crashing down on the steel bar! This was repeated seven times over the next two weeks.

ACTIVITY

5.8

Make a list of ten animals. Get a range of animals in terms of appearance, e.g. different sizes, shapes, skins, limbs, faces.

When you have done this, survey your classmates and ask them to rate each animal in terms of how much they fear them. Decide what kind of rating scale you are going to use.

Your aim is to see whether the animals that look most unlike us are the most feared. This would support the evolutionary theory.

Summarise your findings in numerical form (e.g. averages, graphs). Then describe your findings in words. What do they show? Do they support the evolutionary theory?

HOW SCIENCE WORKS

See Research in Psychology (page 159) for more information on **experiments**.

HINT

Students often make the mistake of thinking that Little Albert himself was hit with a hammer when reaching out for the rat. Watson and Rayner were unethical but not that unethical! Be careful to get details of the study as accurate as possible.

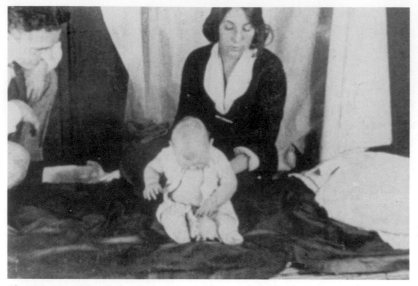

Figure 5.4 *An original photograph showing the Watson and Rayner experiment.*

HOW SCIENCE WORKS

See Research in Psychology, page 171, for more information on **ecological validity**.

HOW SCIENCE WORKS

See Research in Psychology, page 158, for more information on **ethical considerations**.

Results

By the end of the seven trials, the rat on its own was enough to frighten Albert even though it had not done so before. When presented with the rat, he would now cry and try to avoid it. Watson and Rayner had successfully (and deliberately!) conditioned a phobia of rats in the boy.

Five days later, Watson and Rayner tested Albert again. The fear of the rat still persisted. Albert also showed fear reactions for the rabbit, the dog, a sealskin coat, cotton, a Santa Claus mask and even Watson's hair (which was white).

Ten days after the initial conditioning, Albert still showed fear of the rat but it was less marked. One month after the initial conditioning, Albert still showed a mild fear of the rat. At this point, Albert's mother withdrew him from the experiment so he could not be tested further.

Limitations

- **The phobia was conditioned under artificial conditions, therefore the findings may lack ecological validity.** In real life, there would be other variables occurring during a negative event. Watson and Rayner had control over other variables, which is not realistic. In other words, they may have shown that you can condition a phobia in a laboratory but they did not show that it can happen in a more natural setting. Indeed, conditioning may have taken longer in the laboratory. Naturally occurring phobias are thought to occur through one-trial learning but it took seven trials to induce Albert's phobia.

- **Only one child was conditioned with a phobia in this study. This is too small a sample from which to generalise.** We do not know whether it would be easier or more difficult to condition a phobia in other children. We also do not know whether it would work on older children or on adults. In addition, the experiment was only carried out using one stimulus (a rat). Based on the idea of preparedness it may be easier to condition a phobia of rats than other objects. Without testing other objects, Watson and Rayner could not be sure.

- **There are a number of reasons why this study is highly unethical.** Clearly, Albert was caused distress during the experiment as the researchers made him afraid of an animal and other objects on purpose. In addition, because they did not try to counter-condition his phobia, he could have been left with a mental disorder for life. There is also some debate as to whether Albert's mother really knew what she was consenting to.

Applications of Research into Atypical Behaviour

Behaviour therapy for phobias

The reason why psychologists want to explain why atypical behaviours happen is so that they can try to control them. If psychologists know what causes a phobia, then they can try to stop them from happening or 'reverse' them when they do. If the behaviourist theory is right about phobias being learnt then this is actually quite positive. If a phobia can be conditioned then, in theory, it can be counter-conditioned. This is where behaviour therapy comes into play.

Flooding

Flooding is a type of behaviour therapy in which clients are immersed in their fear. As stated earlier, one of the reasons why phobias continue is because people suffering from them continue to avoid the feared object or situation rather than facing it. Flooding works on the principle of facing your fear full-on. For example, a person with a fear of flying may be taken up in an aircraft and flown around for 30 minutes, or a person with a fear of spiders may be locked in a room full of them!

The theory is that the clients will form a new association between the feared object or situation, and overcome their phobia. How? The argument is that initially the client will be full of fear (e.g. racing heart, sweating, feeling sick) as they find themselves in their worst feared situation. However, physically speaking, a body cannot maintain such a high level of arousal (e.g. a heart rate has to slow down otherwise we can kill ourselves). Eventually, the increase in the body's responses has to subside. As the client calms down, they are still in their feared situation (e.g. still flying around, still in a room full of spiders) yet they are feeling more relaxed. On this basis, they should form a new association in, for example, feeling relief while flying in a plane or having a normal heartbeat while in the presence of spiders.

5.9
Questions on the core study

Answer the following questions on Watson and Rayner's experiment to induce a phobia.

1 Give the method used to conduct the study. [1]

2 Identify the sample in this study. [1]

3 State how many trials it took to condition Albert's phobia of rats. [1]

4 Explain why animals (such as the dog and the monkey) and objects (such as the burning newspaper) were neutral stimuli. [2]

5 Outline *one* ethical problem associated with the study. [2]

6 Outline the evidence of stimulus generalisation from the study. [3]

7 Explain why Albert's phobia may not have extinguished itself. [3]

8 Draw a diagram to show the process of classical conditioning in the study. Identify the UCS, UCR, NS, CS and CR in your diagram. [6]

Figure 5.5 *Flooding is one way of attempting to treat a phobia of flying.*

5.10

It is easy to research systematic desensitisation using the Internet.

Try websites such as:

- www.minddisorders.com

- www.guidetopsychology.com

- www.phobialist.com.

Once you have done some research on what systematic desensitisation is, draw up an 'anxiety hierarchy' for a phobia of your choice.

5.11

Imagine you are a behaviour therapist who has to get clients to picture their worst possible situation. What would you suggest that they should think of for each of the following phobias?

- Ophidiophobia – fear of snakes

- Acrophobia – fear of heights

- Chionophobia – fear of snow

- Dromophobia – fear of crossing the road

- Gerascophobia – fear of growing old

- Stenophobia – fear of narrow places

- Linonophobia – fear of string

- Decidophobia – fear of making decisions

- Dishabiliophobia – fear of undressing in front of someone

- Triskaidekaphobia – fear of the number 13.

There is some evidence that flooding works on specific phobias. However, there are concerns about the ethics of immersing people in their worst fears. It is also dangerous for clients with medical conditions, such as heart problems.

Systematic desensitisation

Systematic desensitisation is a more ethical form of behaviour therapy, which can also be used for treating phobias. This is because it conditions clients to form new associations more *gradually* (see Activity 5.10).

Implosion therapy

Implosion therapy is similar to flooding in the sense that it gets clients to face their worst fears. However, it gets around the ethical problem of literally putting them in the situation. Instead, implosion requires the client to *imagine* their worst situation rather than physically experience it (see Activity 5.11).

Your brief is to carry out three interviews with three different people. They could be members of your family or your classmates. The interviewees do not necessarily have to suffer from a phobia but they should have something that they are afraid of which is not typical of other people.

See Research in Psychology for more information on:

- **Ethical considerations**, page 158

- **Structured interviews**, page 162.

You will need to carry out a structured interview in which you ask your interviewees the same questions so that you can look for patterns in their answers.

Your aim is to see if there are any trends in:

1 How their fears/phobias first started

2 The way they respond when confronted with their feared object/situation

3 How they feel about their fear (e.g. Do they see it as irrational?).

What would your hypothesis be? Would you predict certain trends or patterns in your interviewees' answers?

The interviews are likely to be in-depth, so you may find it useful to use audio equipment to record people's answers. This will allow you to analyse them properly afterwards.

Remember, you are asking people questions about something they may feel quite sensitive about. Be careful not to cause them any *distress* when questioning them. You may also want to make sure and reassure them that their responses are *confidential*. Think of how you can ensure this is the case (e.g. by calling them X, Y and Z in any written materials).

Are there any patterns or trends in your interviewees' responses?

Summary

- Many people behave in similar ways. This can be called typical behaviour. However, there are some behaviours that do not follow the norm. People with phobias are an example of this. This is known as atypical behaviour.

- Phobias are intense, persistent, irrational fears. They include fears of being outdoors and away from home (agoraphobia), fears of being in social contact with others (social phobia), fears of being in school (school phobia), fears of heights (acrophobia) and fears of spiders (arachnophobia).

- The behaviourist theory states that phobias are learnt through classical conditioning. This is when the fear response becomes associated with a neutral stimulus. When the neutral stimulus triggers fear, it is described as a conditioned stimulus.

- An alternative to the behaviourist theory is the evolutionary theory, which argues that we are naturally prepared to fear certain stimuli more than others.

- Watson and Rayner's experiment on Little Albert showed how it is possible (although unethical) to use the principles of classical conditioning to induce a phobia of rats in a young child.

- Applications of research into atypical behaviour include behaviour therapy, which can be used to treat disorders such as phobias.

ExamCafé

Revision

Revision Checklist

Check that you can summarise the main points of the Watson and Rayner study by answering the following 'quick questions':

1 What method did they use?
2 Who was their participant?
3 How old was their participant when they first tested him?
4 What kind of stimuli did they test his reactions to?
5 Which stimulus was the only one to trigger a fear response?
6 What was this stimulus paired with to induce a phobia?
7 How many trials did it take to induce a phobia?
8 What was the participant's fear response?
9 What other stimuli did he generalise his fear to?
10 When did the fear response become extinguished?

Summarising the Content

Check that you can match the type of phobia to its definition.

Acrophobia	A fear of being in public spaces away from home
Agoraphobia	A fear of exposure or embarrassment during social contact
Arachnophobia	A fear of attending or being at school
School Phobia	A fear of heights
Social Phobia	A fear of spiders

When describing the behaviourist theory of phobias it is easy to get mixed up between the key concepts of UCS, UCR, NS, CS and CR.

One tip is to think about the concepts logically. If you remember a *stimulus* is 'something' and a *response* is a 'reaction' then it should be obvious that the 'something' causes a 'reaction'. Similarly, if you remember that *conditioned* means 'learnt' and *unconditioned* means 'not learnt' then should be able to label the stimuli and the responses which are natural or conditioned.

Another tip is that if you look at the classical conditioning diagram the concepts appear in reverse alphabetical order. This might help you to remember what occurs where.

Exam Preparation

Planning a Response

Look at the following exam question.

> 1 Describe **one** common phobia. [4]

Look at Candidate A's response to the following exam question.

> 2 Describe and evaluate **one** theory for explaining phobias. [10]

Candidate A

Q2 Evolutionary theory can be used to explain phobias. It says that it is natural and instinctive to fear things, especially things that affect our chances of surviving. This would include potentially dangerous animals, such as insects, rodents and reptiles. It would also include situations that make us vulnerable to attack, such as being in the dark or out in open spaces. The point the theory makes is that these things were particularly threatening to previous generations. If our ancestors feared these things, then they increased their chances of surviving because they played safe. These are exactly the people that lived long enough to reproduce, thus passing their fears on through inheritance. Their genes still exist in people today, which makes them biologically prepared to fear certain things more than others.

The problem with this theory is that it is all about nature and therefore ignores nurture. How can it explain the fact that people can often relate their phobias to a particular incident in their life?

Examiner's tip

If Question 1 came up in the exam, then there a couple of things you need to think about. Firstly, the question asks for a common phobia. You may wonder how common a phobia has to be for it to be considered 'common' – could you get away with describing your auntie's fear of horses? The safest bet is to use one of the five from the specification because the exam board has already identified these as 'common phobias'. Secondly, you need to be aware that there are 4 marks on offer. You need to choose a phobia that you have enough to say about to earn all of the marks. For example, arachnophobia is a relatively specific phobia, which you might struggle to write in detail about. However, if you choose a more complex phobia – such as social phobia – then you have more chance of hitting those 4 marks. For example, with social phobia, you could outline the different situations it occurs in, the reasons for it, and the typical symptoms shown.

Examiner says:
This candidate does a good job of describing the evolutionary theory as an explanation of phobias. However, they have struggled with the evaluation because they cannot make enough points to criticise it. The mistake they have made is to choose to describe the 'alternative theory' from the specification. They have probably not been taught enough about it to be able to evaluate it. It is better to describe the 'core theory' (in this case, the behaviourist theory) if given a choice. Alternative theories can still be included in essays, but they work better under evaluation. This can be seen in Candidate B's response on the next page.

ExamCafé

Q2 One theory for explaining phobias is the behaviourist theory. It says that phobias are learnt following a bad experience with an animal, or object, or situation. Basically, people are classically conditioned to fear something. This means that they learn to associate fear (which starts as an unconditioned response) with a neutral stimulus, like a snake. This is because the snake would have done something to scare them (an unconditioned stimulus). The phobia has been conditioned when the snake becomes a conditioned stimulus and the fear a conditioned response.

The behaviourist theory assumes that phobias are only learnt. This ignores the fact that people may be born with them. This is sort of what the evolutionary theory argues because they say fears have evolved over millions of years. This means we are born ready to fear threatening things, such as snakes. The behaviourist theory is also all about behaviour. It doesn't consider the 'thinking part' of phobias. Some people decide not to develop a phobia, even if they have had a bad experience. It is partly in the mind.

Examiner says:
Although Candidate B's response is not as well written as Candidate A's, it is a more balanced response. It does both of the things required by the question – describing and evaluating – to a good standard.

Understanding Exam Language

Both Unit 1 and Unit 2 will end with an essay that asks you to 'describe and evaluate' something. In the above example, the 'something' was a theory (for explaining phobias). However, sometimes you are asked to describe and evaluate a study. It is not unusual for candidates to get theories and studies mixed up. If you do, you could lose all 10 marks because you are not giving the examiner what has been asked for.

Make sure you are clear that a theory is something that explains a behaviour. It attempts to explain why certain things happen. Meanwhile, a study is an actual piece of research or an investigation. For example, a psychologist may carry out a study (e.g. using an experiment or an observation) to support or to test a theory. Theories are just psychologists' ideas about something, whereas studies try to provide actual evidence.

Criminal Behaviour

Crime constantly features in the news. Many people worry about it and want to know how we can bring crime rates down.

Psychologists have often debated whether people are *born* criminals or *made* criminals. The British justice system seems to work on the basis that people are made criminals because it assumes that it can also make them into good citizens. However, the idea that criminal behaviour is somehow innate still persists today. The biological theory of criminal behaviour would adopt this approach. In other words, the fact that you are a criminal or not is fixed by your biology and has little to do with your experiences and upbringing.

LEARNING OBJECTIVES:

By the end of this topic, you should be able to:

1 Understand the problems of *defining* and *measuring* crime.

2 Understand what is meant by a *criminal personality*.

3 Understand the *biological theory* of criminal behaviour, as well as consider the *social learning theory* as an alternative theory for explaining criminal behaviour.

4 Demonstrate knowledge of Mednick *et al.*'s adoption study into the *genetic basis* of criminal behaviour.

5 Show an awareness of applications of research into criminal behaviour in relation to crime reduction.

Key Concepts

Defining and measuring crime

Crime is not an easy concept to define. In very simple terms, a criminal act is any behaviour that breaks the law. However, some researchers argue that a crime really occurs when someone *intends* to break the law. Other psychologists argue that a behaviour is only criminal if it is intended *and* if it actually causes damage or harm to another person or their property. On this basis, growing drugs for your own use would not be considered criminal, whereas selling drugs for a profit would be.

What counts as criminal behaviour also depends on factors such as time and culture. In terms of time, certain behaviours have become more or less acceptable than in the past. For example, male homosexual behaviour was illegal in the UK up until about 40 years ago, but now homosexual people have the same rights as heterosexual people. Conversely, fox hunting was legal at the end of the last century but since then it has been made illegal.

HINT

You may be asked to give a definition of 'crime' in the exam. Do not worry that it is not an easy concept to define because the examiner has to accept a wide range of definitions.

You may be asked to explain why it is difficult to define crime in the exam. If there are a number of marks on offer, then don't just outline the difficulties. Use examples (e.g. how euthanasia is viewed differently in countries) to help to illustrate your point.

ACTIVITY

6.1

In groups, carry out research into different countries' laws on:

- littering offences
- age of consent for sexual intercourse
- alcohol consumption.

In the same groups, see how many changes to UK law you can list. In other words, how have offences changed over time?

ACTIVITY

6.2

Why do you think people decide not to report crimes?

Write down as many reasons as you can think of. When you have done this, compare your reasons with other people's. What similar ideas did you have?

BUZZWORDS

Criminal personality – A collection of traits that make a person different from 'normal', law-abiding people

In terms of culture, certain behaviours are acceptable in some countries or states but not others. For example, euthanasia is against the law in the UK and many other countries, but has been legalised in countries such as the Netherlands, Belgium and Switzerland. Conversely, abortion is legal in the UK but still illegal in nearby countries such as the Republic of Ireland and Malta.

Even if we agree that it is simpler to define crime as any act against the law, then it is still difficult to actually *measure* this. Official measures of crime rely on accurate recording and reporting by police forces who then pass their crime figures on to the government's Home Office.

There are a number of problems associated with official crime statistics, including the following:

- Statistics count the number of criminal acts rather than the number of criminals, so one crime may have been committed by a number of people (e.g. a gang mugging) or many crimes may have been committed by one person (e.g. a serial killer).
- People may not be aware that they have been a victim of a crime and therefore cannot report it. For example, someone may be pick-pocketed when drunk and assume the next morning that they lost their wallet.
- Victims of crime do not always want to report the crime for a variety of reasons.

Criminal personality

Another problem with defining crime as any act against the law is that this would make most people criminals. Confidential surveys show that nearly every adult has broken the law at some point in their lives. In most cases these are minor offences, such as breaking speed limits or paying the wrong fare on public transport, but they are still acts against the law. However, it is not minor offenders that psychologists tend to be interested in. For obvious reasons, they are more interested in serious offenders who do more damage to society, such as murderers, rapists, arsonists, fraudsters and robbers. These people make up the minority of society rather than the majority. On this basis, psychologists believe they have a different type of personality from 'normal' people. This is often described as a **criminal personality**.

Although a number of psychologists agree on the idea of a separate criminal personality, there is less agreement on the characteristics of this personality. However, common characteristics include:

- impulsiveness
- lacking in feelings of guilt
- pleasure-seeking
- being over-optimistic
- self-importance.

HINT

When you have lists to remember, such as the characteristics of a criminal personality, you can use silly sentences to help you. For example '**imp**s' **g**uilty **p**leasure is **p**ouring milk **over** them**self**ves' may help you to remember **imp**ulsiveness, lacking in feeling of **guilt**, **pleasure**-seeking, being **over**-optimistic, and **self**-importance.

Core Theory: Biological Theory

In the same way that there is some debate about what a criminal personality actually is, there is also a debate about whether it is a product of nature or nurture. In other words, there is a debate about the **heritability** of criminal behaviour.

Biological theory argues that the criminal personality, and therefore criminal behaviour, *is* inherited. This means that a person has already been genetically programmed through their DNA to make them behave in anti-social ways and become a criminal. DNA is made up of genes, and genes are inherited from parents. On this basis, we would expect criminal behaviour to run in families. Indeed, studies do show there are 'criminal families' in which a number of people in each generation appear to commit crimes, whereas there are other families in which there is no evidence of criminal behaviour.

Biological theory would suggest that if an individual's parent is a convicted criminal then that individual would have a *higher chance* of becoming a criminal too. However, the individual will not automatically become a criminal – if for no other reason than the fact that individuals do not inherit all their traits from one parent. Even then, individuals can inherit behaviours which are dominant in a parent (i.e. do show themselves) but are recessive in the individual (i.e. do not show themselves), and vice versa.

If criminal behaviour is genetically inherited, the next question is: What effect do genes actually have? In other words, what do 'criminal genes' actually do to people that means they end up breaking the law?

One theory is that genes have an effect on brain development. Criminal behaviour is seen as 'abnormal', in the sense that it goes against society's norms, rules and laws. It is not surprising then, that the biological theory suggests that perhaps the brains of criminals are also 'abnormal' as well. This is described as **brain dysfunction**.

There are a number of areas of the brain that have been associated with criminal behaviour. The idea is that when they are dysfunctional and not working properly, or damaged in some way, then this increases the likelihood of criminal behaviour. Areas of the brain seen to be dysfunctional in some criminals include:

1 **Pre-frontal cortex.** This area of the brain is underactive in some criminals. It is the part of the brain where humans are conditioned to form an association between fear and anti-social behaviour.

2 **Limbic system.** This area of the brain controls aggressive and sexual behaviour. Scans show increased activity in this area in criminals compared with non-criminals. The amygdala is a specific part of the limbic system and controls emotions, such as when someone responds with sympathy to a sad face. Research shows that the amygdala does not function normally in the brains of many psychopaths.

3 **Corpus callosum.** This is the 'bridge' between the two hemispheres of the brain, which allows the rational side of the brain to communicate with the irrational side. Research on murderers shows that their corpus callosum can be less active than other people's, which means that communication between the two hemispheres of their brain is weak.

ACTIVITY

6.3

Look again at the list of characteristics associated with the criminal personality. For each one, explain how it could lead to a higher chance of someone committing a crime.

BUZZWORDS

Heritability – The proportion of a behaviour that is due to genetic factors

ACTIVITY

6.4

Heritability is one reason why criminal behaviour may run in families.

Discuss other reasons why criminal behaviour can run in families.

BUZZWORDS

Brain dysfunction – The idea that a brain is not operating as normal brains do

Specific parts of the brain are not listed on the specification, so you cannot be asked questions explicitly about them. However, a good answer to a question about brain dysfunction would make reference to parts of the brain rather than the brain in general. Although it is quite difficult to remember different parts of the brain, it might be useful to learn one or two and what their functions are.

HINT

Make connections between the name of the part of the brain and its functions. For example, for the limbic system, you could picture lots of limbs flaying around as people fight or have sex!

BUZZWORDS

Facial features – Features which make up the face, such as forehead, eyes, nose, mouth and chin

4 **Temporal lobe.** This part of the brain is involved in many functions, including language, learning, emotions and memory. Research has shown that brain-wave activity is more likely to be slower in the temporal lobe of aggressive psychopaths compared with that in the normal population.

ACTIVITY

6.5

Look again the areas of the brain associated with criminal behaviour. Copy out Table 6.1, and complete it by explaining how dysfunction in that area of the brain could be responsible for criminal behaviour. The first one is done for you as an example.

Table 6.1

Area of brain	How dysfunction explains criminal behaviour
Pre-frontal cortex	Criminals do not associate anti-social behaviour with fear, so do not worry about the consequences of committing an offence.
Limbic system	
Corpus callosum	
Temporal lobe	

If there is a gene for criminal behaviour, it is possible that the same gene could affect appearance as well as behaviour. For a long time, a small group of psychologists have argued that criminals look physically different from non-criminals (this idea originated in the Victorian period, in the nineteenth century). If this were true, it would fit in with the biological theory as most researchers agree that our physical appearance is mainly determined by our biology.

The **facial features** that have been associated with criminals in the past include:

- asymmetrical faces
- low and sloping foreheads
- glinting or glassy eyes
- high cheekbones
- large, protruding, handle-shaped ears
- crooked, flat or upturned noses
- fleshy lips
- strong jaws
- prominent chins
- lots of hair.

6.6

Look at the photograph of Peter Sutcliffe (Figure 6.1).

Figure 6.1 *Peter Sutcliffe.*

He was an infamous serial rapist and killer in the 1970s and early 1980s.

How many of the facial features associated with criminals do you think apply to Peter Sutcliffe?

To conclude, there is an argument that certain people are born to be criminals and, therefore, criminal behaviour is genetic. The evidence for the genetic basis of criminal behaviour can be seen in family histories, in brain investigation and possibly even in a person's facial features.

Criticisms of the biological theory

There are a number of criticisms of the biological theory of criminal behaviour, including the following.

- **Critics of the biological theory argue that there cannot be one criminal gene that accounts for all criminal behaviour.** It is hard to believe that the same gene is responsible for violent crimes such as rape, for intellectual crimes such as fraud, and for crimes against property such as theft. In addition, crimes do not really 'exist' in the sense that society creates them, so can there really be a gene behind crimes? For example, a person would be considered criminal if they helped a person to die in the UK but not if they helped a person to die in the Netherlands – yet their genetic make-up obviously does not change between those two cultures!

- **Brain dysfunction is only evident in some criminals, so it does not reliably predict whether someone is going to be a criminal or not.** In addition, brain dysfunction may not necessarily be genetic. It could be caused by problems in birth or pregnancy, through illness or injury, or through environmental factors (e.g. pollution or diet). This would still fit in with the biological theory, but it does further show that it is hard to predict exactly what causes criminal behaviour.

- **The idea that criminals have a different set of features from other people is not well supported by evidence. Even when criminals appear to look different, it can be explained by other factors besides genetics.** For example, society may be prejudiced against certain looks and this is why certain types of people end up turning to crime, being arrested or being sent to prison.

- **The biological theory clearly ignores the influence of the social environment on criminal behaviour.** The fact that crime seems to run in families can equally be explained by the theory that children learn their criminal behaviour from their parents and others, and so it continues through generations.

An Alternative Theory: Social Learning Theory

As suggested above, criminal behaviour is just as likely to be learnt as inherited. This is what is argued by the social learning theory.

The social learning theory works on the basis that we learn most behaviours from observing and imitating others. In terms of crime, if a child sees his older brother threatening someone with a knife and getting away with their belongings, the younger brother may be motivated to copy him. However, the theory says that we do not imitate everyone we

ACTIVITY

6.7

Look at the following list of common role models. Try and give an example of a crime that each one might be observed committing.

1 a parent

2 a friend

3 a TV character.

ACTIVITY

6.8

Look at the following examples, and identify the example of vicarious reinforcement in each case.

1 Dean decides to sell drugs because he sees how many luxuries his older brother can afford from drug dealing.

2 Sam went out and mugged a passer-by after he saw his mate get away with somebody's wallet the day before.

3 Leanne wants to go out and steal a car after she saw a television programme on joy-riding, in which the teenagers in the car seemed to get a real thrill out of it.

4 Jayesh plans to burn his school down after coming across a girl on the internet who is getting loads of hits for her video in which she does the same.

observe. Individuals imitate their role models. These are people who individuals admire and respect, and want to be like.

The social learning theory states that we look towards our role models to see how we should behave. Again, we do not automatically imitate everything we see our role models do. Individuals are more likely to imitate behaviours that they see being rewarded. This is known as **vicarious reinforcement**. In other words, an individual is not directly reinforced themselves, but they see others being rewarded. On this basis, they think, 'If I do so-and-so, I will be rewarded too'. For example, if a child sees her father get a lot of adulation and attention after he has beaten someone up, she may be motivated to copy him and go out and fight with other children. If she is directly reinforced after doing this, then she is even more likely to continue with the behaviour, according to the social learning theory.

The social learning theory has played a big part in calls to ban and restrict media that glorifies violence and other criminal behaviour.

Figure 6.2 *Children may learn criminal behaviour from the media just as much as they do from parents and other people around them.*

There is a body of evidence that shows that people, and especially children, are influenced by what they see on-screen and in other formats. This is one of the reasons why there are systems in place such as certification of films, parental guidance warnings on computer games and television watersheds (times when only certain scenes are broadcast).

Core Study: Mednick *et al.* (1984)

One way of investigating the nature–nurture debate is to study people who have been adopted. In theory, if a behaviour is more to do with nature, then an adopted person's behaviour should be more similar to their biological parents' from whom they have inherited their genes. However, if a behaviour is more to do with nurture, then a person's behaviour should be more similar to their adoptive parents' who have brought them up.

The origins of criminal behaviour have been investigated using adoption studies. One of the most extensive adoption studies into criminal behaviour was carried out by Mednick, Gabrielli and Hutchings in 1984.

Procedure

Mednick *et al.* carried out their adoption study in Denmark. They accessed the criminal records of over 14,000 males born between the years of 1924 and 1947. They then compared these men's records with the criminal records of their biological parents and of their adoptive parents.

Results

The results of the study are summarised in Table 6.2 below, which shows the percentage of adoptees who had criminal convictions.

Table 6.2 shows the influence of genetics on criminal behaviour. Compare the first column of figures with the second column of figures. This shows that if a person's biological parents had been convicted of a crime, then they were nearly twice as likely to be convicted of a crime themselves than adoptees whose biological parents had not been convicted of a crime. Similarly, even when an adoptive parent committed a crime this had less influence on adopted children than their actual biological parent committing a crime (14.7% versus 20%).

> **HINT**
>
> The procedure is quite straightforward in Mednick *et al.*'s study. Therefore, it is important to have a detailed knowledge and understanding of the findings, in case you have to describe the study in the exam.

Table 6.2

	Did have biological parents who were convicted of a crime	Did *not* have biological parents who were convicted of a crime
Did have adoptive parents who were convicted of a crime	24.5%	14.7%
Did *not* have adoptive parents who were convicted of a crime	20.0%	13.5%

HOW SCIENCE WORKS

See Research in Psychology, page 166, for more information on **correlations**.

Further analysis showed that there was a particularly strong correlation between biological parents and their sons for property crimes (as opposed to violent crimes). In addition, if a biological parent had three or more convictions, then they were significantly more likely to produce a son who also committed a crime compared with biological parents with no convictions.

Other findings further supported the role of genetic factors in criminal behaviour. If unrelated siblings were raised in the same adoptive family, only 8 per cent of them both committed a crime. This showed that the effect of the adoptive family was quite weak because if related siblings were raised in *different* adoptive families, then as many as 20 per cent of them both committed crimes. This was despite being brought up in different environments. Even more interestingly, if siblings raised in different environments had a biological father convicted of crime, then 30 per cent of them both committed a crime. This shows that their genetic predisposition towards crime was unaffected by the adoptive families they were raised in.

Overall, Mednick *et al.* concluded that there is a strong genetic component to criminal behaviour. However, they did not completely rule out the effect of the environment. This is why adoptees with *both* criminal biological and adoptive parents had the highest chance of a conviction themselves. The effect of the environment added to the effect of genes.

Limitations

- **The study relied on records of criminal convictions that may have been unreliable. As with any criminal records, they rely on crimes being reported or detected, and criminals then convicted.** For example, some of the parents or adoptees may have committed crimes but may not have been caught, so that the statistics may be inaccurate. Similarly, some of the convictions may not have been fair. When we bear in mind that most people admit to committing some offence, it seems unlikely that so many adoptees were really non-offenders.

- **A common problem with adoptions is that most children spend some time with their biological parents before being removed or given up for adoption.** Even though over 90 per cent of the adoptees in the Mednick *et al.* study were adopted before the age of 2, many still spent some of their early lives with their biological parents. This is sometimes described as a 'contamination effect'. A number of

ACTIVITY

6.9

Complete Table 6.3 to show the percentage of siblings where both commit crimes depending on their family situation.

Table 6.3

	Unrelated siblings in same adoptive family	Related siblings in different adoptive families
Percentage of siblings where both commit a crime		

psychologists believe that the experiences we have very early on in our lives are crucial to our development. If we bear in mind that some of the children being studied spent some time with their biological parents, then this may explain the relationship between their behaviour and their biological parents' behaviour.

- **The sample of adoptees was biased because they were all males.** This means it is not safe to generalise and apply the findings to females. It could be that females are more or less likely to inherit criminal behaviour from their parents. Without testing this, the researchers could not be sure how representative their results are.

HOW SCIENCE WORKS

See Research in Psychology for more information on:

- **Biased samples**, page 172
- **Representative**, page 156

Figure 6.3 *Some psychologists suggest that spending even a little time with a biological parent before adoption can result in a 'contamination effect'.*

Applications of Research into Criminal Behaviour: Crime Reduction

The biological theory is not a very popular theory of criminal behaviour because it implies, basically, that it would be difficult to reduce crime. Why? Because it says that people are born criminals and this is fixed by their genes. If it is not possible to change an individual's genetic make-up, then presumably the theory could argue that we should 'lock up criminals and throw away the key'!

Not many societies and governments seem to agree with the biological theory's perspective on criminal behaviour. Most societies invest a lot of resources into trying to reduce crime, which implies that criminal behaviour can be changed. This would suggest that criminal behaviour is more to do with learning and experiences rather than anything else.

ACTIVITY

6.10

Questions on the core study

Answer the following questions on Mednick *et al.*'s adoption study into the genetic basis of criminal behaviour.

1 State how many adoptees were studied. [1]

2 Whose criminal records were the adoptees' criminal records compared with? [2]

3 According to Table 6.2, which group of adoptees had the lowest percentage of criminal convictions? [1]

4 Use Table 6.2 to identify the adoptees who were adopted by parents with no criminal convictions. Calculate the difference in the percentages of convictions between those with criminal biological parents and those without criminal biological parents. [1]

5 Outline what is meant by the 'contamination effect' in adoption studies. [2]

6 Explain how siblings reared apart would both be more likely to commit a crime than unrelated siblings brought up in the same family. [2]

7 Explain why it would be more useful to study identical twins who have been reared apart rather than regular siblings. [3]

8 A common criticism of adoption studies is that they overlook the fact that adoptive parents will often know something of the adoptees' backgrounds. Explain how this may have affected the findings in the Mednick *et al.* study. [4]

ACTIVITY

6.11

Go onto the website www. probation.homeoffice.gov.uk and enter 'reducing reoffending' into the search engine. You should get 'information for offenders' on different rehabilitation programmes. This should be in the form of leaflets.

Use the leaflets to create a spray diagram of the different types of rehabilitation programmes. For each one, give a brief outline of what the programme involves. This outline should say what it is that the programme is trying to *reinforce*.

For example, prisons are about punishing criminal behaviour to reduce the chance of it happening again. Meanwhile, rehabilitation programmes are more about reinforcing appropriate, law-abiding behaviour in people. Psychological techniques can also be used to prevent crime in the first place.

Crime prevention

As mentioned earlier, the media is often seen as a source of criminal behaviour because people imitate anti-social acts they have witnessed on screen or elsewhere. Placing restrictions or bans on what is viewed is one way of trying to reduce 'copy-cat' crimes. However, with the continuing expansion of the internet (which is much more difficult to monitor), this is becoming more difficult.

There is a lot of evidence that criminals 'start young'. On this basis, there are early intervention programmes in place which try to discourage criminal behaviour. For example, these can be delivered through the education system, youth services or social services. The psychology behind early intervention is to stop children learning bad behaviour. Instead, appropriate and co-operative behaviour is reinforced.

People often think of prisons, community orders and fines as punishments. But they are also powerful deterrents. Many people do not commit crimes in the first place because of fear of punishment. In the same way that people are more likely to imitate actions that they see as being rewarded (i.e. vicarious reinforcement), they are also less likely to imitate actions that they see are punished. On this basis, an important part of preventing crime is to make sure that criminals are seen to 'get what they deserve'!

Rehabilitation

The UK justice system does attempt to punish crimes to stop them happening again. However, this is not enough in itself. It also has to teach criminals appropriate behaviour. This is the aim of rehabilitation (see Activity 6.11).

Use of prisons

ACTIVITY

6.12

Imagine you are a criminal psychologist who has been asked to write an article on the strengths and limitations of using prisons to punish crimes. Draw up a list of pros and cons for using prisons. Your article has to give a balanced view, so try to think of as many strengths as limitations. Remember, as a psychologist you will need to go beyond practical considerations (such as cost) and think more about the *psychological* advantages and disadvantages.

Figure 6.4 *Prisons are just one of a number of ways in which we can try to reduce crime.*

Your brief is to investigate whether criminals do look different from non-criminals as stated by some supporters of the biological theory.

To do this you will need to carry out an experiment in which you present participants with a series of criminal and non-criminal faces to see if they can identify the criminal each time. If they can, this would suggest that criminals look different from non-criminals.

What is your hypothesis? Do you think that your participants can identify a criminal by looking at facial features alone?

To carry out your experiment you will need to find some pictures of criminal faces and non-criminal faces. It is relatively easy to find criminal faces by using sources such as newspapers or 'most wanted' internet sites. It is more difficult to be sure whether someone is *not* a criminal. However, it might be relatively reliable to use an internet site where employees are profiled. Remember, ethically speaking you should not use photographs of people for research purposes without their consent. However, if the photographs are available for public consumption then this is acceptable.

You need to decide how many faces you will need for the experiment. If you want some guidance on this, it is recommended that you present faces in groups of three: one face will be a criminal and the other two will be non-criminals. You will need to have a number of sets of faces like this to be able to collect reliable data. Once you have presented your first three faces, you will present another three, and so on. Each time your participants correctly identify the criminal face then record it.

The idea is to investigate how many times a criminal face is identified *more than you would expect on average*. Of course, the participants have got a chance of just guessing the right face and you need to take this into account. If you present three faces, the participant has got a one in three *chance* of getting it right each time anyway. So if you present six sets of faces, you would expect them to identify the criminal face correctly two times (a third of six) just by chance. So will they do better than this, and identify the criminal three, four, five or even all six times? If you present twelve sets of faces, you would expect them to identify the criminal face correctly four times just by chance. So will they do better than this?

You need to carry out your experiment on a number of participants to identify the trend in results. When you have done this, you need to calculate the mean number of times a criminal is identified correctly. You must then analyse whether this is better than what you would expect as a chance result.

What do your findings show? Are people able to identify a criminal face better than they would by chance?

Next, it is time to evaluate your research. It is difficult to control all variables, even in an experiment. What factors may have made your results unreliable?

See Research in Psychology for more information on:

- **Ethical considerations**, see page 158
- **Experiments**, see page 159
- **Hypotheses**, see page 151
- **The mean**, see page 168

Summary

- Criminal behaviour is a difficult area to study as it is not even possible to start with an accurate definition or measure of crime. Because most people have broken the law, a lot of psychological research focuses on the criminal personality. This type of personality applies to a minority of people who are serious offenders.
- The biological theory of criminal behaviour argues that the behaviour is inherited. The genes that cause criminal behaviour may be causing brain dysfunction and may even be responsible for giving criminals distinct facial features.
- The social learning theory offers an alternative to the biological theory. It states that people are not born criminals. It argues that people learn criminal behaviour vicariously by observing their role models being reinforced for crimes.
- Mednick *et al.*'s adoption study showed that adoptees are more likely to inherit their criminal tendencies from their biological parents than they are to learn them from their adoptive parents.
- Applications of research into criminal behaviour include strategies for reducing crime, such as use of prisons, rehabilitation and crime prevention techniques.

ExamCafé

Revision

Key Concepts

Three factors that affect how we define crime are:

- **C**ulture
- **I**ntention
- **D**amage.

You might be able to remember these if you note that their initial letters spell CID – the branch of the police that investigates more serious crimes!

Revision Checklist

For the exam you need to feel confident about:

1 The problems of *defining* and *measuring* crime.
2 What is meant by a *criminal personality*.
3 The *biological theory* of criminal behaviour, including considering the *social learning theory* as an alternative theory for explaining criminal behaviour.
4 Mednick *et al.*'s adoption study into the *genetic basis* of criminal behaviour.
5 The applications of research into criminal behaviour in relation to crime reduction.

Quiz

There are a lot of numbers in the description of Mednick *et al.*'s adoption study into the genetic basis of criminal behaviour.

Write out the following list of numbers. Can you remember what the numbers relate to?

- 4000
- 1924–1947
- 20

- 3
- 30

Summarising Content

The biological theory refers to a number of parts of the brain that may be associated with criminal behaviour. You may find it helpful to download a diagram of the brain and then colour or highlight the parts of the brain that the theory refers to. You could even label the brain with the types of behaviour they affect. This will give you something to visualise in the exam.

Can you solve these anagrams to give you some of the facial features that have been associated with criminals? (Don't look back: that's cheating!)

- *slimmeyratca* faces
- *slygas* eyes
- *turnipdrog* ears

- *ginlops* forehead
- *snotgr* jaws

Exam Preparation

Look at the following exam question.

> 1 Describe **one** problem in measuring crime. [3]

Consider the following exam question.

> 2 Describe the social learning of criminal behaviour. [6]

Below is a candidate's response to the following question.

> 3 Describe and evaluate the biological theory of criminal behaviour. [10]

Student Answer

Q3 The biological theory is on the nature side of the nature–nurture debate when it comes to criminal behaviour. The social learning theory is on the other side of the debate. The biological theory thinks that criminals have brain dysfunction, which means they become aggressive easily and do not have much of a conscience. The biological theory also believes that people end up as criminals because they inherit criminal genes from their families. The genes affect areas of the brain, such as the limbic system and the pre-frontal lobe. Mednick et al. showed that criminal behaviour is genetic because when they studied adopted children they found they were more likely to end up committing crimes if their biological parents had done them too.

Examiner says:
It is good practice to include studies in an essay as research can be used as evaluation. Evidence tends to strengthen an essay.

Examiner's Tip:
Q1. For 3 marks, it might be tempting to offer a number of problems in measuring crime. However, the examiner will only be able to credit you for one, regardless of how many you write about. It is quite difficult to write about one problem in measuring crime in detail but if you choose a broad problem, such as 'people not reporting crimes' you can then go on to explore some of the different reasons why they do not report crimes.

Examiner's Tip:
Q2. Examiners often see many common sense answers when candidates are asked about the social learning theory. Weak responses tend to make references to 'learning from others' and 'copying behaviour', which is not wrong but it is not very technical. Try to use accurate terminology when writing about the social learning theory (e.g. observation, imitation) and especially use the terms referred to on the specification (i.e. 'the vicarious reinforcement of role models'). To earn full marks, it is also important to apply the theory to the behaviour in question. It would very easy – but also a mistake – to describe social learning theory in detail without relating it to criminal behaviours or examples of criminal behaviour.

Examiner says:
It is also good practice to include applications in an essay. This is a useful way of testing a theory – in other words, does the theory work in practice?

But if criminal behaviour is genetic, then why do we have prisons and rehabilitation programmes? Surely there would be no point as genetics suggests that criminal behaviour can't be changed.

If criminal behaviour is genetic, then you might expect criminals to look different as well as behave differently. Psychologists have said that criminals have ears that stick out, big chins and low foreheads. Perhaps because people look like this, they are discriminated against and that is why they end up committing crimes.

Examiner says:
This essay includes a lot of relevant points and detail. However, it would score higher if it was more coherent. Not all points are explained clearly enough, and the essay tends to 'jump around' rather than follow a logical order.

Planning and Structuring an Answer

You should try to find the time to plan essays in the exam. You can use the space on the exam paper to do this (and then cross out your plan afterwards).

You need to remember that an essay will always have 5 marks for description (of a theory or study) and 5 marks for evaluating it. A good 'rule of thumb' is to come up with five features of the theory or study and then five evaluation points. However, if you know that one or some of your evaluation points can easily be expanded on, this will be worth more than 1 mark.

As part of your plan, bullet-point the five things you want to say about the theory or study. Then bullet-point the things you want to say to evaluate it. Look at these points and number them to help you decide what order to present them in.

A lot of candidates tend to do all their description first (and so number their description points 1 to 5) and then the evaluation points come afterwards. This is fine. However, sometimes you may want to evaluate as you go along. An example is if you are describing a study and you outline the sample early on. If you want to criticise the sample, you do not have to do this at the end of the essay. You could consider criticising the sample after you have outlined it. This often makes an essay look more sophisticated and it tends to be easier to follow.

Perception

Cognitive psychology focuses on mental processes and what is happening in the brain. What you are doing at this precise moment as you read these words is known as visual processing. Of the information received by your brain in any one day, approximately 75 per cent comes through your eyes. Of course, most of us have a range of senses – touch, hearing, smell, taste – but visual perception is easily our most dominant and important sense, with a huge part of the cortex at the back of your brain devoted to it. The human eye is clever; for example, it can distinguish between more than 300 different colours. But 'there's more to seeing than meets the eye'. We see in the fullest sense with our brains. Our eyes are just the sense organs, which collect the data. The brain then processes the data to make pictures that usually mean something to us.

LEARNING OBJECTIVES:

By the end of this topic, you should be able to:

1 Distinguish between *sensation* and *perception*, including visual illusions.

2 Describe the role of visual *constancies* in perception.

3 Understand *depth perception* and the use of cues, including
  - linear perspective
  - height in plane
  - relative size
  - superimposition
  - texture gradient.

4 Understand the *constructivist theory* of perception: the role of experience, and the *top-down* explanation based on *perceptual set*.

5 Understand the alternative *nativist bottom-up* theory of perception.

6 Describe and evaluate *Haber and Levin's research* into the role of familiarity in depth perception.

7 Show awareness of applications of research into perception, for example in advertising.

Key Concepts

The ability to see and understand our physical surroundings is for most of us an automatic part of our everyday experience. We take for granted the ability to see colour, shape and movement. We instantly recognise familiar objects; for example, we recognise a chair as a chair, irrespective of the angle from which we see it. We recognise faces even if we forget names. All of this begins at an extremely early age.

ACTIVITY

7.1

Look at the definitions of 'sensation' and 'perception'. Use them to analyse the similarities and differences between the two concepts.

By infancy all the 'building blocks' of visual perception are in place, including:

- the ability to be fooled or get it wrong in visual illusions
- the permanent tools of visual constancies, for example shape and colour
- the use of depth cues.

Before we can perceive our world, we must first be able to sense it. **Sensation** refers to the information or data collected by our sense organs, for example ears, eyes, tongue, nose and fingers. The sensations or information for visual perception are light waves picked up by the eyes. These light waves are sorted out by the retina, or 'film', within the eyes into electrical information. This is then sent across the brain to the visual cortex, or processing centre, at the back of the brain.

Perception is the process through which the visual cortex assembles and combines sensations from the eyes into meaningful images (i.e. sorts individual sensations into the pictures we claim to see).

Sometimes there can be a mismatch between a sensation and our perception. This is called an **illusion**. Our brain plays a trick on us, misinterpreting the sense data supplied by the eyes.

A visual illusion is when people 'see' something which is distorted or false. It can occur when visual cues are misinterpreted by the brain.

A number of basic illusions have been identified:

- **Geometric Illusions** – In geometric illusions it seems that one line or another is somehow distorted and we get it wrong in our minds. There are a number of well-known geometric illusions including the Ponzo illusion (Figure 7.1). When you look at the horizontal lines in between railway lines your brain persuades you that the top one must be further away and therefore wider. However, if you measure them they are identical.

Figure 7.1 *Ponzo illusion.*

- **Ambiguous figures** – This is a picture or drawing that can be seen in more than one way. The best-known example is the Necker cube (Figure 7.2). Stare at the 'x' letters and you will see that they sometimes appear to be at the back, and sometimes at the front, of the cube.

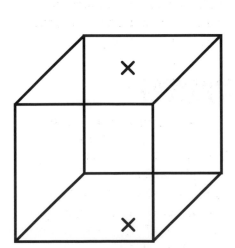

Figure 7.2 *Necker cube.*

COGNITIVE PSYCHOLOGY

7

- **Fictions** – This is simply seeing something which is not actually there. A well-known example is the Kaniza triangle (Figure 7.3). There is no white triangle in the middle of the drawings, but it seems as if there is. It's an illusion!

Figure 7.3 *Kaniza triangle.*

All of these examples of illusion illustrate the point that sensation and perception are different processes. In illusions we perceive things that are not actually true or in other words are not actually sensed (e.g. objects which are not really there, or an image which appears to change when it does not).

We do not need to create illusions to show the power of perception. Everyday perception is full of interesting puzzles, such as how objects, people and animals constantly change their shape as they move about but we still see them as remaining the same size, shape and colour. For example, a car does not shrink in size as it speeds away even though the image of it in the eye grows smaller and smaller. A door does not take on an angled shape when you walk through it even though that's what happens to its shape in your eyes. You know that a bottle of water is still clear even though it looks a different colour under strobe lights.

Visual constancies allow us to see things as remaining the same even though their physical characteristics are constantly changing.

Let's look more closely at two of these constancies.

1 **Shape constancy** – our tendency or habit of seeing an object keep its shape even though we see it from different angles, and the image in the eye is continually changing. For example, when you look down at a rectangular school book it projects that very shape and that's what you say you see. If you tilt the book away from you, it projects a bent shape in your eye but you still see the book in its original shape.

2 **Colour constancy** – Our tendency to see colours as remaining the same despite differences in lighting. For example, if you look into

HINT

It would be useful to be able to sketch at least one of these illusions. It is often easier to demonstrate the difference between sensation and perception if you have something visual to refer to.

ACTIVITY

7.2

Choose an object in your classroom. Choose carefully, as you are going to have to draw it! If it is possible to rotate the object (e.g. a stapler) then do this three or four times. Alternatively, you can look at an object (e.g. a desk) from three or four different angles. Sketch the object each time you rotate it or move around it.

Afterwards, look at your sketches. How different is the shape of the object from different angles? This is what your eye is sensing. It should make you realise how different the sensations are from the actual object you perceive.

BUZZWORDS

Shape constancy – the ability to perceive the shape of an object as constant even if it appears to change through movement

Colour constancy – The ability to perceive the colour of an object as constant even if it appears to change with changes in lighting

your wardrobe with very little light on, all the brightly coloured clothes will look dull but you still perceive them in their original colours and have no trouble picking what to wear. If you look at someone wearing a yellow T-shirt in bright sunlight and then in dull light you know that they are wearing the same T-shirt. Just like illusions, visual constancies illustrate the difference between sensation and perception. Although the sensations on the back of the eye may be changing (e.g. as we move around an object), the perception (of the object) is held constant.

Depth perception also illustrates the difference between sensation and perception. When we sense or look at the environment around us, the image on the back of the eye is two-dimensional – like a photograph. However, the world we perceive in our minds is the three-dimensional one we live in. Depth perception, therefore, refers to the ability of our eyes and brain to add a third dimension, depth, to everything we see. The question is, how does the brain work this all out? What does it take into account in helping us to see three-dimensionally?

Psychologists have identified a number of the depth cues that the brain uses:

1 **Linear perspective** – As you look down a stretch of motorway the outside lines of the road and the white-line markings appear to come together or converge at a distant point. This allows us to interpret the distance of the road, and is known as *linear perspective*.

2 **Height in the plane** – This is also a device or trick used by painters. If the image of an object is higher to the eyes (i.e. above the horizontal halfway line) it is often seen as further away or more distant than objects in the lower part of the painting (see Figure 7.4).

Figure 7.4 *The height of the elephant makes it look more distant than the antelope.*

3 **Relative size** – This is when we expect two objects to be the same size and when we look at them they are not. Our brain interprets this to mean that the bigger one is closer and the smaller one is farther away. For example, it is easy to use relative size with adult human beings as they are approximately the same size. So a goalkeeper looking down the pitch in a football match will be able to work out that the players who appear bigger are closer to him. Players at the other end of the pitch will appear to be smaller. (In Figure 7.4 the antelope appears bigger than the elephant, showing that it is nearer.)

4 **Superimposition** – Put simply, if the image of one object blocks or lies across the image of another object we decide that the first object must be that bit closer to us. The further object will be partially hidden (see Figure 7.5).

5 **Texture gradient** – Imagine you are standing on a beach and are looking along it. The grains of sand and pebbles are pretty clear when you look down at them. However, when you look along the beach they appear to 'blend into one' and give a smoother, less detailed texture. We use this effect to spot nearness and distance (see Figure 7.6).

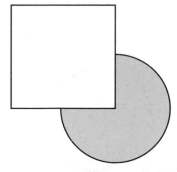

Figure 7.5 *Superimposition.*

ACTIVITY

7.3

You will need to start by getting a photograph of a detailed scene, e.g. a high street, a rural landscape or a sporting event.

Annotate the photograph to show as many different examples of depth cues that you can find.

Are some depth cues more common than others?

Figure 7.6 *Texture gradient.*

Core Theory: The Constructivist Theory of Perception

The **constructivist theory** proposes that we construct our perception of the world not only based on what we see in front of us, but also based on past experience. For example, we recognise the people we share a classroom with partly because we expect them to be there every day anyway. We may not register a new face as quickly because we have no experience of it. It may take us a while to realise that we do *not* know this person.

The constructivist theory supports the idea of **top-down processing**. This means that when the brain is sorting out objects it makes use of past experience, including prior knowledge, cultural features, motivation, expectations and memory. Put simply, what is already in your mind affects what you see here and now. A term associated with this idea is **perceptual set** – a tendency to perceive a scene, situation or object on the basis of what you expect to see.

A number of factors demonstrate the role of perceptual set in processing.

- **Expectations.** You've probably already experienced this when meeting a friend outside the cinema or shops. There may be lots of people milling around but you can pick out your friend easily because you are expecting to see them. You might not notice them somewhere else because you were not expecting them to be there. Look at Figure 7.7 – the middle figure can be a number or letter, you might see one or the other depending on what you have been told.

- **Motivation.** How we are feeling can affect what we see. Research showed that hungry and thirsty people saw pictures of food and drink as brighter than pictures of other objects, but that the difference disappeared when they were allowed to eat and drink.

BUZZWORDS

Constructivist theory – The theory that perception is constructed using past experiences

Top-down processing – When perception is dominated by what we expect to see

Perceptual set – A tendency to perceive something in line with what you expect based on past experience

HINT

If you remember that the brain is above (on top of) the eyes then this may help you to remember what top-down processing is. In other words, the brain has an impact on what we think we are seeing through our eyes.

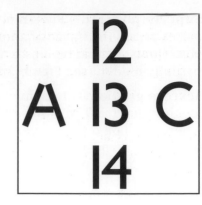

7.4

Think about this:

1 Two people are looking up at the clear night sky. One of them is an astronomer. How might they differ in describing what they see above them, and why?

2 Two people are out on a walk in the countryside. One of them is a keen gardener. How might they differ in spotting things in the hedgerows, and why?

How does this relate to the ideas of top-down processing and perceptual set?

Figure 7.7

Of course, as you have probably guessed already, illusions are 'the proof of the pudding' when it comes to the top-down constructivist theory. Remember, illusions happen because our brains are too clever. It is our brain (with top-down processing) that fools us into illusions when the eyes get it right.

Criticisms of the constructivist theory

The top-down constructivist theory, of course, has its limitations:

- **If perception is based so heavily on individual experiences, then why do people tend to perceive the world in a similar way?** Only rarely do we disagree with people about what we see in front of us. If we do see the world in similar ways, then this suggests that most information is coming from the environment and not 'down' from our minds.

- **If perception requires experience, then how do we explain the newborn baby's ability to perceive their world?** There have been a number of studies carried out on newborns which show that they have some perceptual abilities early on. For example, babies as young as two months appear to recognise faces and complex patterns, and six-month-olds will not crawl over an imaginary cliff edge despite their limited experience of the environment.

- **The effect of illusions actually questions rather than supports constructivist theory.** If we think about it logically, then we should not fall for the same illusion time and time again. If perception is about experience, then we should learn not to be fooled by an illusion second time around. Yet this rarely happens.

The main criticism of the top-down theory is that it tends to ignore the fact that we are born to see, and make sense of, distance, movement, colour and shape. Our natural three-dimensional world is there for us to perceive as a baby, for example.

An Alternative Theory: Nativist Theory

As suggested above, the constructivist theory ignores the role of nature in perception. The nativist theory is the opposite, and believes that instinct and biology play an important role in perception.

The **nativist theory** states that perception is the result of a bottom-up process rather than a top-down process. **Bottom-up processing**

Grade Studio

It is acceptable to evaluate a theory by posing questions; for example: How do we explain the newborn baby's ability to perceive the world? However, if you want to earn higher marks, you should go on to address or elaborate on these questions.

BUZZWORDS

Nativist theory – The theory that perception is a natural and instinctive process

Bottom-up processing – When perception is dominated by what enters through the eyes (rather than what we expect to see)

7
COGNITIVE PSYCHOLOGY

means that perception is *immediate* or *direct* and is data-driven; it starts with independent information from the environment and works its way upwards to an interpretation of that information (i.e. eyes see something first and then the brain registers it).

Imagine the following.

- You are in the passenger seat of a car travelling along a main road and you are just aware of distance because of what has been called the *optic flow* hitting your eyes, the road rushing at you from a distance.
- You turn your head and you see something behind you that a second before was out of sight – but normally that is no big deal and you are not surprised.
- You are looking in a catalogue and see thirteen different kinds of mobile phone and you just know, without really thinking, what they are – even if they are different in shape or colour.
- You are on a football or rugby pitch or tennis court and you just look and know where the ball or player is immediately, or directly, just with your eyes.
- You are at the back of a rock concert hall and you know instantly where you are in the hall without measuring or looking at a seating plan.

All of the above are examples of bottom-up processing. Why? Because we are perceiving the world around us by using the information that is out there in the environment. We perceive the world as it is – it is not based on expectations or misinterpretations. The role of the mind or brain is to simply analyse and integrate the information coming through our eyes. The nativist theory would argue that this happens as naturally as something like breathing. This would explain why we perceive what is happening around us so quickly, and why as humans we tend to see the world in the same way. For example, the nativist theory states that we do not tend to disagree on the colour, shape, position, distance or speed of objects. We have all evolved in the same way so we perceive our world in the same way.

HINT

If you remember that the eyes are below (at the bottom of) the brain then this may help you to remember what bottom-up processing is. In other words, the eyes have the biggest impact on what we see and the brain merely interprets this information after the event.

Grade Studio

You may have to explain the difference between top-down and bottom-up processing in the exam. As well as being able to define each term, make sure you can draw a distinction between them too.

Grade Studio

Remember that you can always use one theory to evaluate another. A link sentence, for example, 'However, another explanation ...' will show that you are aware of an alternative theory as evaluation.

ACTIVITY

7.5

One of the differences between the constructivist theory and the nativist theory of perception is to do with how much of the world we perceive is the same as others do. If perception is based on our own past experiences, we should perceive the world quite differently. If perception is a product of human nature, we should perceive the world in similar ways.

Draw up a table with two columns, and the headings: 'Things we perceive differently' and 'Things we perceive the same'.

Then look at the list of stimuli below. Discuss with other students which of these stimuli would be perceived the same or differently by people and put them in the relevant column in your table.

You should also try to add some of your own examples.

- The time on a clock
- How many people in a football crowd
- The colour of a car
- The shape of a window
- How generous a portion of chips is
- How many bollards there are along a pavement
- How high a mountain is
- How long a garden is
- Whether someone is naked or not
- The speed of a car overtaking you

Does one column have more items in? Which theory does this support? Why?

Core Study: Haber and Levin (2001)

The argument between top-down and bottom-up theories of perception was investigated in an experiment conducted in the USA by Haber and Levin in 2001.

Procedure

Nine male college students, who had been tested for good eyesight, were driven out to a large grassy field surrounded on three sides by trees. The field had been divided and prepared into four separate sections.

- The first section was the arrival area and was empty.
- In the second section, the experimenters had placed, at random distances, fifteen real-world objects which have a known size (e.g. a milk bottle, a door).
- In the third section, they placed fifteen real-world objects which could be of different sizes (e.g. a Christmas tree and a teddy bear).
- In the fourth section, they had placed upright fifteen cardboard cut-outs of three geometric figures (i.e. circles, rectangles, triangles).

Haber and Levin used a repeated measures design. The students were taken in line to the centre of the field through the empty section and asked to face one or other section of the field, in groups of three. They had been given clipboards to record their estimates or guesses about how far away the objects were. When they had all made estimates the groups turned in a new direction and repeated the task until they had looked at all 45 objects in all three directions.

Results

When the data was analysed, it showed an interesting result. The participants' estimates of distance were most accurate for the real-world objects, which were a standard size. Their estimates were good for both near and far objects. However, their estimates for the other real-world objects and for the cut-outs of shapes were not so accurate.

Haber and Levin concluded that it was easier to estimate the distance of familiar objects because the participants were relying on their past experiences. They expected objects such as milk bottles and doors to be certain sizes, and so could work out how far away they were based on their relative size. However, with the other objects they could not use their prior knowledge in the same way. They could not be sure of their size and so could not be sure of their distance.

If the nativist theory was right, then the participants should be able to instinctively judge the distance of any object, familiar or not. The fact that their ability to judge distance relied on experience suggests that the constructivist theory is a more reliable theory of perception.

Limitations

- **It is difficult to draw conclusions from a sample that is not very representative.** The sample of nine was a very small sample which cannot be easily generalised to the rest of the population. The sample was also biased because they were all males and all college students.

- **The task and setting were artificial and unfamiliar.** Judging the distance of randomly placed items does not really relate to real life. Testing city dwellers in a field may also have distorted findings.
- **Although Haber and Levin did use a questionnaire to check how familiar items were to the participants, it is still subjective.** Can we assume that just because something like a milk bottle is familiar to the researchers that participants perceive it in the same way? It may be a coincidence that they were better at judging the distance of those objects.

Application of Research into Perception: Advertising

Research into perception can be useful to people working in the world of advertising. Why? If television and film audiences, magazine and newspaper readers, or internet users are going to buy a product, they have to *perceive* it has something they want or need in the first place. Research has shown that advertisers can influence potential customers' perception of a product in terms of how they present it.

Subliminal advertising

One striking example of advertising is called *subliminal advertising*. A subliminal message is a brief sound or image message that is directed at us without us being aware of it, that is, with less than 50 per cent chance of us spotting it.

The problem or issue is that such a hidden message can actually make us do something because our *unconscious* has heard or seen it all and gets on with it!

The worry about all of this emerged in research in America in the late 1950s. Filmgoers were reported as having bought 50 per cent more popcorn and 18 per cent more Coca-Cola when the words 'Eat popcorn' and 'Drink Coca-Cola' were projected on the screen subliminally for 1/3,000th of a second, which is well below the level of perception for seeing visual information or pictures, i.e. you wouldn't be conscious of it. A second trial, with the words 'Ice cream', was claimed to have led to a rise in sales of ice cream.

But the evidence is not overwhelming. It has been pointed out that since the film being shown was called 'Picnic' and contained several scenes of eating and drinking, perhaps the film itself rather than the hidden messages produced the increase in eating and drinking. In any case, the evidence generated enough anxiety in the USA and UK for governments to debate whether such advertising should be allowed. In the USA, in 1992, Congress took the view that the evidence for the power of subliminal advertising was not convincing. However, the practice was banned in Britain.

In a superstore, research was done into the background music being played and it noted the effect the music had on customers' shopping habits. When it was French music the amount of French wine bought rose substantially. When the music was changed to Italian, more Italian wine was bought.

HOW SCIENCE WORKS

See Research in Psychology for more information on:

- **Experiments,** page 159
- **Questionnaires,** page 161
- **Repeated measures designs,** page 154
- **Representative samples,** page 156.

ACTIVITY

7.6

Questions on the core study

Answer the following questions on the Haber and Levin experiment.

1 Describe the sample of participants in the study. [3]
2 Identify the main difference between the first two groups of objects. [2]
3 State the main way in which the third group of objects differed from the others. [2]
4 Explain which group of objects participants found easiest to estimate the distance of and why. [3]
5 Explain why Haber and Levin's study can be described as an experiment. [3]
6 Identify the experimental design used in the study. [1]
7 Outline the advantage of using the experimental design identified above. [2]
8 Explain how the bias in the sample may have affected the results. [4]

7

PERCEPTION

7.7

Visit the website www.visit4info.com where you can access and watch a variety of television adverts.

Analyse ten different adverts to see how many present more of the emotional content on the left-hand side of the screen and present more of the language content on the right-hand side of the screen.

Keep a tally, and compare your findings with others to see if there are any patterns.

7.8

Imagine you are a psychologist who has been called in by an advertising agency to help with a campaign to sell a series of products. The products are:

- shampoo
- fish-fingers
- trainers
- mobile phone
- chocolate bar.

For each of the above, give details of the context you would advertise them in and explain the reasons for your choices.

See Research in Psychology for more information on:

- **Dependent variables**, page 153
- **Experiments**, page 159
- **Hypotheses**, page 151
- **Independent groups designs**, page 154
- **Independent variables**, page 153.

Advertising for the brain

Research has shown that different parts of the brain are responsible for processing different types of information. Research has also shown that information entering through the left eye goes to the right side of the brain and vice-versa.

Some psychologists argue that the *emotional* part of a television advert should be on the left side of the screen so it can be interpreted by the right side of the brain. Any messages or words should be on the right side of the screen, to be interpreted by the left side of the brain which deals with *language* (see Activity 7.7).

Use of context in advertising

Perception of an object can be affected by the context it is presented in; for example, in adverts.

- The same pair of jeans may look sexier when modelled by a young, glamorous supermodel than when modelled by an older, dowdy woman.
- The same meat pie may look bigger and more appetising on a small plate with a few vegetables than on a huge plate piled with potatoes.
- The same car may appeal more to a female audience if driven by a woman than if driven by a man (see Activity 7.8).

Look at Figure 7.8.

 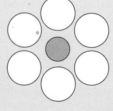

Figure 7.8

The shaded circles are the same size, but people perceive them to be different sizes because of the context they are in. The first circle appears relatively large in the context of the smaller circles but appears relatively small in the context of the larger circles.

Your brief is to use an experiment to investigate whether other stimuli are perceived differently depending on the context they are in.

You will need to use an independent groups design in which you have different participants in each condition. In one condition you will need to present the stimulus in one context, and in the other you will present it in a different context. This is the independent variable. You will also need to decide how you are going to measure your participants' perception of the stimuli. This is the dependent variable. For instance, in the example using the circles, you could ask people to estimate the diameter of the circle.

You can choose your own stimuli, and the different contexts. However, Table 7.1 has some examples to help you.

Table 7.1

Stimuli	Different contexts	Hypothesis
O (a circle)	Present it with numbers or with letters	Participants will be more likely to perceive the circle as a zero when presented with numbers rather than letters.
A turquoise square	Present it with blue squares or green squares	Participants will be more likely to perceive the square as blue when presented with green squares than with blue squares.
An androgynous face	Present it with faces of men or faces of women	Participants will be more likely to perceive the face as a man when presented with women's faces rather than men's faces.

What is your hypothesis?

When you have run your experiment, compare the findings of the two conditions. Was your prediction correct? Is there a significant difference?

Summary

- Perception focuses on visual processing. Approximately 75 per cent of the information being received by your brain in any one day is through your eyes.

- We need to distinguish between *sensation* (the physical process of collecting data) and *perception* (the cognitive process of interpreting data) from the environment via the senses. Illusion happens when we misinterpret data (a mismatch between the data from perception and sensation).

- However, there are visual constancies in perception, such as the size, shape and colour of familiar objects. Added to that is our ability to perceive the depth of objects and scenes from cues that give the visual two-dimensional image a three-dimensional perspective.

- The *constructivist* theory of perception says that experience is key to our visual perception. In other words our brain analyses what we see based on previous experiences, known as top-down processing.

- The *nativist* theory believes that the biological approach is key to our visual perception. We react simply to what we see in front of us, and this just requires bottom-up processing.

- *Haber and Levin's* research into the role of familiarity in depth perception evaluated these two theories. The result showed that the contructivist theory was more likely the correct one as it was easier to estimate the distance of familiar objects because the participants were relying on their past experiences.

- Advertising and the media use the knowledge of how people view things to maximise the message they want to get across. The application is an attempt to manipulate people's perceptions.

ExamCafé

Revision

Revision Checklist

Decide whether the following terms are associated with the constructivist or the nativist theory of perception:

- top-down processing
- bottom-up processing
- perceptual set
- experience
- nature
- motivation
- optic flow
- expectations.

Quiz

If you have understood the text and topic you should be able to make a good effort at the following. Can you suggest definitions for a new Psychology dictionary?

Word	Definition
constancy	
illusion	
linear perspective	
superimposition	
texture gradient	

If you are struggling, go back and check it out in the text.

Summarising Content

For active learning, which may well improve your recall and performance in the exam, you may find it useful to draw up a diagram to illustrate the set-up in Haber and Levin's experiment. This will help you to understand and remember it. It would even be acceptable to use a diagram in the exam as part of your description of a study.

Exam Preparation

It is possible that you may be given a photograph or picture in the exam and asked to describe the depth cues in it. A common mistake is for candidates to just identify the features of the picture in which the depth cues occur (e.g. 'the trees', 'the road', 'the signs'). There will normally be 2 marks for describing the depth cue. The first mark is for naming the actual cue (e.g. superimposition, linear perspective, relative size). The second mark is for describing how the depth cue is used in the picture (e.g. 'the trees closer to us overlap the trees that are further away', 'the sides of the road converge to a vanishing point', 'the sign at the front appears bigger even though it is the same size as the one in the background').

This topic is all about visual perception so it is acceptable to use visual aids to help you to answer questions. A drawing or sketch may also get a mark in itself. For example, you could sketch a picture to illustrate depth cues or constancies.

Planning

Remember, it is common to be asked a question about applications. In this case, the specification states that you should know about research into perception and how it can be applied in the field of advertising.

It is worth being aware that 'applications' questions can be asked in a number of ways. Below are some examples:

Describe **one** application of research into perception.   [4]

Explain **one** way in which advertising is influenced by research into perception.   [4]

Outline how research into perception can be applied in advertising.   [4]

Although the questions are worded differently, all in fact can be answered in the same way. Think about how you would answer them.

ExamCafé

Below is an examination question and a candidate's response.

> Describe and evaluate the constructivist theory of perception. **[6]**

Student Sample Answer

The constructivist theory says that perception is not innate, but is something we have to develop through experience. It says that as we learn about the world by exploring it, we learn how to make sense of it or perceive it. For example, a young baby may learn about depth by being carried around, by reaching out for objects and by bumping into things! As we build up a picture of the world around us, we use this to help us in new situations. In other words, perception is a top-down process where we rely on memories of past experiences to interpret what is around us. Expectations, along with factors such as motivation and emotion, make up our perceptual set: a set way of perceiving the world which might be different from the next person's. This means that we do not perceive the world in the same way as other people, whose experiences are different. This, of course, is one of the main problems for the constructivist theory. It fails to adequately explain why people appear to perceive the world in very similar ways. It also does not explain why we don't always learn from experience – for example, we will fall for the same illusions time and time again. It might be that our perceptual abilities are more instinctive than the constructivist theory recognises, as argued by the nativist theory.

Cognitive Development

Thinking is the way humans deal with and make sense of what is happening to them and happening around them. We use cognitive processes to do this. Put simply, from the moment we arrive on planet Earth as a human baby we begin putting our thinking caps on. However, babies do not think in the same way as we do. This needs to develop and therefore cognitive development is studied as part of Developmental Psychology.

Piaget is seen as the first psychologist to produce a 'route map' of how we develop our ability to discover, think and learn from birth to adulthood. Others, including Vygotsky, disagreed with him and put forward different explanations and theories.

LEARNING OBJECTIVES:

By the end of this topic, you should be able to:

1 Describe how cognitive development occurs in *invariant* and *universal* stages.

2 Understand the stages of cognitive development

3 Understand the key concepts of *Piaget's theory*, for example
   - object permanence
   - egocentrism and the process of de-centring
   - conservation.

4 Consider criticisms of Piaget's theory, for example through other research, and assess *Vygotsky's alternative theory* of cognitive development.

5 Show awareness of applications of research into cognitive development in relation to education.

Key Concepts

Invariant and universal stages

When a baby is born it is already equipped with relatively well-developed senses. It has feelings and expressions that it can use to make wordless communication. The child is an amazingly competent, tiny person set to begin a journey of discovery, thinking and learning which psychologists call **cognitive development**. This development is built on thought processes or *schemas*. Some are present from birth (e.g. sucking) and they follow a pattern of assimilation and accommodation (i.e. they take on board new information and accommodate it with what is already known).

Schemas or thought processes are what every child uses as it interacts with its new, outside world. All the ideas, memories and information about a particular object or thing that a child comes into contact with

BUZZWORDS

Cognitive development – Age-related changes, e.g. how children think and behave differently as they get older

are sorted into patterns in the brain. These are 'mental blueprints' that link things and behaviours. They form the building blocks of thinking, and, like psychological flashcards, children begin to pick these up and recognise them from birth.

For example, children realise that certain actions go best with certain objects – sucking goes best with a nipple, banging goes best with rattles, smiling goes best with mummy's face.

Piaget found that the development of a child's ability to think went through the same stages in a fixed or **invariant** order, like an alphabet or when counting from one to ten. These stages could more or less be tied to the ages of children. He also found that this pattern was **universal** to all children, everywhere. Interestingly, even though different children may experience different cultures, upbringing and types of education, he found that it appeared to have no effect on their pattern of cognitive development.

The stages of cognitive development are as follows:

1   The sensori-motor stage – from birth to about 2 years old

2   The pre-operational stage – from about 2 to 7 years old

3   The concrete operational stage – from about 7 to 11 years old

4   The formal operational stage – from about 11 years old, and onwards.

BUZZWORDS

Invariant stages – The same stages, in a fixed order, that the development of a child's ability to think goes through

Universal stages – The pattern or order of the development of thinking that is the same for all children everywhere

Grade Studio

Some candidates avoid using jargon (i.e. the correct psychological terms). It is best to memorise the correct terms and be prepared to use them correctly wherever you can so as to get used to thinking of them. Make sure that you can distinguish between them easily in your mind. One way of doing this is to find a way of associating terms with definitions. For example, you can remember 'univers**al** stages' by linking it to this sentence: The order of development is the same for **all** children.

HINT

It is not only important to remember the names of Piaget's stages but to get them in the right order too. You can use stories to help you to do this. For example:

A man crashed his **motor** car on the way to work (sensori-**motor**). He was rushed to hospital where the surgeon was **pre**paring to **operate** (pre-**operat**ional). However, on his way across the courtyard, the surgeon tripped and banged his head on the **concrete** (**concrete** operational). He still ended up carrying out the operation but got a **formal** (**formal** operational) warning for doing so.

ACTIVITY

8.1

Think for a moment about the differences between a newborn baby and a twelve-month-old baby, or look at photographs or watch videos of yourself at those ages.

Can you identify three ways in which the infants would react differently to things going on around them? Think about what they like doing, what seems to catch their interest, or what they seem to understand.

Core Theory: Piaget's Theory

It has been said that the huge influence of Piaget's theory on our understanding of cognitive development compares well to the influence of Shakespeare on English literature.

Piaget's theory was the result of his work in the 1920s in Paris, while looking at new intelligence tests. He noticed that children of the same age often got answers wrong in the same way. That is, they were thinking alike, but this changed with age. Piaget observed his three children at home and playing with friends. He kept detailed diaries of things they said and did as they matured. Piaget also invented a number of tasks to experiment on other children's thinking at different ages and stages (see Core Study, page 114).

Finally, Piaget observed how children, including his children's friends, solved problems in their natural settings, such as their cribs, sandboxes and playgrounds, and while playing games such as 'marbles', which was popular at the time. He watched them solve problems and asked them to explain the reasoning behind their decisions. From all this evidence, Piaget went on to put together a general stage theory of cognitive development.

In psychology a stage theory means that

- development follows a fixed (*invariant*) order or pattern
- the behaviour in question, e.g. language, *gets better by the stage*
- the pattern is true for everyone – it is *universal.*

Piaget came to the conclusion that 'children are scientists' who begin to explore the world around them from the moment they first open their eyes and begin to think about it all. Infants are not just passive observers, but are actively involved in making sense of what they see, hear, feel and discover – just like scientists.

Putting two and two together, Piaget went on to propose the idea that most children develop their thinking in clear stages. He came up with four stages of cognitive development.

The sensori-motor stage – from birth to about two years old

In this stage, thoughts and behaviour are generally the same. Babies spend their time examining their surroundings and placing objects into schemas in their minds (e.g. by sucking, shaking, banging, twisting, dropping, and through other actions that often cause mayhem for their parents). The baby gradually learns to make some sense of the information coming in through the senses.

Features of the sensori-motor stage:

1 **Body schema(s)** – The infant recognises that it exists physically (e.g. it can recognise itself in a photograph or mirror).

2 **Motor co-ordination** – The infant learns to co-ordinate different body parts (e.g. hand to mouth for eating, learning how to move knees and hands for crawling).

3 **Object permanence** – The infant knows that an object or person still exists even if they cannot be seen. When a newborn baby cannot see that thing or person, they do not exist for them anymore. Towards the end of the first year, however, perhaps as early as eight months, babies will look for hidden objects because they have developed object permanence.

ACTIVITY

8.2

1 Explain in your own words the three main features of a stage theory.

2 Why do you think Piaget used the word 'scientist' to describe children?

Figure 8.1 *An infant who has not developed object permanence does not look for a hidden toy.*

ACTIVITY

8.3

Use Piaget's concept of object permanence to explain the following three situations:

1 Rajvir's mum tries to play peek-a-boo with a toy rabbit by making it disappear behind the pram. But Rajvir, who is five months old, soon loses interest when she cannot see it.

2 Egor is seven months old. When he drops his food from the highchair he does not bother to look for it and just cries out for more.

3 Caitlin is eleven months old. When her dad puts her toys in the cupboard at the end of the day, she sits and cries for them at the foot of the cupboard doors.

Piaget investigated his own children's lack of object permanence by hiding an object under a cover, for example a doll under a cushion or sheet. Under eight months of age they did not bother to search, but by nine months they got upset by the missing toy and looked under the cushion to find it. He claimed that the change of behaviour meant a development and improvement in the children's thinking. They knew it still existed and they wanted it. In other words, they had an internal mental representation of that object.

The pre-operational stage – from about two to seven years old

At this stage, during which the child starts school, cognitive development gets better by the year. For example, children learn to use symbols, such as words, or mental images, to solve problems. Real thinking is beginning to happen. According to Piaget there are still some things the child does not get right or cannot do, including:

a) **Animism** – Children at this stage treat inanimate objects as if they too are alive just like themselves (e.g. they talk to and about their teddy bear as if it can hear and understand; they tell off a table if they hurt themselves on it).

b) **Reversibility** – A child at this stage is unable to work backwards in their thinking. For example, four-year-old Holly is asked, 'Do you have a sister?' to which she replies 'Yes, Sally,' but when asked, 'Does Sally have a sister?' she replies, 'No'.

c) **Egocentrism** – This means seeing and thinking of the world only from your point-of-view. A child entering the pre-operational stage sees things through their own eyes only and has real difficulty in appreciating someone else's viewpoint (e.g. a parent's). The child cannot put itself in someone else's shoes and see the situation from their viewpoint. Piaget demonstrated this with his 'Three Mountains experiment' on the next page.

At the end of the pre-operational stage, as children move into the concrete operational stage, their egocentrism is no longer active in their thinking. This is generally called de-centring. De-centration means that a child understands more than one feature of a situation or object. For example, they can categorise objects by size *and* colour.

 GradeStudio

In terms of the pre-operational stage, you can only be asked about the concepts of egocentrism and de-centring, so it is important to have a clear and detailed understanding of what these mean. However, if you are asked about the pre-operational stage in general, then there is nothing to stop you from also demonstrating your knowledge of other concepts, such as animism (believing that inanimate objects, such as a teddy bear, are alive and have life-like qualities) and reversibility (thinking that an action can be reversed). Indeed, it might be useful to refer to these concepts if there are a number of marks available.

The 'Three Mountains experiment'

Three papier-mâché mountains were constructed and put on a table. Each mountain had a different object on top (e.g. snow, a hut, a cross). The child was given a chance to walk around and look at the mountains from all angles, then they sat down at one side while a small doll was placed on the other side of the mountains. The child had to choose, from ten picture cards, the one which showed what the doll could see. Most children under seven chose the card of the mountain that matched what they themselves could see. They could only see the scene through their own eyes – an example of egocentric thinking.

Figure 8.2 *The 'Three Mountains experiment'.*

The concrete operational stage – from about seven to eleven years old

A key idea in Piaget's stage theory is that at every new stage the mistakes or shortcomings of the previous stages are removed.

So, at the concrete operational stage the growing child

- overcomes egocentrism
- drops animism, and
- can think backwards.

They also develop new cognitive skills:

- **Linguistic humour** – When children start understanding and enjoying word games and double meanings (e.g. What has an eye and can't see?). Children at this stage will giggle and ask the same people the same question time after time.
- **Seriation** – The ability to put things into rank order (e.g. smallest to largest, youngest to oldest).
- **Conservation** – When children know that the properties of certain objects remain the same (are conserved) even if the objects appear to change. Children at the pre-operational stage don't manage to hold on to or conserve what they see if something appears to have changed in some way. Piaget devised a number of new procedures

ACTIVITY

8.4

Explain why each of the following would not work when a child is still showing egocentric thought.

- Asking the child what *you* can see behind them.
- Playing hide-and-seek with the child.
- Asking the child to think about how their behaviour makes you feel.
- Playing draughts with the child.
- Asking a child to imagine what it is like for another child who cannot read as easily as they can.

or games to test children and conservation (see also Core Study, page 114). Perhaps the best-known example involved a child looking at two identically sized short, fat beakers filled with the same levels of water, then watching the water from one of the beakers being poured into a tall, thin beaker without any spillage. Children under seven said that the tall beaker now held more water because it was taller, those over seven did not (i.e. the older children could conserve volume).

Piaget claimed that the younger children were misled by the idea that a tall beaker must hold more because it is tall. They had no concept of the amount of water staying the same or constant in a different-shaped container.

Piaget did other research using Plasticine. Two identical balls of Plasticine were shown to younger children. One was flattened into a pizza shape but the older children generally knew there was the same amount of Plasticine in the pizza shape as in the original ball. Piaget called this conservation of mass. (See Core Study, page 114, for alternative research evidence on passing the conservation test.)

Figure 8.3 *The volume conservation experiment.*

The reason Piaget called this stage the **concrete operational stage** was because children can conserve and order things provided that the objects are actually present or 'concrete' (e.g. can be seen or held). They begin to be able to solve problems but *only* concrete or practical ones. They still don't do abstract thinking – they are not old enough to reason 'in their heads'.

The formal operational stage – about eleven years old and onwards

By this stage, adolescents develop the new lifelong ability to think about, and solve, sophisticated abstract problems. Piaget believed that it is during this stage that adolescents develop thinking and reasoning typical of adults at their best. For example, a fifteen-year-old can compare several theories about why the dinosaurs disappeared, or the issue of climate change, and so on. Piaget called this kind of grown-up thinking – thinking without physical prompts or objects – *hypothetical thinking*. This involves solving problems logically and perhaps scientifically, and thinking in an abstract way. Hypothetical thinking allows a person to 'see the big picture'. They develop general principles that they can apply to other situations (e.g. some of the big issues discussed in school such as debates about abortion or euthanasia).

Criticisms of Piaget's Theory

- **The cognitive stages are not as fixed or rigid as Piaget proposed.** Some children flick into different stages depending on circumstances, sometimes thinking egocentrically and at other times having grand ideas of right and wrong.

- **There is no guarantee that people develop through all of the stages.** Some researchers argue that only about 50 per cent of adults in fact make it to the formal operational stage at all.

- **Development is not an automatic biological process.** Piaget may have underestimated the role that parents and other people play in a child's intellectual development. Some psychologists believe that we can 'hothouse' children so they develop at a quicker rate. Some argue that Piaget ignored in his research the part played by emotions, for example.

- **Piaget ignored different kinds of thinking.** Not all thinking is an exercise in logic or problem-solving. There is a different kind of thinking, for example, creativity in the arts.

- **Thinking does not develop in the same way for children everywhere.** Aboriginal children, for example, develop concrete operational thinking, which is useful for physical survival, earlier than European children.

- **Piaget only describes the kind of thinking a child can and cannot do, he does not *explain* how the changes in thinking occur.** Some critics would say that this does not make it a proper theory as theories should offer reasons for *why* things happen.

An Alternative Theory: Vygotsky

We have seen that Piaget believed that when it comes to cognitive development there is a kind of biological master plan in the newborn baby. This is an inbuilt timing mechanism, which takes the child forward in time through four predictable stages of development.

Vygotsky developed a different approach. He argued that children are born with considerable thinking abilities, but their cognitive development *takes place within their culture*. The origin of cognitive development does not lie in maturation but in social and cultural influences.

ACTIVITY

8.6

According to Piaget, you would be in the stage of formal operational thinking by now (we hope!). Keep a diary of one day at school or college. Record in it how many times you think you use hypothetical thinking in lessons. Also, make some notes on how you are using hypothetical thinking. Do some subjects require it more than others? If so, why do you think that is? Do you do anything in lessons that you think a child in the concrete operational stage would be able to understand? If so, what and why?

For Vygotsky, a key point is that the child picks up tools for thinking (e.g. language, writing, number systems and ideas from science) and these are developed around them in their home. He called them *cultural tools*. He believed that our culture teaches us *how* to think as well as *what* to think.

Piaget had regarded the child as a 'scientist', following an inbuilt predetermined path of discovery and thinking. Vygotsky, on the other hand, regarded the child as an apprentice – someone who works with a skilled person to learn his or her trade. So, for Vygotsky, the developing child is helped forward in its thinking by the people around them, who have already become thinkers. In other words 'we become ourselves through others'.

Vygotsky emphasised the idea that everyone is born with their own potential for becoming a fully fledged thinking human being, and that other people around us can help us to realise that potential. The term he used for this idea is **zone of proximal development (ZPD)**. It stands for the gap between where we are currently in our development and where we can move on to with the help of others, particularly adults, around us. An example might be a child who has been given a construction kit as a birthday present, and who can only make it up with the help of a parent or older brother or sister. The word that is used to stand for this learning through others is *scaffolding* (a support framework to allow the developing child to get on safely with its learning and thinking – just as scaffolding around a house allows builders to get on safely with the job).

For Vygotsky, everyone's cognitive development happens at an individual pace, helped on by significant people around them in their culture (people at home, among friends, the teacher at school, and even through television). This differs from Piaget's view, which assumed that cognitive development just progresses naturally regardless of who is around.

Core study: Piaget and Conservation of Number (1952)

According to Piaget, pre-operational children of two to seven years old lack the thinking skill to conserve (see pages 110 and 111). Conservation, you will remember, means 'the understanding that certain physical characteristics of objects remain the same even when their outward appearance changes'. The child at this stage of development is influenced by the way things look and is unable to conserve. Piaget devised a number of conservation tasks using volume and shape. Piaget also devised tests for conservation of number.

Procedure

Piaget used a cross-sectional study in his experiment on conservation. In other words, he compared children of different ages. Children were shown, one at a time, two identical parallel rows of counters, with the counters opposite and facing each other one to one. The researcher then changed the layout of the counters as each child watched, stretching one row out but not removing or adding any counters to either row. The children were then asked one at a time which of the two rows had more counters.

ACTIVITY

8.7

Write a poem that summarises Vygotsky's theory. Get in key words, such as culture, apprentice, scaffolding, zone of proximal development and even Vygotsky's name, so good luck!

You may find it easier to attempt this in pairs. If you do manage to come up with a poem it will act as a useful revision aid.

Findings

Children in the pre-operational stage (two to seven years old) tended to say that the rearranged or stretched row had more counters because it was longer. Presumably, they were not able to conserve. Perhaps this was because they could not yet reverse the situation by thinking of what happens if the counters are pushed back closer as at the beginning.

However, children in the concrete operational stage (seven to eleven years old) did largely get it right. They reported that both lines had the same number of counters despite the difference in length of line. They knew that appearances can be deceiving and that unless something is added or taken away the two lines remain as before.

Limitations

- **Piaget was criticised for the way he questioned the children in the experiments.** In his research the child was asked to say whether the two rows of counters were the same. The children were first asked this *before* the researcher played around with the counters, and again after the re-arranging. It has been pointed out that in normal circumstances, (e.g. at home or in class) children are only asked the same question twice if they have got it wrong in the first place. In related research, when the children were asked only once whether the two rows of counters were the same, a far higher number of children got the right answer.

- **Piaget was criticised for the nature of the task.** The task was quite contrived and did not have much meaning to young children. When a game was played to stretch the line using a 'naughty' toy animal who messed up the row, 60 per cent of children in the pre-operational stage could work it out and pass the conservation of number test. The test had been made child-friendly, and it produced results which contradicted Piaget.

- **Piaget used a relatively small sample of children for his experiment.** They may not have been representative of all children. This was especially a problem given the fact that Piaget claimed that his stages of development were universal. How could he be sure without testing a wider variety of children?

Applications of Research into Cognitive Development: Educating Children

Piaget and Vygotsky produced two quite different explanations and theories about how we become thinkers. What they have in common is that both of them have been applied to education and schooling.

One way in which they differ is that Piaget never applied his theory to the classroom, but Vygotsky did. So let's consider them separately.

HOW SCIENCE WORKS

See Research in Psychology for more information on:

- **Cross-sectional study**, page 166
- **Experiments**, page 159
- **Longitudinal studies**, page 166
- **Representative samples**, page 156.

ACTIVITY

8.8

Answer the following questions on Piaget's original research into number.

1 Give the method used by Piaget. [1]

2 State how many rows of counters were involved in the task. [1]

3 Outline how Piaget changed the rows. [2]

4 Explain how the study was a test of conservation of *number*. [2]

5 Outline how pre-operational children responded to the change in the rows. [2]

6 Explain how children in the concrete operational stage perceived the change to the rows. [3]

7 Explain why critics of Piaget argued it was better to ask children only one question in a conservation study. [3]

8 Explain why it might have been better to use a longitudinal study rather than a cross-sectional study in this experiment. [4]

8

COGNITIVE DEVELOPMENT

Piaget's influence on education

1 The concept of *readiness*

This is suggested between the lines of Piaget's theory. It argues that children can only learn what their current cognitive stage allows them to. So classroom materials, subject specifications and ways of learning in class should match the stage and cognitive level of the pupil. Young children, for example, should learn in the classroom through concrete activities and materials; older students should learn by dealing with abstract concepts and hypothetical issues. Young children *do* things to learn while older children have discussions and debates and carry out website research, and all this matches their cognitive development stages.

2 Discovery learning

Piaget's theory seemed to suggest that learning should be child-centred and, above all, active. Children learn best by *doing*. In such a system of schooling the role of the teacher is not to pour knowledge down the throats of the pupils but instead to raise questions and issues and devise activities for the children to get involved in, and in the process to discover, as young 'scientists', things for themselves at first hand. The teacher is a *facilitator*, helping the child find things and learn independently.

3 Peer support

In Piaget's theory this means allowing children in class opportunities for unstructured discussion and collaborative learning. It helps the child de-centre and develop the ability to take the other person's point-of-view.

Vygotsky's influence on education

1 Role of the teacher

Vygotsky disagreed with Piaget and his strict idea of readiness and letting it all happen in due time. He argued that the classroom teacher should actively intervene, to help the child as a learner develop their understanding and knowledge. For Vygotsky, this intervention plays a vital part in children's learning experience. The teacher is at the time the main person in their pupils' zones of proximal development.

2 The spiral curriculum

Vygotsky argued that children are best served in school by what he called the spiral curriculum. This means difficult ideas being presented at first quite simply, and then being revisited at a more advanced level later on (see Activity 8.9).

3 Applying the notion of scaffolding to the classroom

Vygotsky had argued that other people can advance a child's thinking by providing a support framework or scaffold on which the child can climb and achieve (see Activity 8.10).

ACTIVITY

8.9

Choose a topic in maths or science or history and show how you would teach it, first of all to children in Year 6 and later in Year 10. Identify the differences of fact and explanation about the same topic between the two year groups as an example of the spiral curriculum.

ACTIVITY

8.10

Imagine you are an infant schoolteacher. Explain how you would use the idea of scaffolding to teach one of the following areas of the curriculum:

a) spelling

b) addition

c) the concept of weight.

Your brief is to carry out an observation of a child under the age of eleven (i.e. a child in one of Piaget's first three stages of cognitive development). You are aiming to discover whether they do or say things predicted by Piaget's theory, or whether they are more or less advanced than predicted.

Trained psychologists would probably observe children covertly using a non-participant observation.

Ethically speaking, you are not in a position to observe a 'real-life' child, but there are other ways of doing an observation. You could do an equally good job by observing a child on-screen. Indeed, this gets around some of the problems of remaining covert or of causing distress. You could use something like a home video (possibly even of yourself when you were younger). If you don't have access to this kind of thing, then watch out for relevant television programmes. There are many programmes focused on childcare and child-rearing, and your Psychology teacher may even have copies of classics such as Channel 4's 'Supernanny' or the BBC's 'Child of our Time'.

The brief is to collect qualitative data. In other words, your findings will be in words. You simply describe what you see. When do children do things that Piaget would expect? What are they doing? Are there any actions or thoughts that are different from what Piaget would predict? You could see whether very young children search for objects or not, or whether they appear to recognise themselves. You could see whether pre-school children are egocentric in the things they say, or whether they treat objects as 'living things'. You could see whether children of junior age need to solve problems with objects in front of them, or whether they are using linguistic humour.

HOW SCIENCE WORKS

See Research in Psychology for more information on:

- **Covert** and **non-participant observations**, pages 163–164
- **Ethics**, page 158
- **Qualitative data**, page 167.

Summary

- Piaget's theory of cognitive development states that children's minds develop through four invariant and universal stages of development.

- The first stage is the sensori-motor stage (zero–two years) when children's understanding of the world is limited mainly to what they can sense and physically experience. One feature of this stage is object permanence and how children begin to understand that things exist even when they are not actually experiencing them.

- The second stage is the pre-operational stage (two–seven years) when children use symbols and signs to understand the world. Although children begin this stage with egocentric thinking, most will have de-centred by the end of the stage. This means they are able to view situations from another's point of view.

- The third stage is the concrete stage (seven–eleven years) when children can solve problems but by using concrete, physical objects to help them to do so. At this stage they develop conservation in thought. This means that they understand that certain objects' properties (e.g. number, volume, mass) remain the same even when they appear to change.

- The fourth stage is the formal operational stage (eleven+ years) when children can solve problems in a more abstract, hypothetical way.

- Piaget believed that children progress through these stages naturally. However, Vygotsky offered an alternative theory. He argued that children's cognitive development is more a product of their cultural experiences.

- Piaget's theory is supported by a number of his own famous experiments. In one, he showed that young children (in the pre-operational stage) were unable to recognise that there were the same number of counters in a row that had been spread out. This was because they were unable to conserve number.

- There are many applications of research into cognitive development. An obvious one is its use in education. If we know how children's minds develop, it gives teachers some idea of what children should be capable of learning and when.

ExamCafé

Revision

Common Mistakes

There is a lot of difficult terminology in this topic. It is particularly easy to get the terms muddled up between Piaget and Vygotsky. To help, you could draw cartoons of the two psychologists and then write the key terms (with images) on to the characters. For example, you could build a 'conservatory' around Piaget to represent 'conservation' and scaffolding around Vygotsky to represent – you guessed it – scaffolding!

Summarising Content

Copy out the table below, which represents Piaget's four stages of cognitive development. For each stage, write in all the key ideas associated with that stage.

Listed below the table are some key ideas you may want to include. Can you work out where they go?

STAGE OF DEVELOPMENT	KEY IDEA
Sensori-motor	
Pre-operational	
Concrete operational	
Formal operational	

Key ideas:

egocentrism	*de-centring*
use of signs/symbols	*conservation*
object permanence	*animism*
understanding through senses	*hypothetical thinking*
solving problems in abstract form	*solving problems using objects*
reversible thinking	*use of linguistic humour*
recognising oneself	*ability to use seriation*

Exam Preparation

Below is one candidate's answer to the following question.

Describe and evaluate **one** of Piaget's studies into cognitive development.   **[10]**

In the 1950s, Piaget did an experiment using children of different ages. It was to test egocentrism. It did this by setting up a model of three mountains on a table. Each child sat on one side of the table while Piaget placed a doll on another side of the table. The child then had to say what they thought the doll could see. They did this by choosing a photo which showed the scene from the doll's perspective. Young children – around about four – were not very good at the task, and instead chose photographs from their point of view because they were egocentric.

There are some limitations to this experiment though. It was done a long time ago and is now out of date.

Another limitation is the fact that it is a lab experiment. Because the environment and the task are artificial, the findings lack ecological validity.

Critics of Piaget said that the task was not very meaningful to children. Some other researchers went on to test egocentrism differently. They tested it by playing a hide-and-seek game in which children had to hide a doll from some other dolls. When it was tested in this more fun and realistic way then many 4-year-olds could in fact see things from another point of view (i.e. the doll's) and knew where to hide it from the others.

Examiner says:
The experiment is well detailed, including important features such as the aim, the method, the sample, the procedure and the findings. The only obvious thing missing is the fact that older children could de-centre.

Examiner says:
Candidates often make this mistake. Don't assume all older studies are necessarily out of date. It depends on what is being studied. Children's minds are being studied here, and there is no reason to believe that these were any different 50 years ago compared with today. This evaluation point is wrong therefore. However, the candidate does not lose marks for it, it will just be ignored.

Examiner says:
The evaluation gets better here. The evaluation points are expanded on. The alternative study counts as evaluation as it contradicts and questions the original study being described.

Overall, the response is clear, coherent and well balanced. It is also acceptable to describe another study done by Piaget besides the core study on the specification. This does not gain any more marks but neither does it lose marks.

ExamCafé

Language of the Exam

Below are some examples of examination style questions with comments.

Name **one** of Piaget's stages of cognitive development. **[1]**

Examiner says:
Remember if the command word is 'name' then this often only requires a one-word answer or a brief phrase. You do not have to write a sentence. In this case, do not start describing a stage of Piaget's theory. If that is all you do, then you will earn no marks because it is not what is being asked for. If you name a stage and then go on to describe it then you are doing more than is required. The examiner will not give you any more marks, because he or she only has 1 mark to award.

Outline what is meant by egocentrism in Piaget's theory. **[2]**

Examiner says:
The command word 'outline' requires you to do more than just give a brief statement or one-word answer. You would normally be expected to answer in sentences. Your answer needs **two** parts to it (but not necessarily two sentences) to pick up both of the marks. In this case, once you have decided what egocentrism is (to earn the first mark), think how you can elaborate on this to earn a second mark. Sometimes it is useful to offer an example of a concept and this should count as elaboration.

Describe **one** application of research into cognitive development. **[4]**

Examiner says:
The command word 'describe' requires some level of detail and an answer written in sentences. To decide how much detail, look at the marks available. In this case, it is 4 marks, so you should aim to cover four different points or features when describing the application. Also, go carefully, as the question clearly asks for **one** application. If you try to earn the marks by describing more than one application, you will still only get credit for one. The examiners will have been instructed to ignore the others.

Describe and evaluate Piaget's theory of cognitive development. **[6]**

Examiner says:
When a question offers 6 marks for describing and evaluating, it would be 4 marks for describing and then 2 for evaluating. This means that you need to make sure your answer is more descriptive than evaluative. In this case, it is actually quite hard to summarise Piaget's theory for just 4 marks. Think about the four main features you would want to refer to, to earn those marks. Just naming the stages would not really work as this would be a list, not a description. For the 2 evaluation marks you could either offer two criticisms of the theory, or outline one criticism but in more detail.

Non-verbal Communication

What do you think makes humans cleverer than any other species? Yes – you *are* cleverer than any other species! Some species might have and do some pretty clever things; for example, elephants have huge memories, penguins go on long marches, bees are good at waggle dancing – but humans have the biggest package of cleverness. You are showing how clever human beings are right now, by reading printed language. It is said that 'animals signal, but humans speak' and only humans write with a full awareness of vocabulary, tenses, grammar, and so on. We are born to communicate or talk, even if a disability like deafness or blindness means that sign language or Braille is necessary.

Social psychologists are interested in communication because it is the tool for interacting with others. We use communication to influence others and they use it to influence us. Communication is often sub-divided into two main parts: verbal and non-verbal communication. Verbal communication is communication through words (either spoken or written). Non-verbal communication basically covers all other types of communication. This chapter focuses on the latter.

LEARNING OBJECTIVES:

By the end of this topic, you should be able to:

1 Identify some examples of *body language* and *facial expressions* as non-verbal communication.

2 Understand the main ideas of the *social learning theory* including:
   - observation
   - imitation
   - reinforcement
   - punishment.

3 Describe some *cultural variations* in non-verbal communication.

4 Explain the criticisms of the social learning theory and understand the alternative *evolutionary theory* of non-verbal communication, particularly with reference to *survival* and *reproduction*.

5 Demonstrate knowledge of the research by Yuki *et al.* into *interpreting* facial expressions.

6 Show awareness of the applications of research into non-verbal communication, for example in terms of social skills training.

Non-verbal communication – Telling others what we are thinking or feeling or planning by some recognised body movement. It can be conscious (i.e. we are aware of doing it) or unconscious (we are unaware we are doing it)

Body language – Communicating something physically through our body, for example our body movement, gestures, touching, keeping a distance, and so on

Facial expressions – Communicating something through the movement of muscles in the face, for example by moving eyebrows, lips, eyes and so on

ACTIVITY

9.1

To get a real insight into body language as a way of 'talking', test your skills at spotting it, using television.

a) Record a short episode of one of your favourite fictional programmes, such as a soap. While recording it, watch it for the first time *with no sound*, concentrating on the movements, facial expressions, use of eyes, physical contact, distancing, touching and so on. At the same time, try to make sense of the story.

b) Write down your guess at the storyline.

c) Watch the programme again with full sound and compare your notes with the full programme of action and body language, identifying any instances when you guessed the events correctly the first time.

d) As a follow-up you could do an analysis of the communication, by trying to calculate the amount of speech as distinct from body language, to see what the balance was.

Key Concepts

In simple terms, and in a funny way, we are talking about **non-verbal communication** when we say 'Actions speak louder than words'. Actions are gestures and gestures send out messages, such as:

- Someone pointing a finger at you (meaning 'Do it or else!').
- A parent frowning as you try to explain why you are so late home (meaning 'That's a poor excuse.').
- Your friend standing with folded arms and tight lips when you are in trouble with them (meaning 'I thought you were my friend!')

As well as talking with our tongues, we also appear to talk with our bodies through **body language**. In fact, one expert claims that during face-to-face conversation only 7 per cent of the message is conveyed through your words, while 38 per cent is revealed by the tone of your voice, and 55 per cent comes through your gestures, **facial expression** and posture.

Figure 9.1 *Positive body language: creating a good impression.*

Figure 9.2 *Negative body language: creating a bad impression.*

ACTIVITY

9.2

Search through magazines or newspapers for pictures that could be used in a non-verbal communication textbook to illustrate:

- anger
- affection
- uncertainty
- happiness
- surprise.

Compare your pictures with others. Are there any patterns or similarities in the body language or facial expressions used for each emotion?

Body language – a form of non-verbal communication

So, we have seen how we are all in the communication business! Imagine what it would be like if no one returned your greeting as you walked around, if no one met your eyes, if no one acknowledged that you were there and if everyone else seemed to look straight through you.

Communication is the basis for all our interactions with other people, from talking on a mobile phone and texting on the one hand to the way we stand, shake hands and fold arms. The latter behaviours are examples of what is meant by body language.

Next, we will examine some basic types of body language in more detail.

Gestures

Gestures are body signals – actions that send a visual message to someone who is watching, or just nearby. What matters is not what signals we *think* we are sending but what signals are actually being received. For example, a sneeze is a gesture. It tells us about the state of the person (i.e. they have got a cold or perhaps hayfever). Sitting in class with your head propped up on two palms is saying that you are bored. Different cultures have hand or finger gestures for stupidity (e.g. an index finger pointing at the side of the head). There are *technical gestures* which have been invented for a purpose. For example, the police officer moves and stops traffic with arm movements that all motorists recognise. Of course, there are also some very special *coded gestures*, such as sign language for deaf people.

9.3

Demonstrate to others how you would signal rather than say the following:

- Stop!
- Hurry up!
- Be quiet!
- Really?

Now add some of your own ideas. What other common signals are there? Can your fellow students work out the message you are trying to convey?

9.4

Imagine you are standing in a busy street in a town centre. You are there to do a survey. Like most people doing surveys, you are looking for people who are going to be pleasant, and will stop and take part. What are you going to be looking for in terms of posture? What kind of body language is going to suggest that someone is in a good mood? What kind of people would you not stop? How would you identify these people by posture?

Share your ideas with others. How much agreement is there?

Posture

This is where we 'take it from the torso' – it is the way in which we communicate or say something, for example how we communicate feelings about ourselves or others, by the stance we adopt (the way we position ourselves) or how we move or twist our body.

Movements of the head, hands, legs and feet can all tell others what is going on in our mind, such as our mood or our attitude.

Facial expressions

Let's face it – we do a lot of talking in a non-verbal way with our faces and facial expressions! You've heard someone say at some time 'It's written all over your face'. The face is probably the most important part of your body for conveying information, especially about feelings and attitudes. It has been calculated that there are about a hundred different types of smile, for example, but only six or seven other expressions that can be reliably identified, which are as follows:

- surprise
- fear
- anger
- disgust
- happiness
- sadness.

Some researchers have managed to map the movement of the face in the different expressions (it has more than 44 muscles, 22 on each side). For example, someone caught by surprise raises the eyebrows, drops the jaw and horizontal wrinkles appear across the forehead.

Of course, sometimes a person wants to hide what is going on inside them and they mask all that by putting on an opposite expression.

9.5

It is probably true to say that your eyes are the most important part of your face. Think of the things people say, such as, 'If looks could kill' or 'He's giving her the eye'. We also connect the eyes with specific qualities.

See if you can match the following eye movements to the emotion being expressed.

Downward glance	Wonder
Wide eyes	Anger
Narrow eyes	Modesty
Hard staring	Cunning

The social learning theory is one of psychology's more straightforward theories. However, try not to write about it in common-sense terms. You need to show you understand the psychology behind it by using technical terms (such as observation, imitation, role models, and reinforcement) to earn the higher marks.

ACTIVITY

9.6

Make a list of as many different emotions in different situations that you can think of. Beside each, sketch a face with the features drawn in to show the emotion. You can use the six emotions listed earlier, but add others too, such as confused or bored.

Different groups seem to have their own set of display rules. These are expected or normal ways of communicating in different situations. A simple example of such rules might be that boys and men are expected to hide their distress and not cry, for example, when they hit their head on something hard. However, in a football match they can let all their emotions show when their team loses, and cry their hearts out!

Core Theory: Social Learning Theory

You may have already touched on the **social learning** theory (SLT) in the behaviourist theory of attachment and the idea of reinforcers (see Chapter 3, pages 39–40), in the description of the behaviourist theory of atypical behaviour and conditioning (see Chapter 5, pages 66–70), and in the study of criminal behaviour and the idea of imitation and role models to explain crime (see Chapter 6, pages 83–85). SLT makes a reappearance here in thinking about non-verbal communication. It is one of the psychological explanations of body language and facial expressions. It basically argues that non-verbal communication is a learned behaviour rather than a natural, instinctive one.

The social learning theory is about how people look, listen and notice what key people do and say, and how people react to praise for getting something right and being told off for getting something wrong, and so on. The key concepts of SLT are:

- **Observation** – Paying attention and watching, consciously and unconsciously, to the behaviour of the key players around us from infancy right through to adulthood.
- **Imitation** – Making ourselves be like or behave like the people around us, whom we like, love or admire; in other words – how we copy them.
- **Reinforcement** – When we remember the effect of some sense of reward or praise, enough to make us do the same thing again and again, and make it a habit.
- **Punishment** – When we remember the effect of some sense of criticism or disapproval, or even harm. If this is very negative it can stop us repeating a behaviour for good.
- **Role models** – The person or persons who are seen or watched and listened to. These are often influential adults, such as parents, but can be celebrities, older siblings or our peers.

BUZZWORDS

Social learning – How a person's behaviour with, towards and around others develops as a result of observing and imitating others, both consciously and unconsciously

Observation – To watch someone with the purpose of learning about behaviour

Imitation – Doing, saying and behaving the same as the 'model' who was observed doing, saying or behaving (what we call 'copying')

Reinforcement – A process in which a behaviour is strengthened because the consequences are positive

Punishment – Negative consequences following an action

Role model – An individual who other people aspire to be like

9.7

Use the descriptions of the different features of the social learning theory to write a passage on how the theory would explain the development of non-verbal communication. Questions to think about are:

1 What kind of gestures, postures and expressions by others can be observed?

2 How would a child go about imitating these examples of non-verbal communication?

3 How do adults also learn non-verbal communication by observing and imitating others?

4 Who do we learn non-verbal communication from? Who are our role models?

5 How is non-verbal communication reinforced? What are the rewards or benefits of getting it right?

6 How is inappropriate non-verbal communication punished? What might stop us from using a particular gesture or expression again?

Cultural variations – This describes differences (in behaviour) across different countries, societies or communities

Cultural variations in non-verbal communication

If non-verbal communication is a learnt behaviour, as argued by SLT, then how we communicate would depend on our upbringing. One way to test this is to look at different cultures to see if there are differences in the way that people in each communicate. There are indeed significant **cultural variations** or differences in some kinds of body language in different countries.

Cultural variation can be observed in how people greet each other. In France, expect your friend to kiss your cheeks three times when you say hello and goodbye. In Brazil, the custom is to shake hands with everyone in a group when meeting or leaving, or for women to exchange kisses twice if they are married and three times if they are single. In Saudi Arabia, if you are a woman, no body contact is involved at all when meeting others. Of course all such cultural variations are the result of the basic mechanisms of social learning mentioned earlier:

- **Observation** – We see how other people in our community or culture communicate with each other.
- **Imitation** – It is easier to imitate the behaviours we see more frequently or more easily (i.e. those in our immediate community or culture).
- **Reinforcement** – We are rewarded for communicating as expected because people like it when we follow cultural norms.
- **Punishment** – We are reluctant to repeat a behaviour if it has been punished (e.g. we were ignored or ridiculed) or has caused offence, so non-verbal communication that is not accepted by a culture should 'die out' within it.

Of course, if non-verbal communication is not learnt, then we would be arguing that it is natural and instinctive. However, if this was the case then we would not expect to see cultural variations. If non-verbal communication was a product of human nature, then all humans should communicate in more or less the same way regardless of their culture and upbringing.

Criticisms of the social learning theory

- **The social learning theory struggles to explain why certain examples of non-verbal communication may persist even when they have been punished.** For example, a person may be beaten up for a rude hand gesture towards another but still use that gesture. People do not respond very positively to us when we frown, but that does not stop us from frowning. A child may be told off for poking his tongue out but does this necessarily mean that the child will not do it again?

Like a lot of topics in Psychology GCSE, this one explores the nature/nurture debate. Make sure you don't get the terms nature and nurture muddled up if you do use them. Remember that nature relates to something being natural or instinctive. Nurture is about how we help something to grow (in our case human beings) by the way we bring them up and what they learn from us.

- **The social learning theory suggests that people can learn new ways of communicating non-verbally – but this is not always true.** For example, efforts to teach offenders more appropriate body language and more positive facial expressions tend not to work that well. If non-verbal communication was simply a result of learning, it should not be so difficult to teach new behaviours.

- **The social learning theory cannot really explain why children brought up in the same environment can have quite different ways of communicating non-verbally.** For example, two brothers raised by the same parents, in the same community, with the same influences, can have very different ways of expressing themselves.

- **The social learning theory ignores the effect of nature on non-verbal communication.** Looking at the above points we can see this. Perhaps people cannot change the way they communicate because it is innate? Perhaps siblings communicate differently because they are not genetically identical? There is evidence that nature and biology has at least some influence on non-verbal communication. Just as there are cultural variations in non-verbal communication, there are also gestures and expressions which appear to be universal. These include smiling to show pleasure, crying to show distress, shrugging as a defence, and blushing for embarrassment. This would suggest that these examples of non-verbal communication are a product of human nature rather than learning.

An Alternative Theory: Evolutionary Theory

You may have already looked at the evolutionary theory as part of the Atypical Behaviour topic, in which case you will know that it supports the nature side of the nature–nurture debate in psychology. Rather than believing that non-verbal communication is learned (or nurtured) it would seem that it is more to do with human biology.

Evolutionary theory generally argues that human beings, and other animals, are governed by instinct. It is natural and instinctive for animals to want to live long enough to pass on their genes. Therefore, over time, humans and other animals have evolved to pass on behaviours that help them to survive and reproduce.

If we apply the evolutionary theory to non-verbal communication, and particularly to those behaviours that appear to be universal, then we would say that certain forms of non-verbal communication have evolved to help survival and/or reproduction. This was particularly important in prehistoric times when humans had not yet developed the capacity to communicate with words.

In terms of survival, it might be that certain gestures and expressions work by:

- warding off potential enemies or threats
- reducing conflict or threat
- allowing people to co-operate so that they can help each other survive.

In terms of reproduction, it might be that certain gestures and expressions work by:

- allowing people to court (or flirt with) each other
- making a person appear attractive to the opposite sex
- helping people to communicate within a relationship.

> **HINT**
>
> You will not need all of this detailed evaluation for the exam – not even if you are writing an essay. The trick is to try to understand *all* of the evaluation points and then choose two that you understand well. These are the ones you could expand on in an essay.

9.8

Copy out Table 9.1. List at least three examples of non-verbal communication for each feature of evolution. Some examples are given to get you started.

Table 9.1

Feature of evolution	Examples
Warding off potential enemies or threats	Baring your teeth as sign of aggression • •
Reducing conflict or threat	Avoiding direct eye contact as sign of backing down • •
Allowing people to co-operate so they can help each other to survive	Touching people as a sign of liking and reassurance • •
Allowing people to court each other	Eyes widen as a sign of finding someone attractive • •
Making a person appear attractive to the opposite sex	Men stand taller and 'puff out' their chests as a sign that they are strong and good protectors • •
Helping people to communicate within a relationship	Using open gestures as a sign of concern and support • •

Core Study: Yuki *et al.* (2007)

From the 1970s social psychologists showed a growing interest in cultural differences in non-verbal communication. Various studies were carried out and mainly gave evidence for cultural variations. For example, among Americans it was clear that people should be free to show their feelings; in Japan it is more important to control and subdue the display of emotions.

Yuki, Maddux and Masuda, an international cross-cultural team in itself, carried out detailed research under the lovely title: 'Are the windows to the soul the same in the East and the West? Cultural differences in using the eyes and mouth as cues to recognise emotions in Japan and the United States.'

Procedure

The hypothesis being tested was that different cultures pay attention to different facial cues when meeting and talking to each other. In particular, in Japanese culture eyes are more important when expressing and spotting emotions, while in the USA people tend to read emotions on faces by looking at the mouth.

The cross-cultural research involved investigating American students whose culture allowed emotion to be publicly displayed, with a focus on the mouth, and Japanese students whose culture demanded not displaying feelings, with a focus on the eyes.

The participants (118 American volunteer students at Ohio University and 95 Japanese volunteer students at Hokkaido University) completed a questionnaire in which they were instructed to rate on a scale of 1 (very sad) to 9 (very happy) the emotional expressions of six different computer-generated faces or *emoticons*, with combinations of happy and sad eyes and mouths.

At the end of the study the participants were debriefed and thanked.

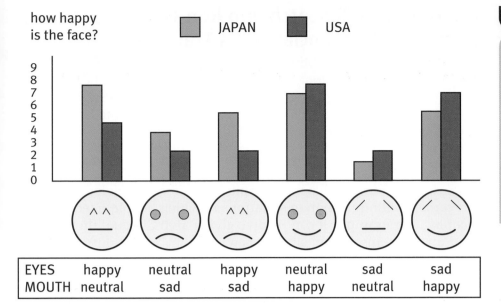

Figure 9.3 *Bar chart to show Yuki* et al.*'s findings.*

HINT

Do not spend time trying to learn the details of Figure 9.3. This is time-consuming and only allows you to reproduce the bar chart in the exam. It is much better if you can describe the results in words. Indeed, if you get a question that asks you to *describe* Yuki *et al.*'s findings, then drawing a bar chart would not be enough anyway.

HOW SCIENCE WORKS

See Research in Psychology for more information on:

- **Dependent variable**, page 153
- **Ecological validity**, page 171
- **Hypothesis**, pages 151
- **Questionnaire**, page 161
- **Representative sample**, page 156

Results

In line with the hypothesis, the two cultures responded differently to the emoticons. The Japanese participants gave higher ratings to faces with happy eyes, the American participants gave the highest ratings when the mouths were happy.

The results show that there are cultural differences in how emotions are expressed and interpreted in faces. This suggests that this aspect of non-verbal communication is affected by upbringing and cultural experiences.

Limitations

- **The research lacks ecological validity.** One of the most obvious problems is that the study used emoticons rather than real-life faces so how much can we generalise the results to every-day encounters? Having said that, Yuki *et al.* also tested participants using real faces later in the experiment and still had similar results. However, even then they were two-dimensional photographs of faces rather than real three-dimensional faces, which could also make a difference. In addition, the artificial conditions may have made participants feel more awkward or inhibited than they would feel in real life.

- **The sample of students was not very representative.** They only represented one narrow age group, for example. It might be that young children or the older generation interpret emotions in faces differently.

- **The dependent variable was measured in a very simple way.** Recognising emotions is a complex process so is it reliable enough to just measure this on a scale of 1 to 9?

Grade Studio

You will notice that some limitations of Yuki *et al.*'s research are more detailed than others. Bear this in mind if you are asked to describe a limitation of Yuki *et al.*'s study in the exam. Look at the marks available at the end of the question. If it is 2 marks, then something like the third limitation point will do. However, if 3 marks are on offer, then you will need more detail as offered in the first limitation.

ACTIVITY

9.9

Questions on the core study

Answer the following questions on the Yuki *et al.* research.

1 Outline the hypothesis being tested. [2]

2 State one factor that the participants had in common. [1]

3 Identify the emoticon that Japanese students rated as most happy. [1]

4 Identify the emoticon that American students rated as most happy. [1]

5 Identify the emoticon that Japanese students rated as most sad. [1]

6 Identify the emoticon that the American students rated as most sad. [1]

7 Outline *two* reasons why Yuki *et al.*'s study could be described as an ethical piece of research. [4]

8 Explain why it was better to use real faces rather than emoticons in this study. [4]

ACTIVITY

9.10

There are many websites that deal with non-verbal communication, and more specifically body language; for example www.bodylanguageexpert.co.uk is a good site. Use this and/or other sites to draw up a list of hints or tips on how to use non-verbal communication to manage conflict. See if you can come up with a 'Top Ten' list.

Application of Research into Non-verbal Communication: Social Skills Training

The study of non-verbal communication has led to a better understanding of how people interact socially, and has helped to identify what makes people better in dealing with others. An important subject to have come out of all the research into body language is 'social skills training' (SST). This works on the assumption that non-verbal communication is learnt, as argued by the social learning theory.

Social skills training – This is the application of our knowledge of non-verbal communication to situations in which people need help in coping. For example, it can involve giving an individual the skill to stand up for themselves in situations where they would normally 'give in' to others, and doing so without using aggressive body language.

Social skills training was first used in helping psychiatric patients to cope, but it has gone on to be widely used in training people in occupations that involve dealing with and getting on with others. It can help them to understand other people's body language and to be able to 'speak' appropriately using their own body language.

Rehabilitation of offenders

Probation teams working with offenders have used social skills training. The theory is that by teaching offenders new ways of communicating (including use of body language and facial gestures), they will be able to manage difficult situations more effectively in the future. For example, their risk of re-offending may be reduced if they can resist peer pressure to commit a crime or if they can avoid getting into conflict with others.

In social skills training the four main mechanisms used to help the offender are:

1 **Modelling** – The trainer demonstrating or acting out the correct behaviour, for example good eye contact, as the offender watches

2 **Practice** – The offender being invited to imitate the model, and sometimes using role-play to build up the desired behaviour

3 **Feedback** – The trainer commenting on the offender's practice performance, sometimes using video of the practice behaviour; good social skills are reinforced

4 **Homework** – Tasks between sessions: the offender transferring the newly acquired skill to real life and to as many real people as possible, and reporting back to the trainer

Managing conflict

As mentioned above, social skills training is now widely used for training employees. Certain groups of employees – in professions such as the armed forces, police force, social services, education and the health service – have to manage conflict quite often. These are situations where others (e.g. patients, pupils, offenders) are being threatening and aggressive. Such situations need to be diffused (see Activity 9.10).

Customer service training

There are many jobs nowadays that involve working with the public. This is always about managing conflict but also about creating a good impression and giving people a good service. This is particularly important when workers come face-to-face with their customers, such as in the retail, catering and leisure industries.

Yuki *et al.* identified some cultural differences in non-verbal communication. Your brief is to investigate if there are any sex differences in non-verbal communication.

You will need to carry out a non-participant observation and, if possible, a covert observation. It would be acceptable to carry out this research in a public place (e.g. a shopping centre, cafe or park) because here the people know they are open to being observed (even if they do not know what for!). It would of course be unethical to 'spy' on people in a place they thought was private.

To make the observation easier, decide on one feature of non-verbal communication that you are going to focus on (e.g. eye contact, touch, open posturing) and also decide how you are going to measure this variable (e.g. duration of eye contact, number of times an individual touches another, number of different types of open posture used). Make sure you think carefully about where you will be doing the observation so that you can make a sensible choice about the variable you are going to test, and how you are going to test it. You also need to think about how you are going to record your data, how long you are going to do the observation for, and how many people you think you need to observe.

You will also need to formulate a hypothesis. What do you predict? Do you expect a sex difference for the variable you are investigating? If so, can you predict the direction of that difference (e.g. which sex will do it more?).

You will need to share your data with others by presenting back what you have found out. Look at your data. If it is quantitative, you will have the option of using graphs or descriptive data. If it is more qualitative, you will need to summarise any patterns in words.

9.11

Imagine you work for a large supermarket retailer. You are in charge of delivering customer service training to new employees. One of your sessions – which lasts one hour – focuses on the use of non-verbal communication in dealing with customers.

Your brief is to draw up a plan of *what* you would teach in that session and *how* you would teach it.

See Research in Psychology for more information on:

- **Covert observation**, page 163
- **Descriptive data**, page 168
- **Ethics**, page 158
- **Graphs**, pages 169–170
- **Hypothesis**, page 151
- **Non-participant observation**, page 164
- **Qualitative data**, page 167
- **Quantitative data**, page 167
- **Variables**, page 153

Summary

- Non-verbal communication describes the way that we use body language and facial expressions to convey meaning to others.
- Some psychologists believe that we learn these gestures and actions, and this is supported by the social learning theory, which basically says we observe and imitate non-verbal behaviours. However, an alternative theory – the evolutionary theory – suggests that non-verbal communication is more instinctive than this, and is linked to survival and reproduction.
- Yuki *et al.*'s cross-cultural study supports the social learning theory as it showed that people interpret facial expressions differently depending on their country of origin.
- The social learning theory is also used in social skills training, which is an application of research into non-verbal communication.

ExamCafé

Revision

Common Mistakes

Non-verbal communication (or body language) is something that people talk about a lot outside of Psychology GCSE. It does not seem as technical as some of the other topics, and so it is easy to write about it in 'common sense' terms. However, you will be doing an examination in Psychology so it is important that you get into the habit of using psychological language when discussing non-verbal communication.

Revision Checklist

What are the key terms that you need to include when describing Social Learning Theory?

Below are examples of key terms with the first letter given but all the others missing.

Can you work out what they are?

o _ _ _ _ _ _ _ _ _ _

i _ _ _ _ _ _ _ _

r _ _ _   m _ _ _ _ _

r _ _ _ _ _ _ _ _ _ _ _

Summarising Content

Write a summary of Yuki *et al.*'s research. Make sure you include all of the following words in your description.

Japan   USA   emoticon   rating   eyes

mouth   cultural differences

Exam Preparation

It is possible that you may be asked about specific examples of body language or facial expressions. For example:

1 Using the following table, tick the correct column to show whether each non-verbal behaviour is an example of body language or a facial expression.   **[4]**

Non-Verbal Behaviour	Body Language	Facial Expression
Smiling		
Crossed arms		
Avoiding eye contact		
Open hands		

Look at the following question.

2 Describe the procedure used in Yuki *et al.*'s study in cross-cultural differences in interpreting facial expressions.   **[4]**

Below is an essay-style question and a candidate's response to it.

3 Describe and evaluate the social learning theory of non-verbal communication.   **[10]**

The social learning theory (SLT) suggests that non-verbal communication is learnt. How is it learnt? The theory says that people learn non-verbal signs from others by observing them and then imitating them. For example, a young boy may show affection by cuddling if that is what he has seen his parents do. He is especially likely to do it again if it is reinforced. For example, if his friends enjoy the cuddle this is rewarding and so more likely to be repeated. Parents are not our only role models. We can also learn non-verbal signs from the wider society. This is how a community or culture may

---

Examiner's Tip:
Q1. Although the specification does not list specific examples of non-verbal communication, it is reasonable for the examiner to expect you to know common ones like those given in the table. Also, you may be asked to give your own examples in the exam too.

Examiner's Tip:
Q2. You will see that this question is only asking you to describe the procedure (or methodology) used by Yuki *et al.* You could get this question for any of the core studies. The kind of details that would earn marks are details identifying the method used, the sample, the variables, the controls, the aim or hypothesis, and ethical considerations. However, you would not get marks for describing the findings (or conclusion) as this is not being asked for. However, if the question asked you to describe the study more generally, then you would have to include the findings as well as the procedure to be able to access full marks.

Examiner says:
This is a sound description of SLT and includes plenty of key terms. Many candidates make the mistake of giving a detailed description of SLT but do not relate it to the behaviour in question. However, this candidate has done a really good job of relating it to non-verbal communication by referring to examples throughout the description.

end up with its own set of symbols (e.g. a 'thumbs up' when something is good, or a V-sign as a rude gesture). What happens is that people imitate the symbols others use and so they become part of everyday communication. However, if people are punished for using certain gestures (like people ignoring or avoiding someone who kisses as a greeting) then that example of non-verbal behaviour may not occur as much.

One positive evaluation point is that cultural differences support the idea of non-verbal communication being learnt. If SLT is right, then we would expect different cultures to have their own set of signs and behaviours because that is what they have specifically learnt. For example, Yuki et al. showed that Japanese and American people use and interpret facial expressions differently. If non-verbal communication was not learnt and was to do with nature instead then we would expect signs and expressions to be universal.

One negative evaluation point is that SLT does ignore the role of biology in non-verbal communication. The evolutionary theory argues that most forms of non-verbal communication are instinctive rather than imitated. It argues that there are many examples of non-verbal communication that occur in every human society, like smiling and blushing. It would be a big coincidence if different cultures – that had nothing to do with each other – just happened to adopt and reinforce the same gestures.

Examiner says:
This is an in-depth and insightful discussion of the theory. Although the candidate has only covered two evaluation points – one positive and one negative – they have expanded on them, showing a high level of understanding. It is quite sophisticated to use evidence as evaluation and to bring in an alternative theory, and the candidate does this effectively.

The Self

'Me, myself, I' – a track with this title was once a big hit. The title focuses on the idea that each of us counts as 'one' when it comes to identity, personality and worth. You have your name, your own birth certificate, and perhaps passport, to prove your identity. You are your own person, and have your own individual and unique memory. This is why the study of the self is often related to the idea of 'individual differentiation'.

Who are you? *What* are you? *How* are you? These are all parts of a bigger question: How is your identity formed? We may, in fact, be not one person but many! For example, we moan that 'I wasn't myself today' or 'I don't know what got into me'. At about fifteen months old infants understand that they are separate from other people; for example, when they are made to look in a mirror they see themselves, not another child.

So, just what is the self, and how and what do we know about it?

LEARNING OBJECTIVES:

By the end of this topic, you should be able to:

1 Understand the idea that individuals are *unique.*

2 Explain the idea of *free will.*

3 Outline the humanistic theory of self, including
   - the concept of *ideal self* and *self-esteem*
   - the idea of *unconditional positive regard*
   - the idea of *self-actualisation.*

4 Explain the alternative trait theory with specific reference to *extraversion* and *neuroticism.*

5 Describe Van Houtte and Jarvis's research into pet ownership among adolescents.

6 Show awareness of applications of research into the self, such as in counselling.

BUZZWORDS

Unique – A one-off, which is not repeated; individual

HINT

The word 'unique' is one used in everyday life but obviously you need to understand it in relation to the self as this is what will be expected in the exam.

Key Concepts

Psychologists believe that our self is our inner being, or who we come to believe we are. Our language is full of 'self' terms; for example: self-help, self-discipline, self-made, self-conscious, self-defence, and so on. Psychologists also insist that human beings are not like the Daleks in 'Doctor Who' – we are not pre-programmed machines that are only able to process information. Every one of us is a **unique** package that comes and goes as they please.

A number of psychologists believe that one of the things that makes us unique is our ability to exercise **free will**. They argue that we are not completely governed by external factors (e.g. the environment), nor internal factors (e.g. genes). In other words, we make choices about what we want to do and how we think about things. This means that we are products of our selves and the self is unique.

Core Theory: Humanistic Theory Of Self

A group of psychologists, known as humanists, put a lot of emphasis on people as individuals. In other words, they see us as unique and as having free will.

The humanistic theory was developed in the 1950s by Maslow and Rogers. The aim was to take on the behaviourist psychologists, who generally taught that all we do has been learnt from others, and also the followers of Freud, who insisted that we are all controlled by our unconscious.

The main humanistic ideas are that

1 Each of us always has the power to decide on our actions.

2 The present is what we should focus on rather than past experiences.

3 We are all motivated to become the best that we can be, to fulfil our potential.

Carl Rogers claimed that our **self-concept** begins to develop in early childhood between the ages of about one and two years, and it is in the hands of parent(s) and others close to us at that early age. The self-concept is basically how we perceive ourselves. How we see ourselves depends on how others reflect back to us. For example, if someone keeps telling

Grade Studio

Many students understand the humanist theory quite well – probably because it seems to make a lot of sense. However, be careful not to describe it in common-sense ways in the exam. It is important to use the proper psychological terms to pick up those higher marks.

you that you are a 'good laugh' then you will see yourself as being fun. Alternatively, if someone keeps telling you that you are ugly, this will affect your perception of your self too. Research has shown that young children tend to see themselves in very physical terms and will often describe what they look like. Older children focus more on their social roles when they describe themselves, talking about who they are, what they do or what they are good and bad at. Teenagers and adults are much more aware of their psychological selves and often describe their traits.

Self-esteem

Your social role means the role or relationship you occupy in connection with other people (hence 'social', as always in psychology). For example, on an average day you move in and out of a number of social roles (e.g. daughter or son, pedestrian or bus passenger, pupil in class, friend at break time, member of sports team after school, and so on). These roles also contribute to a person's view of their actual self: you are a 'polite' bus passenger or a 'kind' son for example.

As well as our self-concept, Rogers also talked about the **ideal self**. This is the person we would ideally like to be. For teenagers and adults, this ideal self is often described in psychological terms (e.g. 'I would like to be better organised', 'I wish I was more understanding'). According to the humanistic theory, it is the difference between the self-concept and ideal self that determines someone's **self-esteem**. If the self-concept and ideal self are incongruent, it means there is a big gap between them. This leads to low self-esteem. In other words, the individual does not value him or herself. Why? Because the person they want to be appears to be far away from the person they think they are. Meanwhile, when someone's self-concept closely matches their ideal self, they have much more reason to value themselves – they are more or less who they want to be.

BUZZWORDS

Ideal self – The person an individual would like to be

Self-esteem – A measure of how much we value ourselves

10

THE SELF

ACTIVITY

10.4

Write out the phrase 'I am ...' twenty times on a piece of paper. Now finish the sentence each time by saying something different about yourself each time.

When you have finished:

a) Count up how many times you describe your physical self – what you look like (e.g. height, hair colour, appearance).

b) Count up how many times you describe your social roles – what you do and who you are (e.g. your family role, your interests).

c) Count up how many times you describe your psychological self – your personality (e.g. how friendly you are, whether you are confident or not).

Is the research right? Do you mainly perceive your self in psychological terms?

10.5

Copy out the following diagram.

- In the eight boxes on the right, write eight things you wish you were better at or more like (e.g. better motivated, more reliable).

- When you have done this, indicate on the line before each box how far along the line you are to achieving your goal. The closer you put a mark to the box, the closer you are to achieving your goal (e.g. being more reliable).

- Now draw a vertical line down through the horizontal lines so that it is exactly half way along them.

- Look to see how many of your marks are to the left of the vertical line. How many are to the right?

If this test is reliable (and it may not be!), the more there are to the right, the better. In terms of Rogers' ideas about the ideal self and self-esteem, why do you think it is seen as better?

BUZZWORDS

Unconditional positive regard – Showing an individual love without expecting certain conditions to be met

So, if someone has low self-esteem, is there anything we can do about it? According to Rogers, the answer is yes. We mentioned earlier that others could affect our view of ourselves, for good or bad. Rogers said that if others show us **unconditional positive regard** then this is the best way to raise self-esteem. Positive regard involves offering love, care, security, respect and other things that make us feel happy in ourselves. If this is also unconditional, then it works even better. Unconditional means there are 'no strings attached' and that you receive positive regard, no matter what you have said or done.

HINT

The humanistic terms seem quite complex when you first come across them. But many of them make sense when you break them down. This might help you to understand them.

For example, 'ideal self' is how you would like your *self* to be *ideally*.

'Unconditional positive regard' is *regarding* (seeing) a person in a *positive* light regardless of the *conditions*.

'Self-actualisation' is *actually* becoming the person you want your*self* to be.

Of course, this is only a way of understanding the terms. In the exam, you will have to find ways of explaining the terms without using the words in the term.

For example, this is the case if parents still love and support their teenage daughter although she was caught shoplifting, or if a wife still cares for and respects her husband even when he has walked out on his job without consulting her. Some people only offer us conditional positive regard and this can be damaging for the self. For example, this is the case when someone promises to be your best friend but only as long as you do not have anything to do with another person.

ACTIVITY

10.6

Get together with other students to write and act out two brief role plays.

1 Create a scenario in which an individual is *not* receiving unconditional positive regard. Make sure you include how that individual feels as a result.

2 Create a scenario in which an individual does receive unconditional positive regard from others. Again, include how that makes the individual feel.

Self-actualisation

So how does unconditional positive regard help raise self-esteem? For Rogers, it was a key part of supporting an individual so they become a whole person. This process is what he called **self-actualisation.** This refers to the development of your unique human potential to become your 'best possible' person. In other words, it is achieving your ideal self. Rogers believed that we all have a tendency to work towards our ideal self, but that we need the help and support of others to do this. Clearly, if others are making us feel good about our actual self (self-concepts) then this is taking us closer to the ideal self. By 'closing the gap' between the self-concept and the ideal self, we are raising our self-esteem.

Maslow came up with a hierarchy of needs that have to be met in turn before we can self-actualise. From birth, we set out on a kind of upward journey of personal growth, as described in Figure 10.1:

BUZZWORDS

Self-actualisation – The idea that each of us has an inborn drive to want to fulfil our potential

10

THE SELF

ACTIVITY

10.7

Maslow developed the idea of self-actualising after studying the lives of a number of exceptional people, such as Einstein, Darwin and Picasso.

1 Create your own modern list of exceptional people and identify against each your reasons for selecting them.

2 Compare your list with others' lists in the group.

3 How do the people on your list stand out as exceptional in terms of self-actualisation?

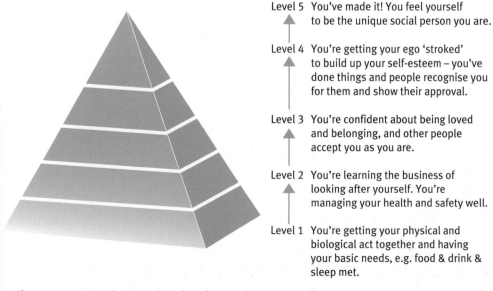

Level 5 You've made it! You feel yourself to be the unique social person you are.

Level 4 You're getting your ego 'stroked' to build up your self-esteem – you've done things and people recognise you for them and show their approval.

Level 3 You're confident about being loved and belonging, and other people accept you as you are.

Level 2 You're learning the business of looking after yourself. You're managing your health and safety well.

Level 1 You're getting your physical and biological act together and having your basic needs, e.g. food & drink & sleep met.

Figure 10.1 *Maslow's triangle – becoming yourself.*

Criticisms of the humanistic theory

The main reason why the humanistic theory is still popular in psychology is perhaps because it sees people as basically good, and believes that people will develop their true potential. However, a number of criticisms of the theory persist, including:

- **Many of the ideas presented by the theory are vague and difficult to measure objectively.** The humanistic theory is subjective by its very nature because it is all about the self. People cannot easily study 'yourself' so it becomes difficult to establish what a person's 'ideal self' is or how much they have 'self-actualised'.

- **It is not a very scientific theory.** This is partly because of the point made above – that ideas are difficult to test and measure if we cannot observe them. It is also because a lot of the evidence for the theory comes from Rogers' own research, which was not very representative. However, Rogers and other humanists would not want to be seen as scientific as they do not think it is appropriate to study people scientifically. They regard people as whole human beings and not animals (as in biological psychology) or machines (as in cognitive psychology).

- **Humanists focus too much on the individual.** Another reason why humanists do not adopt a scientific approach to studying humans is because they believe that people are unique and have free will. In this sense, nobody is predictable – yet the point of science is to try to predict things. Other psychologists argue that if we do not try to predict things about human behaviour (e.g. Who will commit crimes? What will improve memory?) then there is little point in doing psychology.

- **The humanistic theory of the self ignores genetic evidence.** Other psychologists believe that 20 to 60 per cent of a person's intellectual, emotional and social development comes from genetic factors.

An Alternative Theory: Trait Theory

Given the criticisms of the humanistic theory, you will not be surprised to find that there are alternative theories of the self that:

- are more scientific and try to measure personality more reliably
- make more generalisations about people by recognising that we have traits in common with others
- believe that our personality is more a product of genes than how others respond to us.

One such theory of self is Eysenck's trait theory. He believed that personality:

- has a *genetic* basis – we've been born that way
- has a *biological* explanation – our personality is shaped by the activity of a part of the mid-brain called *the reticular activating system* which activates higher parts of the brain.

HINT

The first three limitations are actually all linked to the fact that the humanistic theory is unscientific. You could bring them together into one evaluation point – especially if an exam question asks for one criticism.

Grade Studio

You may be asked to describe an alternative theory in the exam, but not evaluate it. However, you can always use the alternative theory to help you to evaluate the core theory – in this case using a trait theory to evaluate the humanistic theory of self. This is actually quite a sophisticated form of evaluation and should earn you good marks if done well.

ACTIVITY

10.8

Identify and describe what personality traits you might expect to see in the following people:

- a criminal
- a clown
- a college student
- a nun
- a rock star.

Do you think these traits are in-born, and that's why people end up in these 'roles'? Or do you think people adopt these traits?

Figure 10.2 *Does a clown have the same traits as a nun?*

Our personality, according to Eysenck, is shaped by the activity and arousal of parts of our nervous system network. This seems to say that we are the victims of our own biology. We cannot help being an open or closed personality, an agreeable or disagreeable person, and so on – it is just the way we are made.

ACTIVITY

10.9

Rate yourself on the following traits, using a scale from 1 to 6 (6 means that the trait describes you really well and 1 means that it hardly describes you at all).

1)	energetic	2)	quiet
3)	anxious	4)	calm in crisis
5)	sociable	6)	reserved
7)	paranoid	8)	unemotional
9)	big-headed	10)	sensible
11)	sensitive	12)	hardy
13)	optimistic	14)	enjoy own company
15)	worried about what others think	16)	laid back
17)	risk taking	18)	easily led
19)	prone to hypochondria	20)	secure

- Now add together your scores for traits numbered 1, 5, 9, 13 and 17 and call this total A.

- Add together your scores for traits numbered 2, 6, 10, 14 and 18 and call this total B.

- Add together your scores for traits numbered 3, 7, 11, 15 and 19 and call this total C.

- Add together your scores for traits numbered 4, 8, 12, 16 and 20 and call this total D.

If your total for A is greater than your score for B, then this would suggest that you are more extravert than introvert. If your total for B is greater, then this would suggest you are more introverted. Similar scores would suggest that you are neither particularly outgoing nor shy. How well do you think your scores describe you?

If your total for C is greater than your score for D, then this would suggest that you are more neurotic than stable. If your total for D is greater, then this would suggest you are more emotionally stable. Similar scores would suggest that you are an emotional person but not to either extreme. How well do you think your scores describe you?

Extraversion and neuroticism

Eysenck particularly believed that each individual's personality can be assessed by two main traits, and that measures of these traits combine to tell us a lot about the overall personality. One trait is measured on the extraversion scale and tells us, very basically, how outgoing a person is. The other trait is measured on the neuroticism scale and tells us, very basically, how emotionally stable a person is.

Eysenck studied over 700 soldiers who had been psychologically damaged during the Second World War, and he suggested that there are just four basic dimensions of personality:

- **extraversion** – this refers to the degree to which someone is outgoing and sociable,
- **introversion** – this refers to someone who is typically quiet and reserved,
- **neuroticism** – this refers to being anxious or moody, and
- **stability** – this refers to being emotionally stable.

Eysenck devised his own test for measuring **extraversion (E)** and **neuroticism (N)**. By combining people's E and N scores, he identified four main personality types.

Extraversion (E)

If you see someone being very lively and energetic at a school disco it could just be a one-off, but if that person is always the life and soul of a party, and you know they are lively and outgoing at work as well as at parties, you will guess that they are showing the basic extraversion trait generally (see Table 10.1).

Table 10.1

Characteristics of a high score	Characteristics of a low score
Someone who is *sociable*	Someone who is *reserved*
Active	Sober
Talkative	Aloof
Optimistic	Retiring
Affective	Quiet

Neuroticism (N)

If you know someone who is a worrier, who always says, 'But what if?' to any new idea or plan, who gets so worked up about the situation as to make themselves sick, or who always expects things to go wrong, then that person is showing all the traits of a neurotic personality (see Table 10.2).

Table 10.2

Characteristics of a high score	Characteristics of a low score
Someone who is *worrying*	Someone who is *calm*
Nervous	Relaxed
Emotional	Unemotional
Insecure	Hardy
Hypochondriacal	Secure

The diagram below gives examples of the four main personality types (Figure 10.3), we're all there somewhere. Eysenck himself said that 'extraverts make better salespersons, introverts are better accountants' – can you see the point he is making?

One way in which to understand Eysenck's theory is to look at three very normal situations:

1 Think about *school reports* – There is a well-known list of words or phrases or vocabulary, which you will be familiar with already, such as 'punctual', 'always well prepared', 'concentrates well', and 'contributes well to discussion'.

2 Think about your *friends* – There is probably a list of words in your thoughts about them, such as 'dead reliable', 'really good fun'.

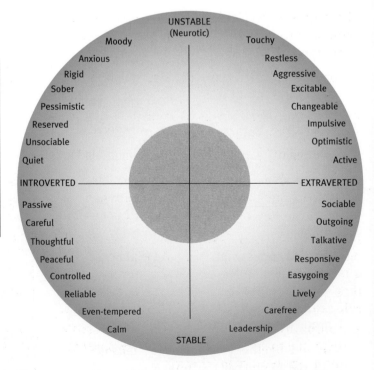

Figure 10.3 *Eysenck's map of four personality types.*

3   Think about the language used in job advertisements, including for part-time work, such as 'good at time-keeping', 'able to get on with other people', 'reliable'.

All these situations use descriptive words that everyone understands. They are all to do with a person's personality, and are meant to describe a *permanent* or *consistent* person, who other people expect to be consistent (i.e. they are *predictable*).

This is what the trait theory is all about (i.e. a person's personality is a combination of traits). 'Trait' means a relatively stable and enduring tendency to behave in a particular way (e.g. be punctual, considerate or helpful). This is the self or identity of the person.

Core Study: Van Houtte and Jarvis (1995)

People love animals and millions of pounds are spent looking after them, feeding them and paying vets' bills. The interesting psychological question, then, is: Are pets good for people?

In 1995, Van Houtte and Jarvis examined the part played by pets in the psychosocial development of pre-adolescent people. The hypothesis being tested was that pet-owning adolescents would report higher levels of autonomy and self-esteem than non-pet owners.

Procedure

A sample of 130 pupils (71 boys and 59 girls, aged between 8 and 13) from Illinois was selected for research based on whether or not they were pet owners. The school gave permission for the study and participants were told what it was all about. They were offered the right to withdraw but all chose to participate. Participants were mainly white American.

The pupils were divided into two groups: pet owners and non-pet owners. However, they were matched on three aspects:

1   marital status of their parents (married, divorced, separated)
2   socio-economic status of their parents (occupation, income, housing)
3   number of brothers and sisters they had.

Questions about pet ownership were also asked, such as kind of pet, length of ownership, looking-after duties and pet's age.

Data was collected from the pupils, pet owners and non-pet owners alike, using questionnaires based on well-known scales that measured autonomy, self-concept and self-esteem, as well as attachment to animals.

- Autonomy was measured on a 4-point scale response to such sentences as 'My parents and I agree on everything'.

Figure 10.4 *Pets: good or bad for you?*

- Self-concept was measured on a 5-point scale response to adjectives, such as 'I am happy'.
- Self-esteem was measured on a 4-point scale response to items, such as 'On the whole I am satisfied with myself'.
- Attachment to animals was measured through a 7-point scale response to a series of statements, such as 'I consider my pet to be a friend'.

In the scales, the range was from 1: strongly agree, upwards to: strongly disagree.

After the tests had been completed the students were debriefed and thanked. Letters were also sent home to parents asking for confirmation about pet ownership.

Results

An analysis of the data found that:

- In general, higher self-esteem was reported in pet owners than in non-pet owners.
- For 11-year-olds, pets were found to positively influence self-concept.
- Higher autonomy was reported by pet owners across all the age groups tested.

Van Houtte and Jarvis concluded that pets may have their greatest impact on children's lives as they move into adolescence. They also put forward the idea that pets can be used to help people suffering from low self-esteem, as a support for others in times of stress, and to enhance feelings of responsibility for elderly people.

The implication is that pets can offer unconditional positive regard for pet owners.

Methodological limitations

The research was imaginative and detailed. However, some issues arise from it, including:

- **There is always potentially a problem with self-report in questionnaires.** The results are only valid if the pupils were honest in their responses. They may not have been lying outright, but it may be difficult for children to have an accurate insight into aspects such as their self-esteem and self-concept.
- **The study used a lot of quantitative data that may not be appropriate when dealing with complex emotional issues.** Some humanists would argue that Van Houtte and Jarvis should not have just tried to score difficult concepts like self-esteem and self-concept. This ignores the depth of these important aspects of the self.
- **The sample was not very representative in a number of ways.** Only teenagers were studied, so the researchers cannot be sure about the effects on other age groups. In addition, the sample was culturally biased because it only used a small number of ethnic minority pupils. In addition, there are other cultures outside of the USA in which pets and animals play a very different role.

ACTIVITY

10.10

Questions on the core study

Answer the following questions on the Van Houtte and Jarvis research into pet ownership.

1 Identify the participants in the research. [1]

2 State the main difference between the two groups of participants. [1]

3 Identify the four dependent variables in the study. [4]

4 Explain the reason for each of the following controls:

a) matching parents' marital status between groups [2]

b) matching parents' socio-economic status between groups [2]

c) matching the number of brothers/sisters between groups. [2]

5 Identify *three* examples of good practice in terms of ethics. [3]

6 Explain why pet ownership may be related to unconditional positive regard. [4]

Applications of Research into the Self: Counselling

People of all ages can have what is called an identity crisis, for example a real soul-searching and head-scratching about who they are, how they feel about themselves, and so on. Adolescents can be confused about their sexuality and sex itself, about getting involved in drugs, and about which route to take at the end of compulsory education. Parents and partners can get into problems with their marriage or relationship, and they may not be happy or getting on well with each other.

This is some of the real stuff of being human rather than a robot. And this is where psychology becomes an *applied science.* Psychology becomes a hands-on subject, dealing with real human issues, and not just explaining but helping. It is where humanistic psychology, described earlier, comes into its own.

Counselling for clients with depression

Rogers made a 180-degree move away from psychoanalysis ('fishing' in the deep recesses of a patient's unconscious) and from behaviourism (actively reshaping a person's thinking and ways of doing things). He developed client-centred therapy – which is therapy that is led more by the client and less by the therapist. This is now better known as counselling and works on the basis that the client knows their self best. Rogers believed that clients themselves have the capacity for, and should be responsible for, change. It followed from this that the counsellor's role was transformed from being the all-knowing expert, telling or directing the client what to do, to being a helper.

The Rogerian way, then, involves these elements:

1   The person doing the counselling avoids giving instructions, and just shows the client that he or she understands what the client is feeling (i.e. offers unconditional positive regard).

2   The counsellor genuinely believes that the client has the capacity to discover a way forward, towards self-actualisation (i.e. the client has a free will).

3   The counsellor shows empathy towards the client, and is able to follow what the client is feeling and lets the client know that.

4   The counsellor, being genuine, allows the client to express themselves as they really are.

So how does the Rogerian way apply to things like depression and careers guidance and relationships?

Read the edited extract on the next page from one of Rogers' counselling sessions with a depressed and fed-up mother.

This is an example of humanistic counselling in relation to depression. Notice that no easy solution is offered and there is no criticism of the mother or the daughter. The client-centred counsellor is helping the client to recognise the situation, and the feelings and frustrations contributing to her depressive state.

Grade Studio

When you are considering the limitations of a core study, always consider the method being used. You should know the pros and cons of each method after studying Research in Psychology. In the exam, you will always get credit by knowing about the disadvantage(s) of a method. However, if you can apply the disadvantage specifically to the study under question then this should earn more marks.

HINT

Remember that the specification does not specify the particular applications you have to look at. The exam can ask you about 'counselling' but you can choose the area in which counselling is used.

HOW SCIENCE WORKS

See Research in Psychology for more information on:

- **Control of variables,** pages 159–160

- **Dependent variables,** page 153

- **Ethics,** page 158

- **Quantitative data,** page 167

- **Questionnaire,** page 161

- **Representative sample,** page 156

10

THE SELF

Client:	I'm really depressed about my daughter. She's 20, she's at university, I'm having a bit of trouble letting her go ... .I have a lot of guilt feelings about her, I want to hang on to her, and it's very hard, lots of empty places with her gone.
Rogers:	The old vacuum, sort of, when she's not there.
Client:	Yes, yes – I'd really like to be the sort of mother who is strong and can say 'go and have a good life' – but I find that really hard.
Rogers:	It's very hard to give up something that's been so precious to you, but also something that I guess has caused you pain when you mentioned guilt?
Client:	Yes, and I know I have some anger towards her that I don't always get what I want. I have needs that are not met – she's my daughter, she's not my mother – sometimes I'd like her to mother me.
Rogers:	So it may be unreasonable, but still, when she doesn't meet your needs you get fed up.
Client:	Yes, and I get very angry, angry with her. (pause)
Rogers:	You're feeling a little tension right now.
Client:	A lot of pain.
Rogers:	A lot of pain.
Client:	A lot of pain.
Rogers:	A lot of pain. Can you tell me anything more what that's about?

ACTIVITY

10.11

You can access information about Relate's counselling services on www.relate.org.uk. There is a lot of information on the website so it might be worth researching it in teams. See how many bits of information you can relate to what you have learnt about humanistic ideas and the self.

ACTIVITY

10.12

Imagine you are doing a presentation to a group of younger pupils to explain how the careers guidance service works in your school or college. Plan the presentation (e.g. as a poster or PowerPoint). Part of your brief is to include information on the principles of counselling and how they would be used to help pupils make decisions about their careers.

Relationship counselling

The same approach has a place in relationship counselling. One of the best known and respected organisations that makes itself available to people having relationship problems (e.g. in a marriage) is known as Relate. The Relate counsellor is trained in the Rogerian method. The basic aim is to make it possible, for example, for couples in a strained relationship and possibly considering divorce or separation, to meet, talk openly, exchange ideas and feelings. It is hoped that in an open-ended way they work things through without being told what to think or feel or do. In 2008, Relate counsellors saw over 150,000 clients at over 600 counselling centres (see Activity 10.11).

Careers guidance

The same approach and method has a place in careers guidance. Every school has a careers adviser as part of what is sometimes called the Connexions careers service. You may already have been in touch with the person, for example about which route to take after education (a job opportunity part-time or full-time, work experience, college and so on). In general, the careers adviser follows the method devised and promoted by Rogers, trying to get the client to clarify in their own mind what is best to do next (see Activity 10.12).

Your brief is to devise a questionnaire to measure a certain aspect of personality. This can be any trait – how outgoing someone is, how friendly someone is, how aggressive someone is – but keep it simple and focus on one trait only. You should use it on at least five people.

What you then need to do is come up with at least five scenarios or statements that allow you to measure that trait. You want to get quantitative data from the questionnaire, so you will need to use closed questions that give some kind of score.

For example, if you were measuring how outgoing someone is you could use the following question:

On a scale of 1 to 10, how much do you like going to parties?

Lots 10 9 8 7 6 5 4 3 2 1 Not at all

Or if, for example, you were measuring how friendly someone is, you could use the following question:

You see a friend of yours crying when you are in a rush to get somewhere. What do you do?

   a) *Stop and sit down with your friend to find out what is wrong.*
   b) *Keep going and hope your friend hasn't spotted you.*
   c) *Keep going because the appointment is important.*
   d) *Check your friend is okay and say you will catch up with them later.*

You would score each response differently.

When you have finished constructing your questionnaire, it is time to put it to the test. Is it a valid questionnaire? In other words, does it measure what it is supposed to measure? The way to assess this is by asking each of your participants whether they think the score is right. For example, if they score high on aggression – is this how they see themselves?

Remember, questioning someone about their personality is quite personal, so bear in mind issues such as confidentiality and right to withdraw.

HOW SCIENCE WORKS

See Research in Psychology for more information on:

- **Closed questions**, page 161
- **Confidentiality**, page 158
- **Quantitative data**, page 167
- **Right to withdraw**, page 158
- **Validity**, page 171

Summary

- The self is a psychological way of talking: it refers to the idea that no two people are completely alike; every one of us is a unique person.
- One vital aspect of our uniqueness is that there is such a thing as *free will*, which means that we should live our life in the light of what *we* think and feel and want, and decide for ourselves.
- The *humanistic* approach suggests that we are each a free agent with the potential to become our best possible person through *self-actualisation*, becoming our *ideal self*, to help us feel good about ourselves and enjoy a healthy *self-esteem*; people who are significant to us help this process by offering us *unconditional positive regard*, loving us 'warts and all'.
- *Trait theory*, on the other hand, confines itself to identifying a number of relatively stable and predictable personality features as a way of referring to our personality.
- *Van Houtte and Jarvis's* study of the impact of pet ownership on adolescent personality provided evidence in terms of self-esteem and a more positive self-concept.
- Research into the self includes the whole industry of *counselling* in areas such as dealing with depression, career guidance and personal relationships.

Revision

Key Concepts

This topic has quite an unusual vocabulary and there's no alternative to the 'sweat and tears' of scribbling down the jargon (e.g. unconditional positive regard or self-concept), and from memory trying to write a definition of each. If you get stuck, look in an index or glossary, and then check it all out in the text.

One interesting way of confirming your study of the self might be to construct your own life-line visually. It might be fun, for example, searching through family photographs of yourself spanning your lifetime, to show your development and the growth of your self, the physical changes over the years, and so on. You might also trawl your memory for events or experiences that you can recall as being important at the time for your growth, and write them up in your life-line chart. This will be your own self-actualising story!

Quiz

Test yourself on the humanistic theory of self by copying out the following passage and filling in the gaps.

The humanist theory believes that each person is an individual and therefore _____. Each person also has _____ _____ and can therefore make their own choices in life. They are essentially 'in charge' of their selves. One part of the self is the _____ _____ and this is how we see ourselves. Another part is the _____ _____ , and this is who we would like to be. The gap between these two parts of the self is a measure of an individual's _____ _____. People need to _____ _____ _____ to grow and develop. When they reach their full potential this is known as _____ _____.

Summarising Content

It is useful to summarise the main points of a core study. You can often use the same headings to do this. Useful headings are:

- Aim/Hypothesis
- Method
- Variables
- Controls
- Ethics
- Sample
- Findings
- Conclusion.

Apply these headings to the Van Houtte and Jarvis study.

Revision

Familiarise yourself with the following important ideas from this topic:

- the components of the self – self-image, ideal-self, self-esteem
- unconditional positive regard – loving someone with no strings attached
- self-actualisation – becoming your best possible person
- personality traits – common features recognised by others
- counselling – helping a client forward through a personal difficulty.

Common mistakes

Remember that an exam question about the self may well test your knowledge of the difference between the component parts that make up the self, so it is vital to be able to show that you know and can define them individually.

However, it is not essential to memorise all the individual features of extraversion and neuroticism, although it might pay you to learn at least three in the high and low scores.

Revision Checklist

For the exam you need to feel confident about:

1. The idea that individuals are unique
2. The difference between self-esteem and self-concept
3. The idea of free will
4. The humanistic theory of self, including
   a) the concept of ideal self and self-esteem
   b) the idea of unconditional positive regard
   c) the idea of self-actualisation
   d) the alternative trait theory with special reference to extraversion and neuroticism
5. Describing Van Houtte and Jarvis's research into pet ownership among adolescents
6. Showing an awareness of applications of research into the self, such as in counselling.

ExamCafé

Exam Preparation

A lot of the concepts overlap in the humanistic theory of the self. For example, self-concept and ideal self make up part of self-esteem, and self-actualisation relies on the idea of using your free will. On that basis, do not be afraid to bring in other key terms to help you describe the one that is being asked about. However, watch out! Read ahead. You do not want to end up spending a lot of time talking about 'unconditional positive regard' on a question on 'self-esteem' if there is a question coming up later on 'unconditional positive regard' anyway!

Look at the following question.

> 1 Describe the findings from Van Houtte and Jarvis's study into pet ownership. **[3]**

> 2 Describe Van Houtte and Jarvis's study into pet ownership. **[6]**

Student answer

Q2 Van Houtte and Jarvis carried out a study using a questionnaire. Their aim was to investigate the effects of pet ownership on self-esteem. Their sample was pre-adolescent children. Some children owned pets and others did not, but they were matched to take into account family background. The children were asked questions about their self-esteem, self-concept, autonomy and attachment to pets. The results showed that children who owned pets were mentally healthier on average – for example, having higher self-esteem. The conclusion was the pets offered unconditional positive regard to their owners, raising self-esteem.

Examiner's Tip:
You will see that Question 1 is only asking you to describe the findings (or results) of the Van Houtte and Jarvis study. You could get this question for any of the core studies. The kind of details that would earn marks are specific references to quantitative data (if appropriate), describing patterns and trends, and drawing conclusions. However, you would not get marks for describing the actual procedure (how the study was done) as this is not being asked for. However, if the question asked you to describe the study more generally then you would have to include the procedure as well as the findings to access full marks.

Examiner says:
This candidate obviously knows the study well, as they have included many accurate details. It would be better if they had offered more explanation (e.g. of the controls) to show understanding of the study as well as knowledge. The command word in the question says 'describe', but this study has really been outlined rather than described. Responses need more depth to access the top mark.

Research in Psychology

Psychologists have very many different areas of study they are interested in, from child development to abnormal behaviour; from investigating the brain to investigating the past. However, whatever their area of interest, they will approach research in similar ways, and follow certain procedures. These procedures can be divided into three main stages of investigation: planning, doing, and analysing the research.

LEARNING OBJECTIVES:

By the end of this topic, you should be able to:

1 Demonstrate understanding of the issues involved in planning research in psychology.

2 Have knowledge of the range of methods available for doing research in psychology, including their relative strengths and weaknesses.

3 Show awareness of how research can be analysed, both in terms of interpretation and evaluation of findings.

4 Have an understanding of the different approaches to planning an investigation.

Planning Research

Before psychologists can carry out their research, there are a number of planning decisions they need to make. One of these is obviously to decide what they are interested in investigating. For example, they may be interested in studying what aids people's memories, or studying how the media reinforces gender differences.

Hypotheses

Before psychologists can do their actual research, most make predictions about what they expect to discover. These predictions are known as **hypotheses**. A hypothesis is a statement of what the psychologist believes will happen at the end of a study. For example, a psychologist may predict that there is a difference in recall of words and images, or a psychologist may predict that children's novels have more male characters than female characters.

There are two main types of hypotheses: an **alternate hypothesis** and a **null hypothesis**.

An alternate hypothesis (sometimes abbreviated to H_1) is a statement that predicts a difference or correlation. The following are examples based around the core studies.

- H_1: 'There is a difference in the way that Japanese and American people interpret emotions in faces.'

BUZZWORDS

Hypothesis – A statement predicting the outcome of research

Alternate hypothesis – A statement which predicts a difference or correlation in results

Null hypothesis – A statement which predicts no difference or correlation in results

11.1

Look at the following aims in psychological research. For each one, come up with an alternate hypothesis that predicts the outcome of the research.

1 Aim: To find out if boys and girls play differently.

2 Aim: To investigate whether children's intellectual ability changes with age.

3 Aim: To research whether there is a relationship between the amount of sleep someone has and how they perform on a task.

4 Aim: To study the reasons why people become serial killers.

HINT

If you link the 'null' in a null hypothesis to the word 'nil' it might help you to remember that it is the one that predicts nothing will happen – no difference or no correlation.

HINT

If you are writing a null hypothesis it helps to begin by saying, 'There is (or will be) no ...'.

Grade Studio

There are often two marks awarded for writing a hypothesis. One will be for getting the stem correct (e.g. knowing whether it is predicting 'a difference' or 'no correlation', and so on). The second mark is for stating the rest of the hypothesis (the variables) in a clear and accurate way. A muddled hypothesis will be limited to 1 out of 2 marks.

- H_1: 'There is a correlation between the number of crimes a parent commits and the number of crimes their sons commit.'
- H_1: 'More people will obey orders from someone dressed in a uniform than someone dressed in civilian clothes.'

Each of the above hypotheses predicts some kind of pattern or trend in the results. That is what alternate hypotheses have in common.

A null hypothesis (sometimes abbreviated to H_0) *contrasts with* an alternate hypothesis because it predicts no pattern or trends in results. In other words, it simply predicts no difference or no correlation.

For example, a H_0 may predict that there is no difference, on average, between how many words and images people can recall. Null hypotheses often start with the phrase 'There is/will be no difference ...' or 'There is/will be no correlation ...'.

Psychologists usually start a piece of research with both a null hypothesis and its alternate hypothesis. This is because one of them has to be right (e.g. either there is a difference in recall or there is no difference in recall between two conditions). What they aim to do is to investigate which is right. They then reject the one that is not supported by the research.

If you look again at the alternate hypotheses from earlier, you will see that their null hypotheses are listed below:

- H_0: 'There is no difference in the way that Japanese and American people interpret emotions in faces.'
- H_0: 'There is no correlation between the number of crimes a parent commits and the number of crimes their sons commit.'
- H_0: 'There is no difference in whether people will obey orders from someone dressed in a uniform and someone dressed in civilian clothes.'

11.2

Write a null hypothesis for each of the following alternate hypotheses.

1 H_1: 'There is a difference in the stress levels of people working in noisy conditions compared with people working in quiet conditions.'

2 H_1: 'There will be a difference between how many words are recalled from the beginning of a list and how many are recalled from the end.'

3 H_1: 'There is a correlation between a participant's driving skills and their map reading ability.'

4 H_1: 'More people will stop to help an older adult than will stop to help a younger adult.'

5 H_1: 'Fewer infants search for a missing object when they are six months old compared with twelve months old.'

Variables

Hypotheses which predict a *difference* have two key **variables**: the **independent variable** and the **dependent variable**. The independent variable is made up of the two conditions (e.g. whether a word or image is presented, whether someone is wearing a uniform or civilian clothes, whether participants are from Japan or the USA). This is what researchers vary themselves – they *manipulate* this variable. The reason why they do this is to see if it has an effect on the dependent variable. Therefore they *measure* (rather than manipulate) the dependent variable (e.g. measure how many words/images are recalled; measure how much people obey; measure participants' rating of faces).

Another way of understanding independent variables and dependent variables is to remember that, in most research, a psychologist will predict that if they do 'so and so' then 'such and such' will happen. The 'so and so' is like the independent variable – the thing the psychologist does. The 'such and such' is like the dependent variable – what they expect to happen. They wait to see the consequences of manipulating the independent variable. The dependent variable depends on the independent variable which is where its name comes from! So imagine a psychologist who predicts that if she gives a group of participants an animal to look after for two weeks it will improve the participants' self-esteem. The independent variable (the 'so and so') is whether someone is given an animal or not (the two conditions). The dependent variable (the 'such and such') is their level of self-esteem. This is what the psychologist actually measures. The psychologist thinks that self-esteem is *dependent* on having an animal to look after or not.

ACTIVITY

11.3

Identify the independent variable and the dependent variable in each of the following alternate hypotheses.

1 H_1: 'There is a difference in how participants in a blue room rate their mood compared with participants in a green room.'

2 H_1: 'Participants would complete more anagrams under noisy conditions rather than under quiet conditions.'

3 H_1: 'Less people will obey orders from someone dressed in a uniform than someone dressed in civilian clothes.'

4 H_1: 'Men are slower drivers than women.'

5 H_1: 'Fewer infants search for a missing object when they are six months old compared with twelve months old.'

HINT

You may be asked to identify an independent variable (IV) or dependent variable (DV) in a source in an exam. It is often easy to identify the variables (the things that will change) but sometimes students get the IV and DV muddled up. Do check by asking yourself: Does the IV you have identified affect the DV you have identified? Double-check by asking yourself: Does the DV depend on the IV? Use a diagram like Figure 11.1 to help you check this.

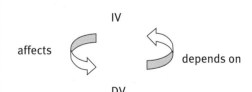

Figure 11.1 *The relationship between IV and DV.*

HINT

Remember that an extraneous variable is like an 'extra' variable or factor. You do not want it to get in the way of results so you try to control it.

ACTIVITY

11.4

Imagine you wanted to conduct an experiment in which you test a group of girls and a group of boys to compare their mathematical ability.

List the extraneous variables you would want to control and say how you would control each one. How many of your controls are examples of standardisation?

The best method to establish whether an independent variable affects a dependent variable is an experiment. This is because in real-life situations it is difficult to isolate a variable and say that is definitely what caused something else to happen. One of the key features of an experiment is that it allows psychologists to control other **extraneous variables**. Why is this important?

Imagine this real-life situation. You are trying to revise for an important exam, and you suddenly realise that you are being distracted by a humming sound in the room. There are a number of different pieces of electrical equipment turned on: a fridge, a television on stand-by, a CD player and a lamp. You want to find out what is causing the humming, in others words you want to find out what the humming (the dependent variable) is affected by (the independent variable). If you turn off all of the pieces of equipment, the humming will stop but you will not know exactly what has caused it. The logical thing to do is to turn off one piece of equipment at a time. This is like manipulating the independent variable: the two conditions are 'on' and 'off'. However, you would keep all of the other pieces switched on (or off). This is like controlling other extraneous variables. If they changed too, it would be difficult to establish the cause of the humming. Keeping other variables constant (or the same) is known as **standardisation**.

Standardisation is a common way of controlling extraneous variables in psychological experiments and other research. Although researchers want the independent variable to change between conditions, they will want other variables to remain constant so that they don't affect the results. For example, they may use standardised instructions or keep timings the same.

Experimental designs

If psychologists decide to use an experiment as their method of investigation, they will also need to choose an **experimental design**. An experimental design describes how participants are allocated to conditions. Most experiments have two conditions; for example, a researcher might be testing whether participants perform better under noisy or quiet conditions. They have two choices. Either they can test all of the participants under both conditions (this is what is known as a **repeated measures design**). In other words, we repeatedly measure or test the same participants (e.g. under both noisy and quiet conditions). The other alternative is to test some participants under the noisy condition and then the remaining participants under the quiet condition. The researcher might do this by alternating the conditions or by randomly allocating each participant to one of the two conditions. The main point is that each condition will have a different group of participants. This is known as an **independent groups design**. In other words, the participants in one condition are independent (different from) the participants in the other condition.

It is not always easy to choose between repeated measures and independent groups designs, because neither is particularly better than the other. The strengths of one tend to be the limitations of the other, and vice versa.

11.5

Imagine you are a psychologist who has been asked to test the effect of an audience on people's ability to do a puzzle.

You have to set up two conditions: an audience condition and a no-audience condition.

1 Outline how this could be done using an independent groups design.

2 Outline how this could be done using a repeated measures design.

3 Explain the advantages and disadvantages of using each type of experimental design in this experiment.

It is common for students to mix up experiments (lab and field) and experimental designs. Sometimes, students just seem to completely forget what experimental designs are. Remember, as soon as you seen that word 'design' you should be thinking about how an experiment is designed in terms of participants and conditions.

Repeated measures designs have the advantage that researchers are comparing the same participants in each condition. This means that any changes in performance or behaviour between conditions are 'real' changes (e.g. due to it being noisy or quiet), and are not due to the fact that the participants have changed. Some researchers also argue that repeated measures is more practical because they do not need to use as many participants as they would do with independent groups.

One of the major sets of problems of repeated measures is what is known as order effects. These are problems that arise because participants are taking part in both conditions. For example, they may underperform in the second condition because they are tired or bored, and not because it is noisy, for example. Alternatively, participants may perform better in the second condition because they are getting more used to the experiment and improving through practice. Whatever the order effect, it can skew the results.

Independent groups designs have the advantage that they get rid of the order effects described above. Since different participants take part in different conditions, they cannot get worse through tiredness or boredom, nor can they get better through practice. However, the disadvantage of independent groups designs is the fact that different participants take part in different conditions. This means that any differences between two conditions could be down to the individual differences of participants. For example, if a group of participants perform better under quiet conditions compared with a group under noisy conditions, how can researchers be sure that the participants in the first condition just aren't better at the task anyway? If the researchers had used the same participants twice (i.e. repeated measures) then they would not have had this problem.

Sampling techniques

Another decision psychologists have to make is: Who are we going to carry out our research on? The people are known as the participants but as a group they can be called the **sample**. A sample is a smaller group drawn from a **target population**. A target population is all the people a psychologist wants to study.

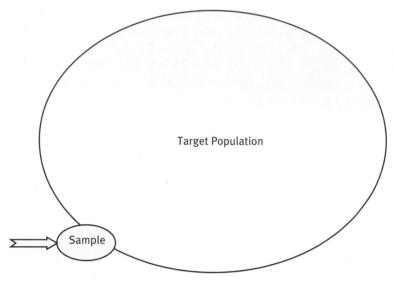

Figure 11.2 *This sample is a smaller selection of the target population.*

Ideally, a sample should be **representative** of the target population. This means that the people in the sample are a good cross-section of the population, representing a range of characteristics, such as age, personality and intelligence. However, sometimes samples are not very representative because of a bias in the sample. For example, if a target population contained both sexes (as most do) then a sample made up of only men and no women could be described as unrepresentative!

ACTIVITY

11.6

Copy Table 11.1.

Table 11.1

Sample	Target population	Reasons why sample is unrepresentative
Inmates from a high security prison	People who have committed offences	
Mothers living in inner city London	British mothers	
Users of the BBC website	Human population	

For each sample, give reasons why it would not be representative of the target population.

Many psychologists are interested in studying human behaviour, so strictly speaking their sample should represent the human population. However, sometimes psychologists are interested in a smaller target population. For example, a psychologist may want to study the attachment behaviours of British infants between six and twelve months old. Their sample does not need to represent different cultures or a wide range of ages therefore.

There are a number of techniques that psychologists use to try to draw a representative sample. One technique that tends to give a representative sample is **random sampling**. Random sampling means drawing participants by chance (e.g. like pulling names out of a hat). In theory, with this technique, everyone in the target population has an equal chance of being selected. Since there is no bias in who is chosen (it is left to chance), this tends to give a good cross-section of people. In other words, it tends to give representative samples. However, because selection is left to chance, there is the possibility of drawing a freak sample. It is highly unlikely, but because there is no control over who is being selected, an unusual sample may be drawn (e.g. if nearly everyone comes from one year group in a random sample drawn from a school's register). Another problem with random sampling is that it is not always very practical, especially when the population is large. For example, it would take some time to compile the names of all of the people in the target population, and even if they were drawn, they may choose not to take part!

Since random sampling is a difficult technique to set up, many psychologists find themselves using other techniques. A common one is **opportunity sampling**. This is a very straightforward method – a researcher simply selects people who are convenient and willing to take part. This may be people in a certain locality, or even friends, family or colleagues. Many psychologists actually use psychology students because they are 'handy' and normally keen to be participants, especially if you pay them or if they can earn credits towards passing their courses! The big problem with opportunity sampling is that it tends not to be representative. For example, people who volunteer themselves for research may be more confident than the average person. Alternatively, they may be very good at the task that is being investigated (e.g. memory tests) and that is why they want to take part. Again, they will be unrepresentative of the average person. Similarly, if psychologists use people they know, then the people may all have similar characteristics – for example, they may come from a similar social class or a limited age range. Therefore, it may not be fair to generalise the results to other social classes or age groups.

To conclude, opportunity sampling is quick and easy to use, but does not give very representative samples. Meanwhile, random sampling is more difficult to use but does generally give representative samples.

HINT

Students often think random sampling is 'grabbing anyone who is around'. Although this sounds quite 'random', remember that it is not. 'Grabbing anyone' is actually what opportunity sampling essentially is. Random sampling is much more technical and mathematical.

BUZZWORDS

Random sample – A sample for which everyone in the target population has an equal chance of being chosen

ACTIVITY

11.7

Test how often random sampling gives a representative sample and how often it gives a freak sample.

1 You can do this by listing all of the names of the people in your class and then putting them into a hat or similar container!

2 Decide how many names to draw out (between 25 and 50% depending on the size of your class). You will draw the sample a number of times (about ten times). Remember to replace the names each time you do this!

3 Each time you do this, decide whether the sample is generally representative or not. Look for a cross-section of characteristics – perhaps sex, ethnicity, tutor groups, ability and personality traits. It is up to you how to judge it.

4 After you have drawn a random sample a number of times, it is time to come to a conclusion. Does random sampling tend to give representative samples?

BUZZWORDS

Opportunity sample – A sample drawn from the target population because they are available and convenient

ACTIVITY

11.8

In pairs, see how many reasons you can think of to show that psychology students are not necessarily representative of a normal population.

Ethical considerations

Another important issue to consider before conducting a piece of research is how participants will be personally affected by taking part. Psychologists should make sure that participants are treated appropriately, and there are ethical guidelines to help them to do this. The main **ethical considerations** are detailed below.

Informed consent and right to withdraw

Participants should agree to take part in research wherever possible. This is known as giving consent. Better still, they should know what the investigation is about. **Informed consent** is when participants not only agree to take part in a study, but also know *why* they are taking part and what is going to happen to them. Sometimes psychologists do not want participants to be aware of the aim of the study otherwise they may behave differently or as expected to. On this basis, it is sometimes acceptable not to reveal the aim. However, participants should always have the **right to withdraw** from a study at any point and should not be pressured to continue. They even have this right if they have given informed consent. There are occasions when a participant may be under investigation without realising it, so they cannot have given consent or know of their right to withdraw. This is normally acceptable when people are observed in public places. This is because in public we might expect to be watched by all sorts of people for all sorts of reasons. However, it would not be acceptable to observe someone when they think they are in a more private setting, such as their own home or a changing cubicle. Some people are not in a position to give their own consent. A good example of this is children who are not considered old enough to understand why they are being studied, especially infants. For this reason, ethical guidelines say that when participants are under 16, parents should give consent for them to take part in psychological research.

Confidentiality

Even if participants are willing to take part in research, it is the psychologist's responsibility to make sure they protect their **confidentiality**. Indeed, because a lot of psychological research is quite personal and sensitive, people will only take part if they know what they say or do is confidential. This basically means that any data collected on people should remain anonymous. Similarly, it would be wrong to take photographs or other recordings during an investigation, otherwise participants would be identifiable. However, sometimes participants have to agree that their data can be shared with other researchers.

Protection of participants

Psychological investigations can potentially have an effect on people's minds and behaviour, as these are exactly the things being studied. Although it is sometimes impossible to guarantee that there will be no effects from taking part in research, there are certain things that psychologists should try to do:

- Participants should not be deceived (e.g. about the aim of the research, about features of the study).
- Participants should not be caused unnecessary distress.

- Participants should not be caused discomfort or embarrassment.
- Participants should not be caused physical harm or be put at risk of harm.
- Participants should generally leave a study in the same state as when they entered.

Not all psychologists agree with the last point because they argue that participants may benefit from taking part in a study. For example, they may actually feel better about themselves afterwards, or they may have learnt a new skill.

Overall, the general guideline is that psychologists should protect and promote a participant's health and wellbeing. If research does not consider the welfare of participants, it can be described as unethical.

Grade Studio

You could be asked to identify an ethical problem with a study in the source in the exam. This may carry as many as 3 marks. If so, you need to identify the actual ethical issue, describe what it means and then apply it to the study in question.

ACTIVITY

11.9

Read the following outline of a psychological study.

> Psychologists conducted a field experiment on the New York subway. They arranged for an assistant to fall over in one of the carriages of a train when it was travelling along. They did this on a number of occasions to see how often he would be helped by the real-life passengers who were riding the train at the same time. Sometimes the assistant pretended to be disabled and other times he pretended to be drunk. The psychologists found that he received less help when he appeared drunk compared with disabled.

Identify different ways in which the above study is unethical.

Doing Research

Once psychologists have planned their research, the next stage is to carry it out. This involves collecting data. Data can be collected through a variety of methods, including experiments, questionnaires, interviews and observations.

Experiments

Experiments are used widely in psychology. They can collect data using a number of techniques (e.g. by observation, by survey) but they have certain features in common. The features of an experiment are:

- The researcher manipulates an independent variable.
- The researcher measures a dependent variable.
- The researcher attempts to control all other extraneous variables that may affect the outcome of the experiment.

BUZZWORDS

Experiment – A method by which the researcher controls variables and measures their effect

11.10

Read through the descriptions of the core studies that use experiments:

a) Terry, pages 25–26

b) Bickman, pages 55–56

c) Watson and Rayner, pages 71–72

d) Haber and Levin, pages 100–101

e) Piaget, pages 114–115

f) Yuki *et al.*, pages 128–129.

For each one, list as many controls as you can identify.

Laboratory experiment – An experiment carried out in a controlled environment

Field experiment – An experiment carried out in a natural environment

Grade Studio

You may be asked to describe what is meant by a laboratory experiment or a field experiment in the examination. This will normally carry 2 marks. This is because not only do you need to explain the 'laboratory' or 'field' part, but you also need to outline what is meant by an 'experiment'.

The key point about experiments is that they are set up and controlled by a researcher. This is so that they can establish cause and effect. In other words, if they have manipulated the independent variable and controlled all others, then they know whether it has an effect on the dependent variable or not. This is the advantage of carrying out an experiment. No other method allows a researcher to reliably establish cause and effect.

There are two main types of experiments:

1   **Laboratory experiment** – This is an experiment carried out in a controlled environment. Many experiments into memory and perception are carried out in laboratories because factors such as noise, lighting and heat can be controlled.

2   **Field experiment** – This is an experiment carried out in a real or natural environment. Although psychologists may not have control over the environment, they still control other key variables (otherwise it would not be an experiment!). Many experiments in social psychology are carried out in the field so that the participants do not guess that situations have been set up. Bickman's (1974) field experiment into obedience is a good example of this (see page 55).

11.11

Draw up a table with two columns. Write the heading 'similarities' over one column and 'differences' over the other column. Use this to identify what laboratory and field experiments have in common, and to identify how they are different.

✔ The strength of a laboratory experiment is that it has a very high level of control. This is because the environment is being controlled as well as many other variables. This makes it easier to establish cause and effect compared with a field experiment.

✔ The strength of a field experiment is that it has higher ecological validity than a laboratory experiment. This is because the experiment is carried out in a natural environment. This means any findings are more applicable to real life.

✘ The weakness of a laboratory experiment is that its findings *lack* ecological validity. This is because the controlled environment is often artificial (e.g. if factors like noise, lighting and heat are held constant this is not realistic).

✘ Another weakness of laboratory experiments is that they tend to have more demand characteristics than field experiments. This is because people tend to know that they are taking part in a laboratory experiment (this is not necessarily true for field experiments, e.g. Bickman). In addition, more things are set up in a laboratory experiment so there are more clues to what the experiment is about. The outcome of this is that participants may work out what the experiment is about and change their behaviour accordingly.

✗ The weakness of a field experiment is that it has less control over variables than the laboratory experiment because the setting is naturally occurring. This makes it harder to establish cause and effect. Uncontrolled variables in the environment may be affecting the dependent variable.

Questionnaires

Since psychologists often want to study the mind, **self report** methods are a very useful method in psychology. Self report methods, not surprisingly, require people to report on themselves! This means that they explain how they are feeling or what they are thinking, or describe what has happened to them in the past. This is the strength of self report methods. They allow psychologists to access aspects of a person that they cannot see.

Questionnaires are one type of self report method. They consist of a list of pre-set questions, which are often written down. These questions are the same for everyone who takes part in the questionnaire survey.

Questionnaires can use **closed questions**, **open questions** or a combination of both.

- Closed questions are questions for which there is a set number of responses. These are often given in the form of multiple-choice answers. It is also common to close a question using options such as yes/no, always/often/sometimes/rarely/never, or a rating scale.
- Open questions are questions for which the respondent chooses their own answers. Such questions can often be answered in some depth.

ACTIVITY

11.12

Draw a spray or spider diagram to show as many different ways of administering questionnaires as you can think of.

Figure 11.3 *A researcher carrying out a questionnaire survey.*

Grade Studio

Do not just learn brief points to summarise the strengths and weaknesses of different methods. You may be asked to describe *one* strength or weakness of a method for 2 marks. In this case, you will need to go into some detail. You cannot earn the 2 marks by offering two points instead. If only *one* thing is asked for, the examiner can only give you marks for one thing.

BUZZWORDS

Self report – When participants report their own experiences

Questionnaire – A set of pre-determined questions which are the same for all respondents

Closed questions – Questions for which there are set responses to choose from

Open questions – Questions for which there are no fixed responses, and participants answer as they please

✔ A strength of questionnaires is that they can be used to access people's thoughts and feelings.

✔ Another strength is that all respondents are asked the same set of questions. This means it is possible to compare answers and look for patterns and trends.

✔ Compared with other self report methods, questionnaires are relatively easy to administer to a large sample quickly. For example, they can be posted on an internet site, or given out to a group of people at the same time.

✘ A weakness of questionnaires is that people may lie or exaggerate as there is often no one there to check their responses. However, others argue that we are more likely to get truthful answers exactly because there is no one there!

✘ Another weakness of questionnaires, especially if someone is not there to administer them, is that respondents may misunderstand questions and therefore not give reliable answers. In addition, with some closed questions, they may not be able to give the response they want. Therefore, they may end up missing out questions, or giving inaccurate responses.

✘ Another problem is that questionnaires do not take individuals into account. By asking everybody the same questions, researchers cannot explore individual responses.

BUZZWORDS

Interview – Face-to-face questioning

Structured interview – An interview with pre-set questions

Unstructured interview – An interview where questions vary depending on the interviewee's responses

ACTIVITY

11.13

Read the following list of open questions.

a) How good would you say your memory is?

b) To what extent do you follow rules?

c) How would you describe your relationship with your parents?

d) How much of an individual are you?

e) Why do you think it is important to practise social skills?

Re-write each of these open questions so that they become closed questions.

Interviews

Interviews are another type of self report method. They are different from questionnaires in the sense that they are always carried out face to face. The psychologist directly asks questions of the interviewee. These questions are often open rather than closed so that more in-depth answers can be given.

There are two main types of interviews.

1 **Structured interviews** are interviews where the questions are pre-determined. This means that everyone who is interviewed is asked the same set of questions.

2 **Unstructured interviews** do not have set questions. Instead the interviewer asks questions based on the interviewees' answers. This means that the interview runs more like a conversation.

Figure 11.4 *A researcher conducting an interview.*

HOW PSYCHOLOGY WORKS

11

- ✔ A strength of interviews is that they can be used to access people's thoughts and feelings.

- ✔ Compared with most questionnaires, interviews have the advantage that people can double-check what questions mean. The interviewer can also clarify interviewees' responses if they are not clear.

- ✘ One weakness of interviews is that people may lie or exaggerate as there is no way of checking the truth. Since the interviewer is present throughout the interview, interviewees may feel obliged to give socially desirable responses rather than their real responses to questions.

- ✘ Another weakness of interviews is that they rely on people being able to explain their thoughts and feelings. Some people do not have the ability to do this because they cannot express themselves clearly. In addition, they may not have a good insight into themselves.

Observations

Figure 11.5 *A researcher carrying out an observation.*

We have considered some of the problems of self-report, such as people not telling the truth or not being able to explain themselves. To overcome this problem, researchers can observe people instead. Although observations can take place as part of an experiment, many observations take place in people's natural environment. This means that psychologists can watch their participants going about their normal behaviour.

There are a number of dimensions to observations.

1 Firstly, observations can be overt or covert. An **overt observation** is one in which participants are aware that they are being observed. In other words, psychologists are open about the fact that they are doing an observation. Meanwhile, a **covert observation** is one in which participants are unaware that they are being observed. Psychologists go 'undercover' to do their observation.

ACTIVITY

11.14
Answer the following questions.

1 What advantages do you think structured interviews have over unstructured interviews?

2 What advantages do you think unstructured interviews have over structured interviews?

BUZZWORDS

Overt observation – To observe people with their knowledge

Covert observation – To observe people without them knowing

HINT

Students often get overt and covert observations muddled. Think of the **o**vert observation being the **o**pen one (both words begin with 'o'). Meanwhile, the **cover**t observation is the under**cover** one.

2 Secondly, observations can be participant or non-participant. This is reasonably self-explanatory. In a **participant observation**, the researcher actually participates (or joins in) with the group of people she or he is studying. However, in a **non-participant observation**, the researcher would observe the group from a distance and not interfere with their activities.

If we combine these different dimensions of observations, it gives us four possible types of observations:

- an overt participant observation
- an overt non-participant observation
- a covert participant observation
- a covert non-participant observation.

ACTIVITY

11.15

Look at the following research aims.

1 A psychologist wants to investigate whether pre-school boys play more aggressively than pre-school girls.

2 A psychologist wants to investigate how much job satisfaction telesales employees get from their jobs.

3 A psychologist wants to investigate how organised football hooliganism is.

4 A psychologist wants to investigate whether non-verbal communication differs in bus queues depending on the location of the bus stop.

5 A psychologist wants to investigate how crowd behaviour at a music festival differs depending on how far spectators are from the stage.

For each of these aims, suggest what types of observations should be used. Attempt to justify your answer.

✔ A strength of overt observations is that they are more ethical than covert observations because participants must have given consent to be observed.

✔ A strength of covert observations is that people will behave more naturally than when they know they are being observed.

✔ A strength of participant observations over non-participant observations is that researchers can actually experience a situation from the participants' point of view, giving more realistic results.

✔ A strength of non-participant observations is that the researcher can be more objective when standing back from the group being observed. When researchers are too involved with a group they may be too subjective.

✘ A weakness of overt observations is that participants are likely to behave differently from normal if they know they are being watched. This is known as the observer effect and can make results less valid.

✘ A weakness of covert observations is that it can be difficult to record data accurately without being discovered. This is especially the case if the observation is a participant observation as well.

✘ A weakness of participant observations is that the researcher can affect the dynamics of the group that they join. The group becomes a different group from normal with their additional member.

✘ A weakness of non-participant observations is that it is easier for a researcher to miss details of an activity when they are separate from it rather than part of it.

✘ A general weakness of observations is observer bias. This is the idea that researchers see what they want to see and interpret behaviours from their own perspective. One solution to this problem is to use more than one observer. This should give inter-rater reliability to any findings.

HINT

You only need to know the strengths and weaknesses of the four main methods on the specification: experiments, questionnaires, interviews and observations. It is enough to be able to describe the other types of studies: case studies, correlation studies, longitudinal studies and cross-sectional studies.

ACTIVITY

11.16

The advantage of one type of observation (e.g. covert) tends to give the disadvantage of the other type (e.g. overt).

Go down the list of strengths and weaknesses of the different types of observations. Rewrite each one, so that the strengths become weaknesses and vice versa.

For example, the first point is that a strength of overt observations is that they are ethical. Therefore, you could rewrite this to say that a weakness of covert observations is that they are unethical because people cannot consent to being observed if they do not know they are being watched. Try to rewrite the others in a similar way.

Types of studies

Experiments, questionnaires, interviews and observations make up the main methods used in psychological research. However, these methods can be used in different ways, giving more specific types of studies.

1 Case Studies

Case studies tend to use methods such as unstructured interviews and observations. They may also involve looking at past records of a person (e.g. medical records, educational records). The key point about a case study is that it is carried out on a small sample. This may be one individual or one group (e.g. an organisation, a community, a family). One other key feature of a case study is that it involves an in-depth analysis of the individual or group under investigation. Quite often the individual or group is studied because it is unusual in some way.

BUZZWORDS

Case study – An in-depth analysis of one person or group

ACTIVITY

11.17

Sketch three scattergraphs to show:

a) a positive correlation

b) a negative correlation

c) no correlation.

2 Correlation Studies

Correlation studies can collect data through a variety of methods (e.g. questionnaires, structured interviews, observations). The important thing to understand about a correlation study is not how it collects data but how it *analyses* data. Correlation studies involve collecting two sets of data from a sample, and then analysing it to see if there is an association between them. For example, is there a correlation between the number of crimes a father commits and the number of crimes that his son commits? Or is there a correlation between people's score on an aggression questionnaire and their score on a verbal ability test? Once a researcher has carried out a correlation study, they can see whether there is a positive correlation, negative correlation or no correlation. If there is a positive correlation it means that as one variable increases then so does the other. For example, as a father commits more crimes his son commits more crimes. If there is a negative correlation it means that as one variable increases then the other decreases. For example, the higher a person scores on an aggression questionnaire, the lower their score on a verbal ability test.

3 Longitudinal studies versus cross-sectional studies

Longitudinal studies can use any of the main methods to collect data, including an experiment. The point is that the method is conducted over a long period of time. This is so that researchers can chart any changes. Longitudinal studies are particularly useful for studying psychological development. For example, a psychologist could test a sample of children every year for the first ten years of their lives to investigate how their cognitive abilities develop. Or a psychologist could assess the relationships between a sample of infants and their carers, and then revisit the infants as adults to assess the quality of their intimate relationships.

The problem with longitudinal studies is that they are time consuming and tend to be expensive because of this. It also takes a long time to collect the final results. This is further complicated if participants in the original sample decide to drop out. For this reason, a number of psychologists choose to do a **cross-sectional study** instead. This involves comparing two groups of people who represent the different stages of development that the psychologist is interested in. For example, if a psychologist was interested in cognitive abilities at different stages, they could compare a group of one-year-olds with a group of two-year-olds and three-year-olds, and so on. The main limitation of this is that the researcher is not actually comparing the same people. This means that any differences could be due to individual differences.

Analysing Research

Once data has been collected, psychologists need to analyse it. This is often to identify patterns and trends. From this, they are able to draw conclusions about their research. However, psychologists also need to be aware of any flaws in their research and how this will affect the findings.

Types of data

There are two main types of data that researchers can collect from an investigation.

1 **Quantitative data** is numerical data. If a psychologist takes a measurement they will have quantitative data.

2 **Qualitative data** is descriptive data. This means it is normally in the form of words. However, it can be in other formats which offer some detail, such as images.

ACTIVITY

11.18

Copy and complete Table 11.2 by ticking a column to show whether each example of data is quantitative or qualitative.

Table 11.2

Example of data	Quantitative	Qualitative
The number of words recalled in two different conditions		
The diary entries of a serial killer		
The case notes on the development of a child abandoned at birth		
The average number of times someone stops to help a stranger		
Participants' ratings, on a scale of 1 to 10, on how close they are to their partners		
A summary of how a teacher treats boys and girls differently in her lesson		
A tape recording of an interview with a patient with a phobia		
How long participants take to recognise an object, in milliseconds		

Descriptive data

Descriptive data is data that summarises patterns and trends in quantitative data. Rather than presenting the raw data (actual scores) it describes them in more general terms. Averages are a good example of this. If a researcher wanted to compare the scores of girls and boys in a mathematical test, they would look at how each group did *on average* rather than looking at each individual score in turn. An average gives the researcher a score that represents the data set that it comes from.

There are three ways of calculating an average:

1 Using a **mode**. The mode is simply the most common score in a data set. It is the average because it is the most popular.

2 Using a **median**. The median is calculated by finding the middle score once a data set has been put in numerical order. If there is an even number of scores in a data set, then you work out which score would fall in the middle. For example, in the data set {3 4 5 8 10 13}, there is no actual middle score, but 6.5 is the median as it falls between 5 and 8.

3 Using a **mean**. The mean is sometimes known as the arithmetic average because you have to do some arithmetic to work it out! To find the mean, add together all of the scores in a data set and this gives you a total. Then divide this total by the actual number of scores in the data set. The final figure is the average score that each participant would get if the total scores were shared out equally.

HINT

The specification states that you should be able to 'describe data collected from investigations'. This data could be in any format – quantitative or qualitative. In an exam situation, it might involve extracting or interpreting data from the source. A good way of practising this skill is to carry out some research and then summarise your data.

BUZZWORDS

Mode – A type of average; the most popular score in a data set

Median – A type of average; the middle score when a data set is in numerical order

Mean – A type of average; the total of a data set divided by the number of scores in it

HINT

It is possible that you could be asked to work out a mode, median or mean in the exam. However, it will be kept simple. It is more likely that you will be asked to **interpret** an average so make sure you understand what it shows you.

ACTIVITY

11.19

Answer the following questions on averages.

1 Why would it not be suitable to use a mode in the following two data sets?

a) {2 3 7 9 15 21 23}

b) {4 13 4 2 25 12 9 4 12 17 12 3}

2 Using the median, decide in which of the following two conditions participants remembered more words on average.

Words recalled in Condition A	Words recalled in Condition B
9	8
8	4
9	4
7	2
3	4
5	9
3	10
5	3
5	8
	9
	1
	9

3 Using the mean, decide in which of the following two conditions participants completed the puzzle more quickly on average.

Condition 1: Time in seconds	35 45 67 72 35 29 22 80 81 59
Condition 2: Time in seconds	50 52 58 48 59 59 50 52 46 51

Tables, charts and graphs

Quantitative data can be represented more visually by using techniques such as tables, charts and graphs. **Tables** are more user-friendly for many people because they set data out in a clear, concise way. For example, see the table below for Mednick *et al.*'s study.

	Did *have* biological parents who were convicted of a crime	Did *not* have biological parents who were convicted of a crime
Did have adoptive parents who were convicted of a crime	24.5%	14.7%
Did *not* have adoptive parents who were convicted of a crime	20.0%	13.5%

Data can be *represented* as a **bar chart**. This works well if data is in categories. For example, see the bar chart below, summarising the results of Yuki *et al.*'s study below.

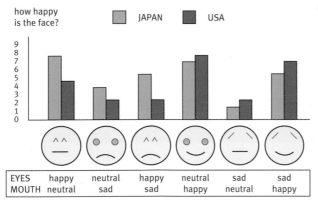

Data can also be represented as a **line graph**. This works well if data is in the form of scores. For example, see the line graph below, summarising the results of Terry's study.

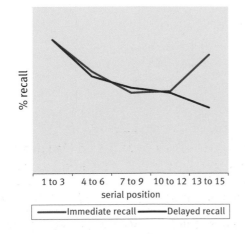

Grade Studio

You may be asked to sketch a chart or graph in the exam. Presentation matters, but accuracy is what the examiner will be looking for. The more accurate your chart or graph, the more marks you will earn. There will also be marks available for labelling the chart or graph, so do not forget that either.

11

RESEARCH IN PSYCHOLOGY

11.20

Answer the following questions on tables, charts and graphs.

1 Look at Table 11.3.

Table 11.3 *The mean scores of women and men on a verbal ability test and a mathematical ability test*

	Women	Men
Verbal ability	65.5	47.3
Mathematical ability	62.3	66.4

a) On which ability was there a greater difference between the sexes?

b) On which ability did men score higher on average?

c) The researchers concluded that 'there was no significant difference in women's verbal and mathematical ability'. Explain what this statement means.

2 Draw a bar chart to represent the findings described below. (Remember to include a title!)

'A psychologist carried out an observation to categorise the different attachment styles of children in a day nursery. Her findings showed that the majority of infants (67%) were securely attached. Of the remainder, 20% showed anxious avoidant behaviour and 13% showed anxious resistant behaviour.'

3 Look at the results in Table 11.4.

Table 11.4 *The number of times students broke the rules in Class A compared with Class B*

Number of rules broken	0	1	2	3	4	5	6	7	8	9
Number of students breaking this many rules in Class A	9	6	4	2	0	1	0	0	1	0
Number of students breaking this many rules in Class B	1	0	3	4	6	6	2	1	1	1

a) Plot the data in the table onto a line graph.

b) Describe what the line graph shows.

Evaluating findings

When evaluating the strengths and weaknesses of different methods, you will see that words such as 'validity' and 'reliability' often come up. These are important concepts in psychological research. For example, if a method is unreliable then the data collected using that method could also be unreliable.

Listed below are some key concepts used to evaluate findings.

- Researchers often question the **validity** of findings. This means they are actually asking whether they are true or real. **Ecological validity** is a specific type of validity. If research has ecological validity it means that findings reflect real-life situations.

- Researchers often also question the **reliability** of findings. Reliability refers to consistency. This means that if results are inconsistent (i.e. different researchers get different results when carrying out the same study) then they are unreliable. Unreliable results may be due to researchers' different perspectives on what is being studied. This is why it is useful to have more than one researcher involved in a study. They can check they agree on what they are observing, or on what is being measured. If there is agreement, then findings have **inter-rater reliability**. More than one person agrees that something has happened.

- **Demand characteristics** are a particular problem when findings come from experiments. People can often work out what experiments are testing using demand characteristics. Basically, they are cues that give away the aim. For example, if as a participant you were asked to complete anagrams under quiet conditions and then under noisy conditions, you would probably guess the effect of noise is being tested. You may then purposely do worse on the anagrams under noisy conditions to help the researcher out. This is responding to demand characteristics and can skew the results.

- The **observer effect** is a particular problem in observations. It occurs when people behave differently because they know they are being watched. This means that their behaviour is not natural, and so the findings are invalid.

- **Social desirability** is a particular problem in self-reports. This is when participants give answers that they think the researchers want to hear, rather than give their true answers. Again, this affects the validity of findings.

BUZZWORDS

Validity – Reflecting the truth

Ecological validity – reflecting a real-life situation

Reliability – Consistency; replicates itself

Inter-rater reliability – When two or more researchers agree on (are consistent in) their findings

Demand characteristics – Cues in an experiment, which give away the aim

Observer effect – When participants behave differently from normal because they know they are being observed

Social desirability – This describes responses that participants give when they say what they believe the researcher wants to hear

11

RESEARCH IN PSYCHOLOGY

BUZZWORDS

Bias – Only viewing things from a certain perspective

Gender bias – Viewing things from the perspective of one gender

Cultural bias – Viewing things from the perspective of one culture

ACTIVITY

11.22

Suggest at least one way of overcoming the following in research:

a) gender bias

b) cultural bias

c) experimenter bias.

ACTIVITY

11.21

Read through the core studies in this book, without reading the evaluation of them.

Try to identify examples of problems with:

- validity
- reliability
- demand characteristics
- observer effect
- social desirability.

Sources of bias

Ideally, the data presented as the results of a study should be free of **bias**. This is because people want data to be objective. We tend not to be interested in results that are basically a person's opinion rather than fact. For example, we may want to know that females *really* do have better verbal skills than males, not that someone believes they do.

Although many psychologists try hard to be objective, it is easy for biases to 'creep in'. This is because they are people themselves and are studying other people for their research.

Common biases include:

1 **Gender bias** – This occurs where one gender is favoured over another. This can happen if findings are based on studying one sex more than another, or if a researcher's perspective on findings is affected by their own gender. For example, a lot of early research on obedience was based on samples of men. It was later discovered that this did not represent women very well, as they tended to have higher rates of obedience. Another example would be a female psychologist who assumes that attachment is stronger between mother and baby rather than father and baby because of her own experiences.

2 **Cultural bias** – This occurs when one culture is favoured over another. This can happen if findings are based on studying one culture or another, or if a researcher's perspective on findings is affected by their own cultural experiences. For example, a lot of early research on non-verbal communication was carried out in the USA. Based on this, some researchers wrongly suggested that certain gestures were universal, even though they had not studied people in other countries. Another example would be a psychologist testing depth cues in African cultures using pictures only familiar to Westerners.

3 **Experimenter bias** – This occurs where one theory is favoured over another. Psychology is renowned for its many different approaches to studying human thought and behaviour. This means that different psychologists prefer different explanations – whether it be biological, cognitive, behaviourist or something else. The point is that psychologists will have certain expectations of what causes something to happen, and this may affect how they interpret their findings. For example, an experimenter who believes gender is a product of nature may overlook evidence that suggests otherwise. An experimenter who believes that there are cultural differences in non-verbal communication may exaggerate the differences they see. An experimenter who believes that men who had secure attachments make better husbands may give them higher ratings on a task. It is not that psychologists are cheats who 'fiddle' their results. The point is that psychologists are only human too, and when they carry out research – even experiments – they may have certain expectations about what they are going to observe or measure. If the observations and measurements are not rigorous enough, then findings are open to interpretation.

Planning an Investigation

When you have learnt about the different concepts for Research in Psychology, you will also need to be able to apply them. This means actually doing research yourself. Hopefully this book will encourage you to do your own investigations. This is really good practice for the Unit 3 examination where you have to plan your own investigation. There are more details on this in the Exam Café at the end of this chapter.

Summary

- In planning research, psychologists usually formulate a hypothesis, identify variables to be studied and controlled, choose an experimental design, select a sample of participants, and consider ethical issues.

- In doing research, most psychologists will use an experiment, a questionnaire, an interview or an observation. They may also consider methods such as case studies, correlation studies, and longitudinal or cross-sectional studies.

- In analysing research, psychologists need to decide on the type of data to collect. They need to decide on how this data is interpreted (descriptive data, and tables, graphs or charts are commonly used). Results also need to be evaluated, with validity, reliability and bias being key considerations.

ExamCafé

Revision

Research in Psychology is different from other topics because it is made up of lots of small concepts, rather than whole theories or studies. Because it contains so much detail, it is easier to get things mixed up. It is made worse by the fact that there are lots of similar concepts: two types of hypotheses, two types of variables, two types of experimental designs, two types of sampling methods, four types of methods, four types of studies, three types of averages, etc. For this reason, it is important that you know the difference between the two types of hypotheses, the two types of variables, and so on.

Fortunately, in most cases, the names given to concepts make sense so that they 'do what it says on the tin'. For example, an independent groups design uses different (independent) groups of participants in conditions, whereas a repeated measures design repeatedly measures the same participants (by using them in each condition). Similarly, an opportunity sample gets its name from the fact that you use any participants you have the opportunity to use, whereas random sampling is choosing participants at random (i.e. by chance). See if you can apply this logic to other categories of concepts, such as averages, variables and methods.

Revision Checklist

An important part of Research in Psychology is the main methods and their strengths and limitations. It is useful to summarise these in a table, such as Table 11.5 below. The first method has been summarised for you. Can you finish off the rest?

Table 11.5

METHOD	DESCRIPTION	STRENGTHS	WEAKNESSES
EXPERIMENT	The researcher manipulates the IV, measures the DV, and controls other variables. Can be done in a lab or in the field.	• High level of control. • Can establish cause and effect.	• Lab experiments lack ecological validity. • Field experiments can lack control. • Problems with demand characteristics.
QUESTIONNAIRE			
INTERVIEW			
OBSERVATION			

Key Terms

There are a number of key terms used in Research in Psychology. Sometimes the ideas are straightforward but the terms are quite difficult to get right! You need to be able to define terms as you may be asked about them in the exam. Even if you are not asked about them, it looks impressive when you use them. However, you must make sure you use them appropriately.

Look at the key terms below and match them to their correct definition.

Ecological validity	*Consistency and replicability*
Demand characteristics	*People behaving differently when watched*
Reliability	*Only seeing things from a certain perspective*
Social desirability	*Giving the response the researcher wants, rather than the truth*
Bias	*A true reflection of a real-life situation*
Observer effect	*Cues in an experiment which give away the aim*

Exam Preparation

The Research in Psychology paper is different from the other two papers. One key difference is that it is made up of a lot of short questions. You should not be asked a question worth more than 4 marks. Many questions are worth fewer than this. A number of questions will simply ask you to 'identify', 'give' or 'state', such as:

1 Identify the sampling method used in the study.   **[1]**

2 Give the mean number of times the doll was hit.   **[1]**

3 State the name of one experimental design.   **[1]**

These questions would carry 1 mark, and require just one statement, or even one word in some cases.

Even higher scoring questions are likely to use simple command words, such as 'outline' or 'describe'. For example:

1 Describe an advantage of using a field experiment   **[2]**

2 Outline **one** reason why the researcher used standardised instructions.   **[3]**

The highest scoring questions could use 'explain' as a command word. For example:

1 Explain the difference between a structured and unstructured interview.   **[3]**

2 Explain **one** ethical problem with the study in the source.   **[3]**

3 Explain how you would carry out the investigation.   **[4]**

There are some benefits in having an exam paper that is made up of lots of short questions:

- It gives you the opportunity to show the breadth of your knowledge and understanding.
- If there is a question you find difficult or are not sure how to answer, you will not lose a lot of marks because of it.
- You are not expected to go into a lot of detail about any one idea.

Do bear this last point in mind in the exam. Some students write too much for the marks available. Make sure you do not waste time giving more than is asked for.

ExamCafé

Section A

Section A on the Research in Psychology paper starts with a source outlining a study.

Some of the questions are easy to prepare for because they are independent of the source. This means that you do not necessarily have to look to the source to answer them. For example:

1 Describe what is meant by an observation. **[2]**

2 Outline what is meant by the term 'gender bias'. **[3]**

3 Name **one** sampling method psychologists can use in research. **[1]**

4 From the options below, identify the definition of 'ecological validity':

Consistency in results. ☐

True reflection of real life. ☐

Being unbiased. ☐

Tick one of the above boxes to show your answer. **[1]**

Other questions are more difficult to prepare for because they will be based on information in the source, and you will not know what is going to be in the source before the exam! However, you can still practise these kinds of questions by applying them to other studies you already know. This means you will have some idea of where to look for the information in a description of a study.

Below are some examples of source-dependent questions.

1 The study has a number of problems associated with the ethical issues listed below:

- avoiding deception

- avoiding distress

- gaining consent

- protecting confidentiality.

Complete the table on the next page by choosing a different ethical issue from the list to match the problem described. **[3]**

ETHICAL PROBLEM	ISSUE
	The participants did not know that they were taking part in a study
	The participants really believed the confederate was in trouble when he was not
	Participants who did not help may have felt guilty afterwards

2 Identify the independent variable in the study in the source.   [1]

3 Name the method used by the psychologist in the source.   [1]

4 Outline **one** reason why the researcher used standardised instructions.   [2]

Section B

In Section B of the Research in Psychology paper, you will be given a short brief and then asked to design an investigation based on this. As with the source in Section A you will not know what the brief is, so there is a limit to how much you can prepare for this section. However, if you have had the opportunity to carry out some of your own research as part of your course, this section will be easier. You will be able to design an investigation from experience. Ideally, you would have had a go at carrying out an experiment, questionnaire, interview and observation as these are the four methods that your brief can focus on.

Although the brief is unpredictable, we can predict what the questions will focus on. Questions will ask about some of the following points:

- The hypotheses of your investigation
- The sample you would use
- Ethical considerations
- Control of variables
- The procedure you would use
- Strengths of the method used
- Weaknesses of the method used
- Analysis of findings.

Make sure you read all of the questions in Section B before answering any, so that you have an overall view of what you are being asked to do.

Examiner's Tip:
There is a lot of planning time built into this exam paper, so use it wisely by 'sketching out' your investigation before answering questions.

Exam**Café**

The type of questions you can be asked are demonstrated below.
A candidate's response with comments is also given.

You have been asked to carry out a **questionnaire** to investigate whether
19-year-olds in education get more depressed than 19-year-olds in work.

a) Outline a null hypothesis for your investigation.　　[2]

There is no difference in the rates of depression
between 19-year-olds in education and 19-year-olds in
work.

Examiner says:
A clear and concise response.
The stem is right for a null
hypothesis and the variables are
correctly identified and ordered
after this.

b) Describe how you would select the participants for your
investigation.　　[3]

I would go to a local university for the participants in
education. I would choose a workplace where quite a lot
of young people are working, such as a call centre. When
I got to both places, I would randomly select people to
take part in investigation. I would do this by getting the
names of all the people prepared to do the questionnaire,
and then draw them from a hat.

Examiner says:
Another good response. The
candidate has given realistic
and relevant places to draw the
sample from. They have also
included a sampling method
showing sound technical
knowledge.

c) Outline *one* ethical issue in carrying out an investigation into
depression.　　[2]

One ethical problem is protection of participants. This is
because people may get upset having to think about their
mood state, especially if they are depressed. They may
not want to think about it too much.

Examiner says:
The candidate has approached
the question well. First they
identify the ethical issue, and
then they apply it to their
investigation.

d) Explain how you would deal with the ethical issue you have outlined in (c) when carrying out your investigation. **[2]**

I would deal with the issue by making sure that participants know they have the right to withdraw from the questionnaire at any point. I would write this in a briefing at the top of the questionnaire before they start.

Examiner says:
The candidate has obviously chosen an issue that they know how to address. This is why it is sensible to read all the questions in Section B before answering them, as some may rely on others.

e) Briefly describe how you would use a questionnaire in this investigation. **[3]**

I would make sure the questionnaire was on paper so that it could be answered in private. I would use closed questions with a rating scale of 1 to 6. This is so that I could actually measure rates of depression objectively. For each question, the participants would have to say how they felt about a statement. A low rating would mean they were depressed and a high rating would mean they were not.

Examiner says:
This is an excellent response to the question. It includes a lot of technical details, design decisions are justified and are explicitly applied to the investigation brief. It is worth pointing out that there are other ways of answering this question. For example, you may want to give examples of questions, or may want to say how you would administer the questionnaire.

f) Explain *one* strength of using a questionnaire to investigate rates of depression in 19-year-olds. **[2]**

Questionnaires can be confidential because I wouldn't need to be there to ask the questions. This is useful here because asking people about their feelings is quite personal and they may not tell the truth if they are questioned face-to-face, like in an interview.

Examiner says:
A good finish to a pleasing set of responses that show this candidate has a good overview of their investigation. The candidate earns both marks as they have identified a strength of questionnaires and then linked it to what they are investigating.

Accessibility problems – Problems associated with retrieving information in storage

Acrophobia – An extreme fear of heights

Agoraphobia – An extreme fear of being in public spaces away from the safety of the home

Alternate hypothesis – A statement which predicts a difference or correlation in results

Androgyny – A type of gender where an individual shows high levels of both masculine and feminine traits

Arachnophobia – An extreme fear of spiders

Attachment – An enduring bond formed with a significant other

Attention – A process that makes people aware of information in the memory

Atypical behaviour – A behaviour which is considered abnormal, usually because it applies to a minority of people

Authoritarian personality – A personality type which is prone to obedience

Authority – A level of status or power

Availability problems – Problems associated with information no longer being stored

Bar chart – A chart that summarises data by using bars to represent the different frequencies of categories

Behaviourists – A group of psychologists who believe that human behaviours are learnt rather than natural

Bias – Only viewing things from a certain perspective

Body language – Communicating something physically through our body, for example our body movement, gestures, touching, keeping a distance, and so on

Bottom-up processing – When perception is dominated by what enters through the eyes (rather than what we expect to see)

Brain dysfunction – The idea that a brain is not operating as normal brains do

Capacity – This refers to the amount of space in the memory

Case study – An in-depth analysis of one person or group

Chromosome – A part of a cell that contains genetic information

Classical conditioning – Learning by association, so that certain stimuli are associated with certain responses

Closed questions – Questions for which there are set responses to choose from

Cognitive development – Age-related changes, e.g. how children think and behave differently as they get older

Colour constancy – The ability to perceive the colour of an object as constant even if it appears to change with changes in lighting

Conditioned response (CR) – A response which has been learnt (or conditioned) through association

Conditioned stimulus (CS) – Something that triggers a learnt response; something we have been conditioned to respond to

Confidentiality – Protecting the identity of participants by not revealing names and other details

Consensus – When everybody agrees on something

Conservation – The logical rule that quantity does not change even when things are re-arranged; the ability to understand that changing the form of an object or substance does not change the amount or volume

Constructivist theory – The theory that perception is constructed using past experiences

Correlation study – A study that analyses two sets of data for a relationship

Covert observation – To observe people without them knowing

Criminal personality – A collection of traits that make a person different from 'normal', law-abiding people

Critical period – The first three years of a child's life, when attachment has to take place or there will be long-term consequences

Cross-sectional study – A study where two or more groups are compared, to investigate changes or differences

Cultural bias – Viewing things from the perspective of one culture

Cultural variations – This describes differences (in behaviour) across different countries, societies or communities

Culture – A way of life made up of a set of rules, standards and expectations

Decay – This is the fading of information over time until it is forgotten

Deep processing – Coding information for meaning

Defiance – Resisting orders or commands from people in authority

Demand characteristics – Cues in an experiment, which give away the aim

Denial of responsibility – Blaming actions on a higher authority rather than accepting blame oneself

Dependent variable – Something that is measured to see if it has changed (after an independent variable has been manipulated)

Deprivation – When a child has formed an attachment to a caregiver, but this attachment is broken through separation

Depth perception – Refers to the ability of our eyes and brain to add a third dimension (depth) to everything we see

Displacement – A process in which information is 'shunted out' of storage by new information, and so becomes forgotten

Dispositional factors – Factors associated with an individual's personality

Duration – This refers to how long information lasts in the memory

Ecological validity – Reflecting a real-life situation

Electra complex – A conflict that occurs when girls unconsciously desire their father but worry about losing their mother's love

Encoding – The process in which data is changed into another format

Ethical considerations – Issues of research that take into account the welfare of participants

Evolution – A process by which species adapt to their environment in order to survive and reproduce

Evolutionary theory – The theory that animals have evolved over time and instinctively behave in ways that allow them to survive and reproduce

Experiment – A method by which the researcher controls variables and measures their effect

Experimental design – A way of allocating participants to conditions in an experiment

Experimenter bias – Setting up an experiment and/or interpreting the results to fit a certain idea or theory

Extraneous variable – A variable (which is not the independent variable) but could affect the dependent variable if not controlled

Facial expressions – Communicating something through the movement of muscles in the face, for example by moving eyebrows, lips, eyes and so on

Facial features – Features which make up the face, such as forehead, eyes, nose, mouth and chin

Femininity – A gender term associated with female traits/roles

Field experiment – An experiment carried out in a natural environment

Free will – The ability to make your own decisions, uninfluenced by other factors

Gender – A psychological term that tells us whether an individual is masculine, feminine or androgynous

Gender bias – Viewing things from the perspective of one gender

Heritability – The proportion of a behaviour that is due to genetic factors

Hormone – A chemical produced by the body that affects cells and organs

Hypothesis – A statement predicting the outcome of research

Ideal self – The person an individual would like to be

Illusion – The effect of misinterpreting data

Imitation – Doing, saying and behaving the same as the 'model' who was observed doing, saying or behaving (what we call 'copying')

Independent groups design – An experimental design in which participants are different in each condition

Independent variable – Something the researcher changes or manipulates

Information processing – The idea that information is processed through a number of stages

Informed consent – When participants agree to take part in a study and also know what the aim of the study is

Input – The process of data entry

Insecure ambivalent attachment – When a child and caregiver have a relationship in which the child can be clingy and demanding, yet awkward with the caregiver at the same time

Insecure avoidant attachment – When a child and caregiver have a relationship in which the child is quite independent of the caregiver

Instinctive – Natural and automatic

Inter-rater reliability – When two or more researchers agree on (are consistent in) their findings

Interview – Face-to-face questioning

Invariant stages – The same stages, in a fixed order, that the development of a child's ability to think goes through

Laboratory experiment – An experiment carried out in a controlled environment

Line graph – A graph that summarises data using a line to show changes in the frequencies of scores

Longitudinal study – A study carried out over a period of time

Long-term memory – The memory store that has unlimited capacity and unlimited duration, and where information is permanently stored

Maintenance rehearsal – A process that basically involves repeating information so that it stays in storage, either temporarily or permanently

Masculinity – A gender term associated with male traits/roles

Mean – A type of average; the total of a data set divided by the number of scores in it

Median – A type of average; the middle score when a data set is in numerical order

Mode – A type of average; the most popular score in a data set

Monotropy – An attachment to one primary caregiver

Nativist theory – The theory that perception is a natural and instinctive process

Neutral stimulus (NS) – Something that would not normally trigger a reaction

Non-participant observation – To observe people from a distance

Non-verbal communication – Telling others what we are thinking or feeling or planning by some recognised body movement. It can be conscious (i.e. we are aware of doing it) or unconscious (we are unaware we are doing it)

Null hypothesis – A statement which predicts no difference or correlation in results

Obedience – Following orders or commands from people in authority

Observation – To watch someone with the purpose of learning about behaviour

Observer effect – When participants behave differently from normal because they know they are being observed

Oedipus complex – A conflict that occurs when boys unconsciously desire their mother but fear their father finding out

Open questions – Questions for which there are no fixed responses, and participants answer as they please

Operant conditioning – Learning by consequences. If the consequences of an action are rewarding, we learn to do them again. However, if the consequences are negative, we tend not to repeat the action

Opportunity sample – A sample drawn from the target population because they are available and convenient

Output – The process of using data after it has been retrieved

Overt observation – To observe people with their knowledge

Participant observation – To observe people whilst joining in their activities

Perception – The cognitive process of interpreting data once it has been sensed

Perceptual set – A tendency to perceive something in line with what you expect based on past experience

Phobia – An atypical fear response, given the object or situation

Privation – When a child forms no attachment to a caregiver

Punishment – Negative consequences following an action

Qualitative data – Descriptive data

Quantitative data – Numerical data

Questionnaire – A set of predetermined questions which are the same for all respondents

Random sample – A sample for which everyone in the target population has an equal chance of being chosen

Reinforcement – A process in which a behaviour is strengthened because the consequences are positive

Reliability – Consistency; replicates itself

Repeated measures design – An experimental design in which participants take part in each condition

Representative – An accurate reflection of a larger group

Retrieval – The process in which information is located and taken out of storage

Right to withdraw – When participants are allowed to stop participating in a study or can stop the study altogether

Role model – An individual who other people aspire to be like

Sample – A smaller group selected from a larger population

School phobia – An extreme fear of attending and being in school

Secure attachment – When a child and caregiver have a relationship based on trust and security, and the child wishes to interact with its caregiver

Self report – When participants report their own experiences

Self-actualisation – The idea that each of us has an inborn drive to want to fulfil our potential

Self-concept – A person's view of their actual self (what they think they are like)

Self-esteem – A measure of how much we value ourselves

Sensation – The physical process of collecting data from the environment via the senses

Sensory store – The store where all immediate information is briefly held unless it is paid attention to

Separation protest – When an individual shows upset and distress on separation from an attachment figure

Setting – The physical environment in which something takes place

Sex – A biological term that tells us whether an individual is male or female

Shallow processing – Only coding information based on its physical characteristics

Shape constancy – The ability to perceive the shape of an object as constant even if it appears to change through movement

Short-term memory – The memory store that has limited capacity and limited duration, and where information becomes conscious

Social desirability – This describes responses that participants give when they say what they believe the researcher wants to hear

Social learning – How a person's behaviour with, towards and around others develops as a result of observing and imitating others, both consciously and unconsciously

Social phobia – An extreme fear of being exposed or embarrassed during social contact

Standardisation – A way of controlling extraneous variables; to keep variables the same across conditions

Storage – The process in which information is held, ready to be used at a later date

Stranger anxiety – When an individual shows anxiety and distress in the presence of an unfamiliar person

Structured interview – An interview with pre-set questions

Table – A way of presenting data by summarising it under headings

Target population – The entire set of people researchers want to generalise their results to

Top-down processing – When perception is dominated by what we expect to see

Typical behaviour – A behaviour which is considered normal, usually because it applies to the majority of people

Unconditional positive regard – Showing an individual love without expecting certain conditions to be met

Unconditioned response (UCR) – A response which is natural and does not need to be learnt

Unconditioned stimulus (UCS) – Something that triggers a natural (unconditioned) response

Unique – A one-off, which is not repeated; individual

Universal stages – The pattern or order of the development of thinking that is the same for all children everywhere

Unstructured interview – An interview where questions vary depending on the interviewee's responses

Validity – Reflecting the truth

Variable – Anything that is open to change

Vicarious reinforcement – When someone's behaviour is reinforced (strengthened) because they observe how another person is rewarded for the same behaviour

Zone of proximal development – The gap between where a child is in their learning and where they can potentially get to with the help and support of others

Index

Note: Bold terms are Buzzwords and bold page numbers indicate where they are defined.

A
accessibility problems 17–18
acrophobia 65
adoption study, criminal behaviour 85–7
Adorno et al., authoritarian
    personality 54–5
advertising 101–2
agoraphobia 64
Ainsworth, attachment types 44
alternate hypothesis 151
ambiguous figures 94
androgyny 2
animism 110
arachnophobia 65
armed forces, obedience 58
attachment 33
    behaviourist theory 39–40
    Bowlby's theory 36–9
    Hazen and Shaver study 40–2
    key concepts 33–6
    research applications 42–4
attention 19
atypical behaviour 63–4
    behaviourist theory 66–70
    evolutionary theory 70–1
    key concepts 63–5
    research applications 73–4
    Watson and Rayner study 71–2
authoritarian personality 54–5
authority 49
    power of authority figure 52–3
availability problems 17–18

B
bar chart 169
behaviour therapy, phobias 66–70, 73–4
behaviourist theory
    attachment 39–40
    classical conditioning 66–9
    criticisms of 69–70
    operant conditioning 69
behaviourists 66
bias 172–3
Bickman's obedience study 55–7
biological approach
    criminal behaviour 81–3, 85–7
    sex and gender 3–6, 7–9
body language 122–3
bottom-up processing 98–9
Bowlby's theory of attachment 36–9
boy raised as girl, study of 7–9
brain dysfunction 81–2

C
capacity of memory 19, 20
care of children
    in the family 44
    in hospitals 42–3
    in nurseries 43
careers guidance 146
case studies 165
    methodological limitations of
        charts 169–70
chromosome 3
classical conditioning 66–9
    Watson and Rayner study 71–2
closed questions 161, 162
cognitive development 107
    conservation of number 114–15
    key concepts 107–8
    Piaget's theory 108–13
    research applications 115–16
    Vygotsky's theory 113–14
colour constancy 95–6
concrete operational stage of cognitive
        development 111–12
conditioned response (CR) 66
conditioned stimulus (CS) 66
confidentiality 158
conflict management 130
consensus, impact on obedience 53
conservation 111–12
conservation of number 114–15
**constructivist theory of
        perception 97–8**
context in advertising 102–3
corpus callosum 81
correlation 151–2
correlation studies 166
counselling 145–6
covert observation 163, 164, 165
crime, defining and measuring 79–80
crime reduction 87–8
criminal behaviour 79
    biological theory 81–3
    key concepts 79–80
    Mednick et al. study 85–7
    research applications 87–8
    social learning theory 83–5
criminal personality 80
critical period, attachment 36, 38
cross-sectional studies 114–15, 166
cues as memory aids 27–8
cultural bias 172

cultural differences in non-verbal
        communication 126, 128–9
cultural setting, effect on obedience 52
cultural variations 126
culture 52
customer service training 131

D
data analysis 167–70
data collection 159–65
data types 167
de-centring 110
decay 19, 21–2
deep processing, memory 23–4
defiance 50
demand characteristics 27, 54, 171
denial of responsibility 50
dependent variable 153
depression, counselling for 145–6
deprivation 37–8
depth perception 96–7
descriptive data 168
Diamond and Sigmundson study 7–9
discovery learning 116
displacement 19, 21
dispositional factors 54
dispositional factors theory 54–5
distance of objects, judgement of
        100–1
duration of memory 19, 20

E
**ecological validity 51, 54, 72, 129,
        160, 171**
education
    equal opportunities in 9–10
    influence of Piaget and
        Vygotsky 115–16
egocentrism 110
Electra complex 6
encoding 16
equal opportunities 9–10
ethical considerations 158–9
evaluation of findings 171
evolution 4–5
evolutionary theory 127
    non-verbal communication 127–8
    phobias 70–1
experimental designs 154–5
experimenter bias 173
experiments 159–61
extraneous variable 154

extraversion 142
Eysenck's trait theory 140–3

F **facial expressions 122**
facial features 82
fears *see* phobias
femininity 2
fictions 95
field experiments 160, 161
five factor model of personality 143
flooding 73–4
foetus, development of 3
formal operational stage of cognitive
    development 113
free will 136
Freud's psychodynamic approach 6–7

G **gender 2**
gender bias 172
gender development, biological
    approach 3–6
gender roles 2, 4, 5–6, 7–8
genetic basis for criminal behaviour
    81–3, 85–7
geometric illusions 94
gestures 123, 126–7
graphs 169–70

H Haber and Levin perception
    study 100–1
Hazen and Shaver attachment
    study 40–2
height in the plane 96
heights, irrational fear of 65
heritability 81
hormones 3–4
humanistic theory 136–40
hypotheses 151–2

I **ideal self 137**
illusion 94
imagery, memory aid 28
imitation 125
implosion therapy 74
independent groups design 154–5
independent variable 153
information processing 15–16
informed consent 158
input 16
insecure ambivalent attachment 35,
    36, 40

insecure avoidant attachment 35,
    36, 40
instinctive 39
inter-rater reliability 171
interviews 162–3
introversion 142
invariant stages 108

K Kaniza triangle 95

L **laboratory experiment 160**
levels of processing theory,
    memory 23–5
limbic system 81
line graph 169
linear perspective 96
linguistic humour 111
'Little Albert', early phobia study 71–2
long-term memory 18–21
longitudinal studies 166

M **maintenance rehearsal 19**
masculinity 2
Maslow, self-actualisation 139
mean and **median 168**
media violence and watersheds 84–5
Mednick *et al.* study, criminal
    behaviour 85–7
memory 15
    accessibility and availability
        problems 17–18
    key concepts 15–16
    levels of processing 23–5
    multi-store model 18–23
    research applications 27–8
    Terry's study 25–7
Milgram's study of obedience 50, 51,
    52, 53, 54
mind mapping 28
mode 168
monotropy 36
multi-store model, memory 18–23

N **nativist theory of perception**
    98–9
nature–nurture debate
    criminal behaviour 81, 85–7
    non-verbal communication 126–7
neuroticism 142
neutral stimulus (NS) 66
non-participant observation 164, 165
non-verbal communication 121, **122**

evolutionary theory 127–8
key concepts 122–5
research applications 130–1
social learning theory 125–7
Yuki *et al.* study 128–9
null hypothesis 151, 152

O **obedience 49**
Bickman's study 55–7
dispositional factors theory 54–5
key concepts 49–50
research applications 57–8
situational factors theory 51–4
object permanence 109–10
observations 125, **163–5**
observer bias 165
observer effect 171
Oedipus complex 6
offender rehabilitation 88, 130
open questions 161, 162
operant conditioning 69
opportunity sampling 157
order effects, repeated measures
    design 155
organisational hierarchy 57
output 16
overt observation 163, 164

P parental relationships,
    psychodynamic approach 6–7
participant observation 164, 165
participants in experiments, protection
    of 158–9
peer support in learning 116
perception 94
    constructivist theory 97–8
    Haber and Levin study 100–1
    key concepts 93–7
    nativist theory 98–9
    research applications 101–2
perceptual set 97
personality
    and obedience 54–5
    theories of 140–3
pets, effect on self-esteem 144–5
phobias 64–5
    behaviour therapy for 73–4
    classical conditioning 68, 71–2
    evolutionary theory 70–1
Piaget's theory 108–13
    conservation of number 114–15
    criticisms of 113

influence on education 116
posture 124
pre-frontal cortex 81
pre-operational stage of cognitive
    development 110–11
prisons
    keeping order in 58
    pros and cons of using 88
privation 36–7
protection of participants,
    experiments 158–9
psychodynamic approach 6–7
punishment 125

Q qualitative data 167
quantitative data 167
questionnaires 161–2

R random sampling 157
readiness concept 116
rehabilitation of offenders 88, 130
reinforcement 125
relationship counselling 146
relative size 96
reliability 171, 172
repeated measures design 154, 155
representative sample 156
research in psychology 151
    analysing research 167–73
    conducting research 159–66
    planning an investigation 173
    planning research 151–9
retrieval 16
reversibility 110
right to withdraw 158
Rogers, Carl
    counselling 145–6
    self-actualisation 139
    self-concept 136–7
    social role 137–8
role model 125

S sampling techniques 156–7
scaffolding 114, 116

schemas 107–8
school phobia 64
secure attachment 35
the self 135
    humanistic theory 136–40
    key concepts 135–6
    research applications 145–6
    trait theory 140–3
    Van Houtte and Jarvis study 144–5
self-actualisation 139
self-concept 136–7
self-esteem 137–8
    pet owners study 144–5
    and unconditional positive regard 139
self report 161
sensation 94
sensori-motor stage of cognitive
    development 109–10
sensory store 19
separation protest 34
seriation 111
setting, effect on obedience 51–2
sex 1–2
sex and gender 1–3
    biological approach 3–6
    Diamond and Sigmundson study 7–9
    psychodynamic approach 6–7
    research applications 9–10
shallow processing 23–4
shape constancy 95
short-term memory (STM) 18–21
situational factors theory 51–4
social desirability 171
social learning 125
social learning theory (SLT)
    criminal behaviour 83–5
    non-verbal communication 125–7
social phobia 64
social role 137–9
social skills training 130–1
spiders, irrational fear of 65
spiral curriculum 116
stability, emotional 142
stage theory 109

standardisation 154
stimulus generalisation 69
storage 16
stranger anxiety 34
structured interview 162
studies, types of 165–6
subliminal advertising 101
superimposition 97
Sutcliffe, Peter 83
systematic desensitisation 74

T table 169
target population 156, 157
temporal lobe 82
Terry's study, multi-store model 25–7
texture gradient 97
three mountains experiment 111
top-down processing 97
trait theory 140–3
TV commercials study 25–7
typical behaviour 63

**U unconditional positive
    regard 138–9**
unconditioned response (UCR) 66
unconditioned stimulus (UCS) 66
unique 135
universal stages 108
unstructured interview 162

V validity 171, 172
Van Houtte and Jarvis study, pets and
    self-esteem 144–5
variables 153–4
vicarious reinforcement 84–5
Vygotsky's theory 113–14, 116

W Watson and Rayner study, learning
    of phobias 71–2

Y Yuki *et al.* study, non-verbal
    communication 128–9

**Z zone of proximal
    development 114**